# PREFACE

These are still the early days of the digital economy. But already it is clear that it has had, and will continue to have, globally transformative impacts on the way we live, work and develop our economies. As the world strives to implement the 2030 Agenda for Sustainable Development – our universal blueprint for building peaceful, prosperous societies on a healthy planet – harnessing the great power of information and communications technologies can be one of the keys to success, including by opening new pathways of development and helping countries gain access to the global store of knowledge. The developing world itself is showing great leadership in technological innovations that can spur their own growth while benefiting the world.

At the same time, we know that large parts of the developing world remain disconnected from the Internet, and many people lack access to high-speed broadband connectivity. Policymaking at the national and international levels needs to mitigate the risk that digitalization could widen existing divides and create new gaps. Moreover, since increased reliance on digital technologies, such as cloud computing, three-dimensional printing, big data and "the Internet of things", is certain to influence most industries and global value chains, it is essential to start assessing opportunities and pitfalls alike, and to prepare for what is coming.

The enormous scope and considerable uncertainty associated with the next digital shift call for more facts, dialogue and action by all stakeholders The analysis contained in the *Information Economy Report 2017: Digitalization, Trade and Development* contributes to this process and proposes ways in which the international community can reduce inequality, enable the benefits of digitalization to reach all people and ensure that no one is left behind by the evolving digital economy

António Guterres
Secretary-General
United Nations

# FOREWORD

The world is at the dawn of the next technological revolution. It will be multifaceted and its implications transformational. Digitalization will create opportunities for entrepreneurs and businesses, while also bringing enormous benefits to consumers. However, at the same time it will disrupt existing practices, expose incumbents to competition, change skills requirements of workers and result in job losses in some countries and sectors.

The *Information Economy Report 2017* looks at some of these trends, and examines how information and communications technologies are having an increasing impact on global trade and development.

Like previous large-scale economic transitions, the benefits will be immense, but they will not materialize through a smooth, cost-free process. The net outcome will depend on policies undertaken at both national and international levels to build countries' capabilities to take advantage of these transformations.

The international community has a huge responsibility to ensure that no one is left behind in this transformation process. Given the very rapid evolution of the digital economy, many developing countries will need to develop or strengthen their capabilities in a wide range of policy areas, including in all key aspects of e-trade readiness: connectivity, payment solutions, trade logistics, Internet security and legal frameworks.

This year's *Information Economy Report* aims to augment our collective understanding of the way the digital economy works and its implications. It aims to help intensify policy dialogue and peer learning about the issues involved among developing and developed countries alike. And countries with more resources will need to reach out and assist those with less; current efforts are inadequate.

UNCTAD is committed to playing a constructive role in this context. We do this through in-depth research, as evidenced in this *Report*. In addition, our new Intergovernmental Group of Experts on E-Commerce and the Digital Economy will provide a new forum for policy dialogue, and our eTrade-for-all initiative can be leveraged to ensure that technical assistance is offered in more effective ways through smart partnerships and enhanced transparency.

It is my hope that this holistic approach will help us to respond to the desire of people in developing countries to connect to the new world of technological progress, and to benefit from the prosperous future they deserve.

Mukhisa Kituyi
Secretary-General of UNCTAD

UNITED NATIONS CONFERENCE ON TRADE AND DEVELOPMENT

UNCTAD

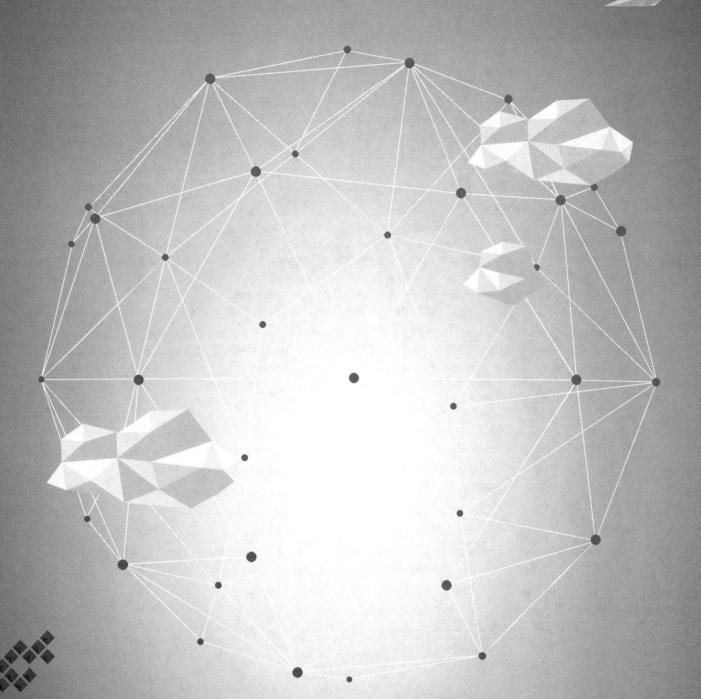

INFORMATION
ECONOMY REPORT 2017

DIGITALIZATION, TRADE AND DEVELOPMENT

UNITED NATIONS
New York and Geneva 2017

# NOTE

Within the UNCTAD Division on Technology and Logistics, the ICT Analysis Section carries out policy-oriented analytical work on the development implications of information and communications technologies (ICTs) and e-commerce. It is responsible for the preparation of the *Information Economy Report*. The ICT Analysis Section promotes international dialogue on issues related to ICTs for development, and contributes to building developing countries' capacities to measure the information economy and to design and implement relevant policies and legal frameworks. The Section is also managing the *eTrade for all* initiative.

In this Report, the terms country/economy refer, as appropriate, to territories or areas. The designations employed and the presentation of the material do not imply the expression of any opinion whatsoever on the part of the Secretariat of the United Nations concerning the legal status of any country, territory, city or area or of its authorities, or concerning the delimitation of its frontiers or boundaries. In addition, the designations of country groups are intended solely for statistical or analytical convenience, and do not necessarily express a judgement about the stage of development reached by a particular country or area in the development process. The major country groupings used in this Report follow the classification of the United Nations Statistical Office. These are:

Developed countries: the member countries of the Organisation for Economic Co-operation and Development (OECD) (other than Chile, Mexico, the Republic of Korea and Turkey), plus the European Union member countries that are not OECD members (Bulgaria, Croatia, Cyprus, Lithuania, Malta and Romania), plus Andorra, Liechtenstein, Monaco and San Marino. Countries with economies in transition refers to those in South-East Europe and the Commonwealth of Independent States. Developing economies in general are all the economies that are not specified above. For statistical purposes, the data for China do not include those for Hong Kong Special Administrative Region of China (Hong Kong, China), Macao Special Administrative Region of China (Macao, China) or Taiwan Province of China. An excel file with the main country groupings used can be downloaded from UNCTADstat at: http://unctadstat.unctad.org/EN/Classifications.html.

Reference to companies and their activities should not be construed as an endorsement by UNCTAD of those companies or their activities.

The following symbols have been used in the tables:

Two dots (..) indicate that data are not available or are not separately reported. Rows in tables have been omitted in those cases where no data are available for any of the elements in the row;

A dash (–) indicates that the item is equal to zero or its value is negligible;

A blank in a table indicates that the item is not applicable, unless otherwise indicated;

A slash (/) between dates representing years, e.g. 1994/95, indicates a financial year;

Use of an en dash (–) between dates representing years, e.g. 1994–1995, signifies the full period involved, including the beginning and end years;

Reference to "dollars" ($) means United States dollars, unless otherwise indicated;

Annual rates of growth or change, unless otherwise stated, refer to annual compound rates;

Details and percentages in tables do not necessarily add up to the totals because of rounding.

The material contained in this study may be freely quoted with appropriate acknowledgement.

UNITED NATIONS PUBLICATION

UNCTAD/IER/2017

Sales No. E.17.II.D.8

Print ISSN 2075-4396

Online ISSN 2075-440X

ISBN 978-92-1-112920-5

e-ISBN 978-92-1-362787-7

FEB 0 6 2018

# ACKNOWLEDGEMENTS

The *Information Economy Report 2017* was prepared by a team comprising Torbjörn Fredriksson (team leader), Cécile Barayre, Pilar Fajarnes, Scarlett Fondeur, Sabrina Ielmoli, Diana Korka, Smita Lakhe, Marta Pérez Cusó and Marian Pletosu under the supervision of Angel Gonzalez Sanz, Chief, Science, Technology and ICT Branch, and the with overall guidance of Shamika N. Sirimanne, Director of the Division on Technology and Logistics.

The report benefited from major substantive contributions by Anupam Chander, William Drake, Christopher Foster, Mark Graham, Michael Minges. Timothy Sturgeon, Kati Suominen and Desirée van Welsum. Additional inputs were provided by Hassiba Benamara, Katia Cerwin, Claudia Contreras, Poul Hansen, Jan Hoffmann, Martin Labbé, Teresa Moreira, William Natta, Maria Prieto, Félipe Sandoval and Frida Youssef.

Valuable comments on a draft version of the report were received from experts attending a peer review meeting in Geneva in July 2017, including Nick Ashton-Hart, Dimo Calovski, Paul Donohoe, Mohamed Es Fih, Cristopher Foster, James Howe, Marie Humeau, Michael Kende, Min Jae Kim, Michael Lim, Andreas Maurer, Susan Schorr, Marie Sicat, David Souter, Thomas van Giffen, Felix Weidenkaff and Anida Yupari. Additional comments were received at various stages of production of the report from Mario Acunzo and Simone Sala.

UNCTAD is grateful to national statistical offices for their sharing of data and for responses received to UNCTAD's annual survey questionnaire on ICT usage by enterprises, and on the ICT sector. Eurostat, GSMA Intelligence, the International Labour Organization, the International Telecommunication Union, the Oxford Internet Institute and the Universal Postal Union also shared data for this report, which is highly appreciated.

The cover was done by Magali Studer. The graphics and desktop publishing were done by Stéphane Bothua. The infographics were done by Natalia Stepanova and the *Information Economy Report 2017* was edited by Praveen Bhalla.

Financial support from the Governments of Finland and the United Kingdom is gratefully acknowledged.

United Nations

UNCTAD/IER/2017/Corr.1

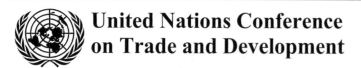

**United Nations Conference on Trade and Development**

Sales No. E.17.II.D.8
23 October 2017

English only

**Information Economy Report 2017:**
**Digitalization, Trade and Development**

**Corrigendum**

**Chapter II, page 16**

*For* Cross-border B2C e-commerce: $7 billion in 2015 *read* Cross-border B2C e-commerce: $189 billion in 2015

*For* Global Internet traffic 66 times higher in 2019 than in 2015 *read* Global Internet traffic 66 times higher in 2019 than in 2005

**Chapter IV, page 62**

*For* Strong cognitive, adaptive and creative skills *read* Strong non-cognitive, adaptive and creative skills

---

GE.17-18664(E)

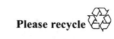

Please recycle

# CONTENTS

## Boxes

## Box figure

## Tables

# LIST OF ABBREVIATIONS

| | |
|---|---|
| AI | artificial intelligence |
| B2B | business-to-business |
| B2C | business-to-consumer |
| B2G | business-to-government |
| BPO | business process outsourcing |
| CBDF | cross-border data flow |
| EDI | electronic data interchange |
| EU | European Union |
| FTA | free trade agreement |
| G-20 | group of 20 (countries) |
| G-7 | group of 7 (countries) |
| GATS | General Agreement on Trade in Services (of WTO) |
| GCIG | Global Commission on Internet Governance |
| GDP | gross domestic product |
| GPS | global positioning system |
| GVC | global value chain |
| ICT | information and communications technology |
| ILO | International Labour Organization (or Office) |
| IoT | Internet of Things |
| ISIC | International Standard Industrial Classification of All Economic Activities |
| IT | information technology |
| ITU | International Telecommunication Union |
| LDC | least developed country |
| M2M | machine-to-machine |
| MNE | multinational enterprise |
| MSME | micro, small and medium-sized enterprise |
| OECD | Organisation for Economic Co-operation and Development |
| OTA | online travel agent |
| RFID | radio frequency identification |
| RTA | regional trade agreement |
| SDG | Sustainable Development Goal |
| SME | small and medium-sized enterprise |
| TDF | transborder data flow |
| TISA | Trade in Services Agreement |
| TPO | trade promotion organization |
| TPP | Trans-Pacific Partnership |
| UNCTAD | United Nations Conference on Trade and Development |
| UPU | Universal Postal Union |
| WTO | World Trade Organization |

# OVERVIEW

## Digital technologies are changing the economy, with implications for development

The world is on the cusp of a new digital era. With dramatically reduced costs of collecting, storing and processing data, and greatly enhanced computing power, digitalization is transforming economic activities around the world. It is expected to affect value chains, skill requirements, production and trade, and will require adaptations of existing legal and regulatory frameworks in various areas. This has major implications for the implementation of the 2030 Agenda for Sustainable Development, presenting significant opportunities, but also challenges, for developing countries. The *Information Economy Report 2017* examines the evolution of the digital economy and its potential consequences for trade and development. Although the speed of digital transformation differs among countries, all of them will need to adapt policies in several areas.

The report shows that the digital economy is creating new opportunities for trade and development. It is helping smaller businesses and entrepreneurs in developing countries to connect with global markets more easily, and is opening up new ways of generating income. Information and communication technologies (ICTs), e-commerce and other digital applications are being leveraged to promote entrepreneurship, including the empowerment of women as entrepreneurs and traders, and to support productive activities, decent job creation, creativity and innovation. Furthermore, mobile and digital solutions are contributing to facilitating greater financial inclusion. And small firms in developing countries with sufficient connectivity may be able to access various cloud services and obtain crowd finance in online platforms.

However, such development gains are far from automatic, and there are certain development challenges associated with the evolution of digitalization. Many developing countries, especially the least developed countries (LDCs), are inadequately prepared to capture the many opportunities emerging as a result of digitalization. Moreover, there is a risk that digitalization will lead to increased polarization and widening income inequalities, as productivity gains may accrue mainly to a few, already wealthy and skilled individuals. Winner-takes-all dynamics are typical in platform-based economies, where network effects benefit first movers and standard setters. Indeed, the world's top four companies by market capitalization are all closely linked to the digital economy: Apple, Alphabet (Google), Microsoft and Amazon.com. There are also concerns over how data flows can be harnessed while at the same time addressing concerns related to privacy and security.

The rapid pace at which the digital economy is evolving is a result of the technologies and innovations that were developed over several decades and that are becoming more pervasive. High-speed broadband access to increasingly powerful computing and storage capacity, and drastically reduced costs of ICT equipment and data management, have facilitated the process of digitalization. Key technologies underpinning the evolving digital economy include advanced robotics, artificial intelligence, the Internet of Things (IoT), cloud computing, big data analytics and three-dimensional (3D) printing.

## The digital economy is evolving fast but at very different speeds

The digital economy is expanding in several ways. Global production of ICT goods and services now amounts to an estimated 6.5 per cent of global gross domestic product (GDP), and some 100 million people are employed in the ICT services sector alone. Exports of ICT services grew by 40 per cent between 2010 and 2015. Worldwide e-commerce sales in 2015 reached $25.3 trillion, 90 per cent of which were in the form of business-to-business e-commerce and 10 per cent in the form of business-to-consumer (B2C) sales. UNCTAD estimates that cross-border B2C e-commerce was worth about $189 billion in 2015, which corresponds to 7 per cent of total B2C e-commerce. Sales of robots are at the highest level ever, worldwide shipments of three-dimensional printers more than doubled in 2016, to over 450,000, and are expected to reach 6.7 million in 2020. And by 2019, the volume of global Internet traffic is expected to increase 66 times from what it was in 2005.

At the same time, monitoring the digital divide remains important. Although the number of Internet users grew by 60 per cent between 2010 and 2015, more than half of the world's population remains offline. Broadband connectivity in developing countries, when available, tends to be relatively slow and expensive, limiting the ability of businesses and people to use it productively. Only 16 per cent of the world's adult population uses the Internet to pay bills or purchase items. And while more than 70 per cent of the population in several developed countries already buys goods and services online, the equivalent share in most LDCs is less than 2 per cent. Meanwhile, most micro, small and medium-sized enterprises (MSMEs) in developing countries are ill-prepared to take advantage of the digital economy, and may thereby miss opportunities to boost their productivity and competitiveness. Small firms generally use the Internet much less than large ones for selling online. Only 4 per cent of all 3D printers are used in Africa and Latin America, and the use of robots is also very limited in most developing countries, with the exception of some countries in Asia where they are used quite extensively. As the digital economy evolves further, there is a greater need to ensure that as many people and businesses in developing countries as possible are able to engage in and benefit from it.

### The digital economy is transforming trade, jobs and skills

Digital technologies have a bearing on the prospects for MSMEs, especially those in developing countries, to participate in global trade. They allow enterprises to cut costs, streamline supply chains and more easily market products and services worldwide. Increased trade at reduced costs can have positive spillovers effects on the economy as a whole, for example through enhanced competition, productivity and innovation, as well as improved access to talents and skills. But to derive such benefits from digitalization, MSMEs will need to overcome various barriers.

Many small firms in developing countries remain limited in their digital involvement in relevant value chains, reflecting inadequate connectivity, limited awareness of the benefits of digitalization, skills gaps and other barriers. It will be important for digital systems to be designed in ways that facilitate the effective integration of smaller firms in value chains. The use of online platforms is growing, especially in sectors facing strong global competition and involving many buyers and sellers. Smaller producers are more likely to benefit from participating in global platforms if they serve a well-defined niche market rather than competing in mass markets.

The evolving digital economy has been accompanied by the rise of "trade in tasks" mediated by online labour platforms. This is creating new income-generating opportunities for people in developing countries who have adequate connectivity and relevant skills. These platforms are enabling web designers, coders, translators, marketers, accountants and many other types of professionals to sell their services to clients abroad. Annually, some 40 million users access these platforms looking for jobs or talent. However, at the same time, a large oversupply of job-seekers on such platforms may weaken their bargaining power, and thus may create tendencies towards a race to the bottom in terms of wages and other working conditions. Some experts caution against the risk of "cloud work" and "gig work" leading to the commodification of work. Further research and policy dialogue will be important to ensure that this expanding segment of the economy provides quality and decent jobs.

Increased digitalization and automation is leading to new types of jobs and employment, changing the nature and conditions of work and altering skills requirements, as well as affecting the functioning of labour markets and the international division of labour. The ability of countries and enterprises to exploit new digital resources will become a key determinant of competitiveness. The overall effects of digitalization remain uncertain; they will be context-specific, differing greatly among countries and sectors. This makes it increasingly important for countries to ensure they have an adequate supply of skilled workers with strong cognitive, adaptive and creative skills necessary for "working with the machines".

### Rapid technological change presents a multifaceted policy challenge covering many areas

Policymakers are facing a bold task in keeping up with the rapid pace of technological change amidst a high degree of uncertainty about the shape of the future. The policy challenge is also contextual, varying greatly in terms of countries' readiness to engage in and benefit from the digital economy, with LDCs being the least prepared. For these countries, formulating relevant policies and implementing adequate measures will be particularly important, not least to avoid falling behind even further as the digital economy evolves, as well as to seize new opportunities. Countries also vary in their capacity to formulate, implement and monitor policies related to the digital economy. Ensuring that no one is left behind in the digital economy therefore necessitates a much expanded global effort to provide adequate support to these countries in particular.

The policy challenge is multifaceted. First, there is a wide spectrum of policy areas that should be addressed in a holistic manner, such as infrastructure, education and skills development, the labour market, competition, science, technology and innovation and fiscal issues, as well as trade and industrial policies. This requires effective cross-sectoral collaboration both within the government and with other stakeholders. Governments should seek to seize opportunities presented by the digital economy in support of relevant sustainable development objectives. Coordinating cross-sectoral policies is challenging for any country, but especially for those with very limited resources. Second, in order to formulate evidence-based policies and strategies, there is a need to help developing countries, and especially LDC, build their capacity for collecting more and better data on relevant aspects of the digital economy. Third, formulating policies for the digital economy is most urgently needed for those countries that currently are at a relatively low level of readiness to engage in it, and have limited experience with digitalization.

The *Information Economy Report 2017* touches upon a number of policy areas, one of which relates to connectivity. In many developing countries, adequate and affordable ICT connectivity is still insufficient for MSMEs to compete effectively online. Policy measures needed to address this situation, both at the national and international level, include efforts to ensure that policy frameworks and regulations secure an open, transparent and fair telecommunications market to attract additional investment. Measures to make broadband use more affordable include infrastructure sharing, effective spectrum management and the avoidance of high taxes and import duties on telecom/ICT equipment and services.

Another critical area concerns education and training. All countries will need to adjust their education and training systems to deliver the skills required in the digital economy. This is vital not only for young people entering the labour market, but also for existing workers who need to be retrained and prepared for a future of lifelong learning that equips them for jobs and provides skills flexibility and adaptability. Priorities may vary by country. For instance, LDCs may need to focus on promoting digital literacy among a growing number of students and workers, as well as on building a base of ICT specialists. Policies should also

expand the opportunities for workers and teachers to upgrade their skills, promote alternative means of developing non-cognitive skills, adapt teaching methodologies and capabilities, and seek to make future skills more attractive to students and workers. In addition, attention should be given to the social and political dimension of technological change, innovation and job creation. Proactive redistribution policies could help mitigate the risk of increased polarization and income inequality. Social protection systems that support workers when they are between jobs or not working regularly are currently available only to about a quarter of the world's population.

Countries should also explore ways to integrate digital solutions in export promotion. In most countries, current export and trade promotion and capacity-building efforts are insufficiently adapted to help MSMEs engage in the digital economy Trade promotion organizations (TPOs) should embed digital tools in their services offered to small businesses. For instance, online platforms could be better leveraged to present businesses internationally and reach desired communities, as well as to facilitate data collection and analysis, and assess customer needs. With the growing importance of online marketing channels, there should be a greater use of e-market solutions and social media platforms in events or trade shows, and in other efforts to facilitate e-commerce. Public-private partnerships (PPPs) can be useful in such a context.

Policymakers need to deepen their understanding of the issues at the interface of trade logistics, digitalization and e-commerce. An increasing number of products are delivered digitally, rather than physically, and the expansion of e-commerce in physical products implies rapid growth in shipments of small parcels and low-value goods, sometimes referred to as a "tsunami of parcels". Policymakers should explore and harness relevant opportunities to embrace cross-border e-commerce, and create conditions (e.g. alignment of standards), procedures and resources that would enable e-commerce to thrive, keeping in mind the best interests of MSMEs. New technologies may help overcome some logistical bottlenecks. For example, they can help navigate traffic by calculating the fastest routes or identifying the most fuel/time-efficient pick-ups. Trade facilitation experts and city planners may leverage 3D printing in order to reduce the need for long-distance transportation of final products.

The digital economy relies increasingly on the generation, storage, processing and transfer of data, both within and across national boundaries. Access to data and its analysis are becoming strategically important to enhance the competitiveness of companies across sectors. Policymakers need to balance the need for companies to collect and analyse data for innovation and efficiency gains, on the one hand, and the concerns of various stakeholders with respect to security, privacy, and movement and ownership of data, on the other. In this context, they should work nationally, together with industry and consumer groups, as well as internationally. The current system for data protection is fragmented, with varying global, regional and national regulatory approaches. In addition, many developing countries still lack legislation in this area altogether. Instead of pursuing multiple initiatives, it would be preferable for global and regional organizations to concentrate on one unifying initiative or a smaller number of initiatives that are internationally compatible.

As trade in both goods and services is increasingly affected by digitalization and conducted over the Internet, it becomes important for trade policymakers to factor in how the Internet itself is governed and operated. The way in which trade policies are developed differs greatly from the manner in which Internet policies are governed. While the former involves State-to-State negotiations in closed rooms, Internet governance is characterized by multi-stakeholder dialogues in open settings. This report highlights different options for trade policymakers to engage with actors in the Internet community to ensure that future agreements influencing trade in the digital economy are operationally feasible and politically sustainable.

## International support and collaboration on a massive scale is needed

To prevent the evolving digital economy from leading to widening digital divides and greater income inequalities, and to ensure that more people and enterprises in developing countries have the capacity to participate effectively in it, the international community will need to expand its support on a massive scale. The current level of support is unsatisfactory. Indeed, the share of ICT in total aid for trade declined from 3 per cent in 2002–2005 to only 1.2 per cent in 2015. Proactive efforts are therefore warranted. One way to capitalize on existing knowledge and maximize synergies with partners is to tap into UNCTAD's *eTrade for All* initiative. UNCTAD has also launched a project to help LDCs assess their readiness to engage in and benefit from e-commerce and other activities in the digital economy. This will also help them identify areas in which targeted support is needed the most.

Given the transformative impact of the digital economy, both developed and developing countries will be looking for ways to adapt their policies and strategies. In this context, it is important to avoid reinventing the wheel, where possible. Instead, countries should seek to collaborate and exchange experiences about both the benefits they have reaped from digitalization and the costs and problems encountered. It is expected that the new UNCTAD Intergovernmental Group of Experts on E-Commerce and the Digital Economy will provide a valuable forum for member States to engage in such multilateral policy discussions and to explore good practices in relevant policy domains.

# AN EVOLVING DIGITAL ECONOMY

The role of information and communications technologies (ICTs) in the implementation of the 2030 Agenda for Sustainable Development is gaining importance. With reduced costs of collecting, storing and processing data, and greatly enhanced computing power, digitalization is transforming more and more economic activities around the world. However, the pace at which the digital economy is evolving varies considerably. Some countries have quickly embraced digital technologies, but most of them lag far behind in their readiness to engage in the digital economy.

Although the speed of digital transformations differs, they present both opportunities and risks for countries at all levels of development. The impacts depend on the readiness of countries, enterprises and people to take advantage of digitalization. This chapter provides an introduction to some of the main features of the evolving digital economy and its development implications, and offers a roadmap to the remainder of the Report.

# AN EVOLVING DIGITAL ECONOMY

## Opportunities

**Empowerment of women**

**Greater participation in global market & value chains**

Small businesses access to export markets

Financing & business information

**New digital era**

The digital evolution has major implications for the implementation of **the 2030 Agenda for Sustainable Development**

**The impacts depend on:**
- ▶ the readiness of countries
- ▶ the enterprises and people to take advantage of digitalization

## Risks

**Widening digital divides** with increased income inequality

**Elimination of jobs** and tasks due to **automation**

**Consumer protection, data privacy & cybercrime**

## Key technologies
underpinning the evolving digital economy

The ability to exploit the new technologies will increasingly:

**drive competitiveness**

**bring more benefits** from the digital economy

**Robotics**

**Artificial Intelligence**

**Internet of Things (IoT)**

**Cloud computing**

**Big data analytics**

**3D printing**

**More analysis & dialogue needed**
Uncertainty associated with the next digital shift calls for more analysis, more dialogue and more action by all relevant stakeholders.

## A. THE EVOLVING DIGITAL ECONOMY MATTERS FOR DEVELOPMENT

The world economy is increasingly affected by digital technologies, with potentially profound disruptions to industrial organization, skills development, production and trade, and will thus require appropriate regulatory frameworks. In its '*Overall Review of the implementation of the Outcomes of the World Summit on the Information Society*', the General Assembly of the United Nations committed to harnessing the potential of ICTs to achieve the 2030 Agenda for Sustainable Development, noting that ICTs could accelerate progress across all 17 Sustainable Development Goals (SDGs).[1] Different ICTs and the digitalization of economic activities are of direct relevance to several of these goals, as highlighted in various reports.[2]

Digitalization of economic activities and transactions can help to overcome certain barriers to more inclusive development. For example, ICTs, e-commerce and other digital applications can be leveraged to promote entrepreneurship – including the empowerment of women as entrepreneurs and traders (SDG 5, target b) – productive activities, creativity and innovation, as well as the creation of decent jobs. They can also encourage the formalization and growth of micro, small and medium-sized enterprises (MSMEs), including through access to ICT-enabled financial services (SDG 8, target 3). Digital solutions can be leveraged to increase access by MSMEs in developing countries to financial services (online and mobile payments) and markets (e.g. leveraging virtual marketplaces), and enable their integration into value chains (SDG 9, target 3). Moreover, e-commerce will become increasingly important for achieving SDG 17, target 11 – to significantly increase the exports of developing countries, and to double the share of global exports of the least developed countries (LDCs) by 2020.

Unsurprisingly, the impact of digitalization on economies and societies is the focus of several international policy dialogues and processes. UNCTAD Member States, at the Ministerial Conference in July 2016, decided to set up an Intergovernmental Group of Experts on E-Commerce and the Digital Economy, and the Group of 20 (G-20) issued a Digital Economy

Ministerial Declaration in April 2017.[3] E-commerce and digital trade also feature in discussions related to the Ministerial Conference of the World Trade Organization (WTO) to be held in December 2017. More broadly, e-commerce and e-business remain central aspects of the follow-up to the World Summit on the Information Society.[4]

A major concern is the prevalence of various "digital divides" in both access and use of ICTs, notably between the rich and poor (across and within countries), between urban and rural areas, as well as by gender (see chapter II). Significant variations in the readiness of countries to take part in and benefit from the digital economy enhance the risk of these gaps widening, and of greater income inequality. Among the LDCs, only one in six people currently use the Internet, and digital exclusion remains a reality.

Nonetheless, high-speed broadband access to increasingly powerful computing and storage capacity, as well as drastically reduced costs of ICT equipment and data management, are fostering the growth of the digital economy. And this has direct and indirect positive and negative consequences for countries at all levels of development. The next section highlights some of the key technologies driving the evolving digital economy.

## B. KEY TECHNOLOGIES UNDERPINNING THE DIGITAL ECONOMY

There is no widely accepted definition of the "digital economy", but Bukht and Heeks (2017) have developed a useful approach. This distinguishes between core, narrow and broad scopes (figure I.1). The core and narrow scopes relate to the ICT producing sector, and encompass various digital services (e.g. outsourced call centre services) and platform economy services (e.g. Facebook and Google). The broad scope includes the use of various digital technologies for performing activities such as e-business, e-commerce, automation and artificial intelligence (AI) (referred to collectively as the "algorithmic economy"), the "sharing economy" (e.g. Uber and Airbnb) and online labour platforms (e.g. Upwork and Amazon Mechanical Turk). All these aspects are discussed in this Report.

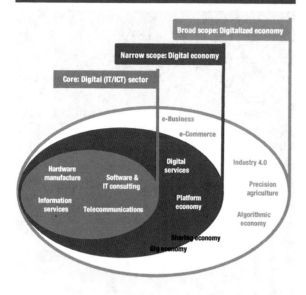

**Figure I.1.    A representation of the digital economy**

Broad scope: Digitalized economy

Narrow scope: Digital economy

Core: Digital (IT/ICT) sector

e-Business

e-Commerce

Hardware manufacture

Software & IT consulting

Information services

Telecommunications

Digital services

Platform economy

Industry 4.0

Precision agriculture

Algorithmic economy

Sharing economy

Gig economy

*Source:* Bukht and Heeks, 2017: 13.

This evolving digital economy is the result of the development and adoption of new technologies and innovations over several decades. The major landmarks include the arrival of mass market personal computers (PCs) in the mid-1980s, the maturing of digital design tools and robotized manufacturing equipment in the 1990s, the boom in outsourcing and offshoring in the 2000s, and the growing ability of multinational enterprises (MNEs) to better use what were once disparate corporate information technology (IT) systems, and improve interoperability and coordination. Today, supply-chain integration is taking place as part of the development of digital business systems, though at a relatively slow pace in many developing countries (see chapter III). The "third industrial revolution," based on ICTs, set the stage for the fourth revolution.

This latest revolution is emerging from a combination of technologies, which are becoming more pervasive across mechanical systems, communications and infrastructure. An expanding variety of ICT devices, and especially software, have become increasingly important in manufacturing, services, transportation and even agriculture (e.g. precision farming).[5] The underlying technologies and processes have far-reaching implications for the organization of work, production and trade, extending existing organizational and geographic fragmentation into knowledge-intensive business functions and job categories (chapters III and IV). For global manufacturing

firms, digitalization is influencing all segments of the supply chain, from inbound logistics and supplier management to internal processes and customer management (UNCTAD, 2017b). The full impact of the digital economy will only be apparent if and when all these features mature, and become integrated and widely used. However, various factors, such as data security risks, data localization pressures, as well as data collection and privacy concerns, may significantly slow down its development.

The following subsections examine key technologies that are underpinning the evolving digital economy. They include advanced robotics, artificial intelligence (AI), the Internet of Things (IoT), cloud computing, big data analytics, three-dimensional (3D) printing and electronic payments. While most developing countries are at a very early stage in their use of these technologies, it is important for them to gain a better understanding of their possible implications. Furthermore, several of these technologies are being tapped to support efforts to achieve the SDGs.

## 1.    Advanced robotics

Industrial robots have been available for decades, but only recently have they become more sophisticated, agile and flexible. The mass production revolution of the early twentieth century brought in dedicated machines for repeated operations. Over time, the flexibility and speed of industrial robots and computer numerically controlled (CNC) machinery have increased and the costs have declined. Today, machinery can rely on relatively simple algorithms to adjust production processes automatically. With the rise in affordable computing power and the advent of low-cost sensor technology, the collection and sharing of operational data within and even across factories have made "predictive maintenance" possible, thus preventing processing errors or machine breakdowns.

As robots become smarter and more agile, the scope for digital automation is enhanced. Robots might replace some work previously undertaken by people, but they may also work alongside workers to increase their efficiency and assist them. Through AI or machine-learning algorithms, robots are becoming increasingly sophisticated, with the ability to make "predictions and decisions in an increasingly automated way, and at large scale" (Brynjolfsson, 2016). While the implications are hard to predict, the trend towards automation and robotization is giving rise to various concerns, not least about the impact on jobs and skills (see chapter IV).

## 2. Artificial intelligence

Artificial intelligence refers to the capability of machines to imitate intelligent human behaviour. This may involve performing various cognitive tasks, such as sensing, processing oral language, reasoning, learning, making decisions, and demonstrating an ability to manipulate objects accordingly (OECD, 2016a). Intelligent systems combine big data analytics, cloud computing, machine-to-machine (M2M) communication and IoT in order to operate and learn (OECD, 2015). With AI software, robots can behave more and more independently from the decisions of their human creators and operators.

Currently, AI is confined to relatively narrow, specific tasks, far from the kind of general, adaptable intelligence that humans possess. But the importance of AI is expanding in the world, and is already incorporated into many products and services – from online search and translation services to real-time traffic predictions and use in self-driving cars. There is wide scope for applying AI to supporting achievements of the SDGs. For example, IBM is using its AI solution, Watson, to address development challenges in Africa in the areas of agriculture, health care, education, energy and water through the Project Lucy initiative.[6]

## 3. Internet of Things: From embedded sensors to smartphones

The Internet of Things (IoT) concerns the extension of connectivity beyond people and organizations to objects and devices (UNCTAD, 2015a). Today, sensors are being embedded at low cost not only in robots and production equipment, but also in operator wearable devices, industrial vehicles, buildings, pipelines and household appliances. This has been made possible by the falling prices of sensors that can continuously transmit small volumes of data with very low power requirements (Kshetri, 2017). Wireless transmission allows remote devices to easily link to larger systems.[7] Since data are collected continuously in real time, from multiple sources and in multiple points in the system, vast amounts of data can be accumulated.

IoT devices are sending information to be stored and processed in the cloud, and they are streamlining processes and information flows. Estimates suggest some 25 billion IoT devices may be deployed by 2020

(ITU and CISCO, 2016). Most investment in IoT will be in the manufacturing sector, which is expected to reduce costs as a result of increased efficiencies and better risk management (Deloitte, 2014). Sensors and global positioning system (GPS) tracking will enable "real-time monitoring of the [movement] of physical objects from an origin to a destination across the entire supply chain including manufacturing, shipping, distribution, and so on" (Xu et al., 2014: 2238).

The Internet Society (2015b: 62) notes several ways in which IoT can support sustainable development:

> The application of sensor networks to environmental challenges, including water quality and use, sanitation, disease, and health, climate change, and natural resource monitoring, could have significant impact beyond resource management. The data derived from such applications also could be used in research contexts, assisting local scientists and universities in making unique contributions to the broader body of global scientific knowledge and providing an incentive for local academic talent to stay in country to conduct research.

Thus, digital technologies, such as IoT, and the data obtained from their use, can provide new sources of knowledge, innovation and profits *if* utilized correctly and effectively. However, there are also trade-offs from these developments. For example, companies and product designers want consumers to make use of the technologies in order to be able to collect very detailed information about their preferences and interests, what they buy and do, and where and when. This allows the companies to innovate and offer new, better and/or more customized products and services. But at the same time, watchdogs, regulators and consumers are concerned about the implications for security, privacy and the use of personal information, sometimes without the consumers' knowledge or consent, or for purposes they may not have intended or to which they may not have consented (box I.1).

| Box I.1. | **Privacy and security concerns related to the Internet of Things** |
| --- | --- |

The use of IoT devices raises particular privacy and security issues. They silently listen, watch and record location and activity in the household, the workplace, and/or in public places to assist individuals with their lives or help companies or governments improve their goods or services or tailor advertisements. This information gathering poses risks for individual privacy if the information is misused or falls into the wrong hands. Even devices that communicate data about machines, such as information about the operation of an engine for diagnostic purposes, might betray personal information, such as what time of day a car is used and where it is driven. The absence of a traditional user interface in many IoT devices means that the usual process of notice and choice is often unavailable (Peppet, 2014).

Internet-enabled devices also raise security concerns. Because they collect sensitive information and are increasingly embedded in our surroundings, they may be an attractive target for people with malicious intent, either to gather information illegally or for unlawful use, or to manipulate the devices (e.g. the brakes or steering of a car). Competition to sell IoT devices quickly and cheaply, and to allow easy set-up, may mean that producers do not pay sufficient attention to security aspects when the device is delivered. This means that IoT devices sometimes lack easy processes to update software to patch up security vulnerabilities as they are discovered.[a] In 2016, for example, hackers exploited the security vulnerabilities of Internet-enabled home cameras and other IoT devices to deliver a distributed denial-of-service attack that temporarily slowed down much of the Internet in the United States (Shackelford et al., 2017).[b]

*Source:* UNCTAD.

[a]  The United States Federal Trade Commission (2015:ii) has noted that IoT presents a variety of security risks by: "(1) enabling unauthorized access and misuse of personal information; (2) facilitating attacks on other systems; and (3) creating risks to personal safety".

[b]  See also "A new era of internet attacks powered by everyday devices", *New York Times*, 23 October 2016.

## 4.  From mainframes to cloud computing

The shift towards cloud computing can be seen as a step change in the relationship between telecommunications, businesses and society as a result of massively enhanced processing power, data storage and higher transmission speeds, accompanied by sharp price reductions (UNCTAD, 2013a). For example, the average cost of a hard drive with 1 gigabyte storage capacity fell from more than $400,000 in 1980 to $0.02 in 2016.[8] In simple terms, this enables users to access a scalable and elastic pool of data storage and computing resources as and when required. Cloud computing often involves transferring data and computing to a server controlled by a third party.

The externalization and aggregation of computing resources and data storage in the cloud are essential aspects of the evolving digital economy. The cloud allows data to be pooled and analysed in vast quantities. It also reduces the costs to small businesses of accessing IT hardware and software, and precludes the need for developing IT skills in-house. In terms of globalization, cloud solutions provide a more convenient way for firms to integrate their operations and management into applications available across multiple sites and devices. The advantage of the cloud is evidenced by the ever increasing flow of data entering the cloud each day. However, as in the case of IoT, a growing reliance on cloud computing and data is prompting fears over security, privacy, movement and ownership of user data (UNCTAD, 2016a). It can also give the companies that control the data considerable market power, causing concerns about potential market dominance.

## 5.  Big data analytics: Making sense of chaos

A truly novel aspect of the digital economy is the aggregation of large amounts of data in the cloud.[9] Digitalization allows data to flow from all corners of industry and society, not only from sensors built into production lines, but also from electric meters, security cameras, customer service call logs, online clicks, point-of-sale registers, status updates on social media, and post reactions (such as "likes"). Access to and analyses of data are becoming crucial for the competitiveness and expansion of companies across sectors. Manufacturers and exporters increasingly depend on data analytics, not only because they have digitized their operations, but also because they use support services that require access to data, such as shipping and logistics, retail distribution and finance. This makes the handling of data an economy-wide concern.

Big data is a radically new resource that is opening new doors for analysis, value creation and the application of AI (Loebbecke and Picot, 2015; Kenney and Zysman, 2015). It can be "mined" for insights that enable data-driven decision making (Brynjolfsson, 2016) by businesses, government agencies, and any person or organization with access to the data and the means to carry out further analysis. It can lead to new levels of understanding of business and social dynamics.

There are different ways in which big data can support sustainable development, especially when combined with mobile technologies (Kshetri et al., 2017). In sub-Saharan Africa, for instance, large sets of data on soil characteristics are mined to help determine fertilizer needs and increase productivity.[10] Bridge International Academies, with a presence in several developing countries, utilizes big data and algorithms to enhance early childhood and primary education.[11] With cloud-based (on-demand) services, data gathering and analysis are becoming more affordable. Even small companies can rent cloud-based, pay-per-use data services, instead of having to buy expensive hardware and software systems and hiring in-house data analysts.

However, beyond having access to adequate connectivity and competitive prices, the right skills are needed in order to be able to derive development benefits from mining big data. Data scientists and data engineers, data architects and data visualization specialists must also be business savvy to help enterprises capture business opportunities from the analyses obtained (chapter IV). At the same time, there is a need to address concerns (noted earlier) relating to data privacy, data ownership and security.[12]

## 6. Three-dimensional printing

Three-dimensional (3D) printing is expected to significantly alter production and trade patterns. With software guiding the printing process, 3D printing makes it possible for items to be made when and where they are needed. 3D printers layer only as much material as is needed. This "additive manufacturing" process contrasts with the old, "subtractive" one of cutting, drilling and bashing metals and plastic.[13] The technology is likely to affect international trade, leading to an expansion of trade in designs and software and less trade in final physical products.

Some developing countries are already using 3D printing in manufacturing. In India, for example, the largest two-wheeler maker, Hero MotoCorp, uses 3D printers, robotic arms and computerized warehouses to make almost 7 million motorbikes a year in three factories, with hopes of expanding to 20 world markets by 2020.[14] In Myanmar, some farmers use a 3D printer of the social enterprise, Proximity Designs, to create parts for a sprinkler system and the internal mechanics for a solar pump.[15] And in the United Republic of Tanzania, recycled plastic bottles are being used as the printing material for 3D printers,[16] for example to 3D-print prosthetics.[17]

According to some estimates, 3D printing may generate up to $550 billion in economic gains across industries per year by 2025 (Cohen et al., 2014). The technology has the potential to lower costs of materials, enable rapid prototyping and shorten supply chains; the 3D printing of parts, where they are also assembled into final products, eliminates the time and costs of transportation, distribution and inventory management. By eliminating tooling, the cost for truly customized and extremely low-volume production, including of prototypes, is dramatically lowered. Fast, low-cost prototyping can speed up the innovation process, and also support "on-demand" manufacturing of products for which there is only low or occasional demand. The effects will vary among different industries, but are expected to be the most pronounced in production with materials suitable for additive manufacturing, where economies of scale are low, customization needs are high and automation levels relatively low (Laplume et al., 2016).

There are also a number of challenges. Firstly, to take advantage of 3D printing, countries will need to provide appropriate education in relevant areas of science, technology, engineering and mathematics. Secondly, 3D printing may disrupt traditional manufacturing and reduce the demand for workers in countries with strong manufacturing industries (Lanier, 2014). Thirdly, 3D printing may raise issues related to copyrights, industrial designs, trademarks and patents. There are also questions concerning the appropriate level of protection of intellectual property rights (IPRs) so as not to stifle innovation (Bechtold, 2015). Fourthly, the lack of industry standards is a concern: there are no clear product or safety standards or standards for the materials and testing methods for 3D-printed products. Fifthly, there are concerns about environmental effects from 3D printers, and the risks that 3D printers could be used to produce firearms.[18] As the industry matures, these and other issues could make 3D printable products seem unsafe for consumers, which might curtail their use.

## 7. Digital payment systems

Digital payment systems refer to the use of debit and credit cards, online and mobile payments, and of systems based on distributed ledger technologies, such as blockchain. In general, digital payments make transactions faster, reduce frictions and lower transaction costs, offering productivity gains and enabling firms to engage in trade (David et al., 2003). They free banks and merchants from the financial and non-financial costs of manual acceptance of payments, record keeping, counting, storage, security, delays, transparency of payment tracking, the risk of non-payment at cash-on-delivery, recipient security and transportation of physical currency. They can also help developing-country governments address critical challenges, including tackling black markets and tax avoidance, as well as supporting the financial inclusion of underbanked populations.

The uptake of debit and credit cards as well as innovative online and mobile payment methods has grown over time. In 2014, credit and debit cards accounted for more than half of all e-commerce payments in value terms. However, their share is expected to drop to 46 per cent by 2019, as e-wallets and other alternative payment methods (such as mobile money) gain in importance (WorldPay, 2015). In developed regions, digital payments are dominated by credit and debit cards, followed by e-wallets. In developing countries, by contrast, credit cards are rarely the most important payment method for e-commerce, and the uptake of digital payments is often low.

For example, in Egypt, around 90 per cent of e-commerce transactions are paid by cash-on-delivery,[19] and in LDCs the reliance on cash is even more pronounced (UNCTAD, 2017c and d). In China, the preferred payment method for business to consumer (B2C) e-commerce is Alipay, an escrow-based system used by 68 per cent of all online shoppers in that country. In Kenya, mobile money, or accessing financial services via a mobile telephone, is more commonly used than credit cards for e-commerce, although cash on delivery remains the main method. In a CIGI-IPSOS-UNCTAD global survey of Internet users,[20] 79 per cent of the Kenyan respondents expressed mobile payment as their preferred method of paying for goods and services purchased online.

For cross-border purchases, e-wallets appear to be particularly popular as a method of payment. A 2016 survey of cross-border e-commerce shoppers across 26 countries found that e-wallets (such as PayPal) were the preferred choice for 41 per cent of the respondents, followed by credit cards (33 per cent) and debit card/bank transfer (18 per cent) (International Post Corporation, 2017). A major obstacle to cross-border transactions is the lack of interoperability of payments systems.

In the future, distributed ledger technologies such as blockchain may increasingly be used for cross-border payments. This technology can make online payments safe, and being peer-to-peer, it is less expensive than intermediated payment platforms.[21] While few Internet users currently prefer this method of payment,[22] it is gradually being adopted as it improves security, accelerates settlement, reduces the size of

the minimum viable transaction and executes digitized versions of traditional contracts (so-called "smart contracts").[23] Its properties enable cross-border micro-transactions, including remittances, which would otherwise not be made due to high fixed costs or lack of trust among parties.

## 8. The importance of interoperable systems and platforms

A central feature of the evolving digital economy is the role of interoperable technology systems and platforms. The complexity of the technologies and embedded products and services means that no single company (or country) can control all system elements. Over time, ICTs, including electronic control of mechanical systems, have developed as a set of nested modules and platforms, ranging from discrete functional elements (modules) to high-level tools, hardware systems and software environments (technology systems), upon which developers can create a variety of higher level goods and services for end users (product platforms) (figure I.2). And because system elements can be altered and upgraded without the need to redesign the entire ecosystem, there is no apparent limit to the depth or complexity of the digital economy. A given product platform, such as a smartphone, which itself has emerged from a complex platform ecosystem, has in turn been harnessed as a mobile platform for the delivery of higher level product platforms, such as mobile social networking and online retail (figure I.3). Platforms are also central to what is referred to as the "sharing economy" (box I.2).

**Figure I.2. Module and platform layering in the digital economy**

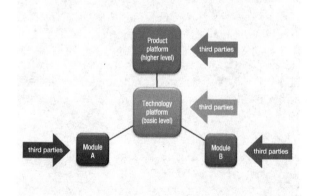

*Source:* UNCTAD, 2017e.

**Figure I.3.    Platforms and interoperable systems in mobile telecommunications**

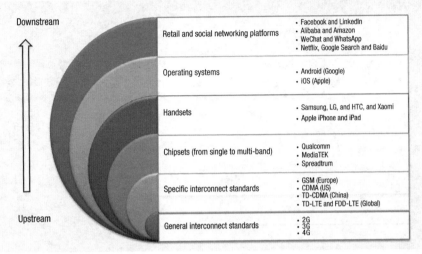

| | |
|---|---|
| Retail and social networking platforms | • Facebook and LinkedIn<br>• Alibaba and Amazon<br>• WeChat and WhatsApp<br>• Netflix, Google Search and Baidu |
| Operating systems | • Android (Google)<br>• iOS (Apple) |
| Handsets | • Samsung, LG, and HTC, and Xaomi<br>• Apple iPhone and iPad |
| Chipsets (from single to multi-band) | • Qualcomm<br>• MediaTEK<br>• Spreadtrum |
| Specific interconnect standards | • GSM (Europe)<br>• CDMA (US)<br>• TD-CDMA (China)<br>• TD-LTE and FDD-LTE (Global) |
| General interconnect standards | • 2G<br>• 3G<br>• 4G |

Downstream → Upstream

*Source:* Thun and Sturgeon, 2017.

**Box I.2.    Platforms and the "sharing economy"**

Most of the so-called services relating to the "sharing economy" use digitally enabled platforms to achieve more efficient utilization ("sharing") of physical assets (e.g. house, car, physical space, machinery, tools, appliances, clothes, shoes, bags/accessories) or time (e.g. for tasks such as cooking, cleaning, assembly of furniture, do-it-yourself jobs or running errands). Generally an exchange of money is involved, and often the creation of some form of employment. To some extent this takes place in the "large" aggregator companies that provide the technologies and the platforms, but also in the "person companies" that they enable (e.g. people renting out their physical assets or selling their time on demand).

These digital platforms – often accessed through mobile apps – bring together and aggregate demand and supply in ways that were not possible before (being faster, cheaper and more easily coordinated), including in geographical areas/service sectors where lower density tended to make this more complicated. They therefore create new business opportunities. Transaction and search costs, as well as "friction" are reduced by connecting those offering assets or services with those wishing to consume them. These platforms are effectively new "market places" that instantaneously match supply and demand on a massive scale, both for location-bound work (e.g. Uber, TaskRabbit) and online location-independent work (e.g. tasks though Upwork or Amazon Mechanical Turk).

*Source:* UNCTAD.

At each level of these ecosystems, third-party vendors provide products and services that allow platforms to be customized and enhanced for different needs and markets. This creates potential market opportunities for those vendors (e.g. the makers of smartphone applications, better known as apps), and also enhances the value of each platform. In turn, it attracts more users to the platform, which then attracts more vendors in what is known as "network effects".[24] The result is a broad ecosystem of overlapping systems and platforms consisting of platform owners and users (Parker et al., 2016). For example, Uber's platform connects drivers to riders, and Amazon connects buyers to product vendors. Whoever controls the platform also controls the distribution channel, and this can give the dominant platform (and data) owner considerable market power. As on 31 March 2017, the world's top companies by market capitalization were Apple, Alphabet (Google), Microsoft and Amazon. com, while Facebook was the sixth largest company.[25]

A look at the locations of headquarters of the top players in the evolving digital economy shows an extremely high level of concentration (figure I.4). Even within North America, a handful of postal codes in and around Silicon Valley in California and Seattle in Washington State, host most of these headquarters (Van Alstyne, 2016). Asia, led by China, follows at a rapidly growing second place. By contrast, companies in Africa and Latin America accounted for less than 2 per cent of the total market capitalization value of digital economy companies, with a market capitalization of more than $1 billion. An UNCTAD analysis of the top MNEs in the world, confirmed the strong geographic concentration of MNEs directly involved in the digital economy or "digital MNEs" (UNCTAD, 2017b): as many as 63 per cent were headquartered in the United States in 2015, compared with only 19 per cent of other top MNEs.[26]

---

**Figure I.4. Geographical concentration of headquarters of "digital MNEs" with a market capitalization of more than $1 billion, by region, 2016**

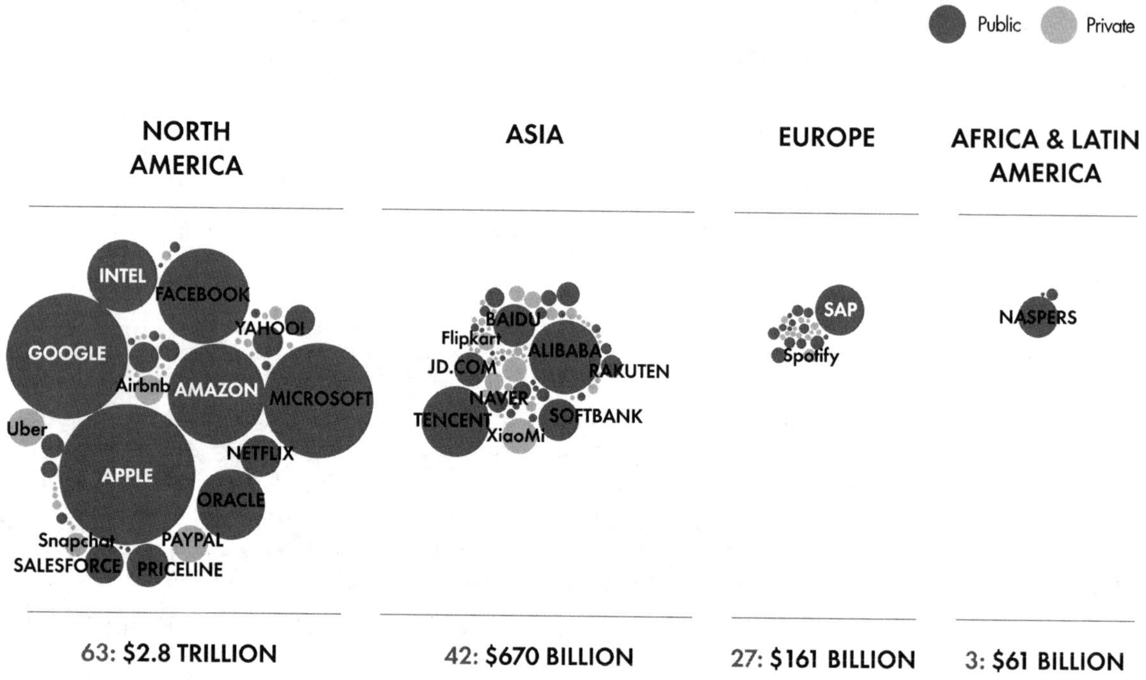

● Public  ● Private

NORTH AMERICA — 63: $2.8 TRILLION

ASIA — 42: $670 BILLION

EUROPE — 27: $161 BILLION

AFRICA & LATIN AMERICA — 3: $61 BILLION

*Source:* Van Alstyne, 2016.
*Note:* Public refers to publicly listed companies. Private refers to privately owned companies.

---

In summary, the evolving digital economy is characterized by the emergence of a platform-based ecosystem of digital products and services that are evolving through a combination of widespread and continuous measurement and data collection by the IoT, data flowing from sensor-laden factory automation systems and ubiquitous, Internet-connected user devices. This is generating "big data" pools that can be mined and analysed for patterns and correlations that would otherwise remain hidden. The results can be fed into systems where machine learning and automated decision-making are used to upgrade system elements and even an entire system. Platforms hosted by players such as Alibaba, Amazon, Apple, Facebook, Google, Microsoft, SAP and others already have big data and AI at the centre of their business models. The capability for analysis will expand when larger swaths of society are connected via the IoT and further improved AI comes into more mainstream use.

The cycle of data streaming from connected factories and users, data pooling in the cloud, big data analysis and machine-learning algorithms will, in turn, generate cycles of platform upgrading and system-level leaps in productivity and innovation. This is especially true if machines make decisions about the structure and operation of the digital economy itself. In such cases, the loop from data generation to machine learning will be completed, and the entire ecosystem of interoperable systems and platforms might leap further ahead (see figure I.5).

The next section discusses possible implications for different stakeholders.

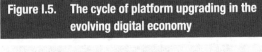

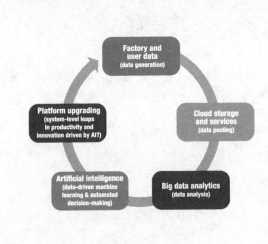

*Source:* UNCTAD, 2017e.

*Note:* The question mark in the platform upgrading box is meant to indicate that autonomous system-level platform upgrading is still speculative and not yet possible in the larger scale systems underpinning the digital economy.

# C. WHO STANDS TO GAIN FROM THE EVOLVING DIGITAL ECONOMY?

These are still early days of the digital economy. Much of the new landscape is yet to take shape or is in the process of being developed, while some digital innovations exist only within the confines of a few high profile companies. In most developing countries, and particularly in the LDCs, the level of digitalization is still very low (chapter II). Nevertheless, it is important to begin assessing possible impacts of the digital economy, and how governments and enterprises may prepare for what is yet to come.

A better understanding of the enabling conditions and implications of digitalization for the economy and society is urgently needed in order to maximize potential benefits and opportunities, and cope with various challenges and costs. Effects from digitally induced transformations will differ between countries at different levels of development, as well as between different stakeholders. For example, it is estimated that as much as two fifths of the economic value from IoT will accrue to developing countries, and that the

greatest benefits will be reaped in cities, worksites, factories and shipping, where there are concentrations of large populations and greater economic growth (McKinsey Global Institute, 2015). Other organizations expect that the development impacts of IoT will be the greatest in health care, water and sanitation, agriculture, livelihoods, climate change and pollution mitigation, natural resource management and energy (ITU and CISCO, 2016).

An optimistic vision of the evolving digital economy might emphasize the ubiquity and democratization of information. It could also highlight the shortening of supply chains with the advent of on-demand manufacturing (e.g. 3D printing). From this perspective, the evolving digital economy could be seen as ushering in a new, equitable and environmentally sustainable growth model based on the maximization of human empowerment and well-being rather than on maximization of profits, and resource extraction and utilization.

Companies that engage in digitalization can make their organizations more efficient, reach and serve customers more easily, speed up product development, and invent products and services at lower cost and without the need for extensive system-level expertise or in-house IT management skills. From a developing-country perspective, small firms and start-ups with sufficient connectivity may be able to access various cloud services to build products and obtain crowd finance in online platforms. With AI built into design software analytical tools for subsequent integrations, business development or customer service, business opportunities could multiply. As such tools can lower the cost of market entry, potential benefits for economic development may increase.

On the other hand, there are concerns that widespread use of new technologies will result in greater job losses, widen existing income inequalities and lead to a further concentration of power and wealth. In countries belonging to the Organisation for Economic Co-operation and Development (OECD), where technology is the most widespread, the income gap between the rich and poor has widened, from 7:1 in the 1980s to 9.5:1 in the early 2000s (OECD, 2014a).

With the increased scope for computerization, automation and the use of AI, more occupations and tasks risk disappearing, even as output and productivity rise and bring relatively greater returns to capital. This could potentially lead to further job losses (*Foreign Affairs*, 2016; see also chapter IV). And the effects of the digital economy may disrupt entire industries. A study of five industries in South-East Asia found that various digital technologies will have disruptive effects on all of them (table I.1).

| Table I.1. | The most disruptive technologies for five sectors in the Association of South-East Asian Nations, 2016 |
|---|---|
| **Sector** | **Main disruptive technologies** |
| **Automotive and auto parts** | Electrification of vehicles and vehicular components |
| | Advancements in lightweight materials |
| | Autonomous driving |
| | Robotic automation |
| **Electrical and electronics** | Robotic automation |
| | 3D printing |
| | Internet of Things |
| **Textiles, clothing and footwear** | 3D printing |
| | Body scanning technology |
| | Computer-aided design (CAD) |
| | Wearable technology |
| | Nanotechnology |
| | Environmentally friendly manufacturing techniques |
| | Robotic automation |
| **Business process outsourcing** | Cloud computing |
| | Software automation |
| | Knowledge process outsourcing |
| **Retail** | Mobile and e-commerce platforms |
| | Internet of Things |
| | Cloud technology |
| | Big data analytics |

*Source:* ILO, 2016.

For consumers, there are also risks to consider. For example, big data and AI could enable instantaneous and/or individualized price discrimination, where prices are adjusted constantly and in real time based on a consumers' behaviour, perceived need for the product or service, and willingness to pay. Analyses of shopping and purchasing histories, in the context of millions of prior purchases from shoppers with similar habits, can give firms a very high level of detailed information that could weaken consumers' bargaining power (Shiller, 2014).

For users of connected applications that send data to higher level platforms, the loss of privacy and bargaining power constitutes another risk. Many smartphone apps – such as easy-to-use map navigation, music streaming services and online purchase and reservations services – have already proved their worth to users. Although many of these services are provided free of charge, consumers end up paying the price of giving firms and apps developers detailed information about their whereabouts, preferences, relationships and personal habits, sometimes unknowingly.

Moreover, as more economic activities go digital, companies, organizations, governments and individuals will need to pay more attention to how they protect their online data and devices. Connecting private communications networks, industrial systems and public infrastructure to the Internet makes them vulnerable to hacking, identity theft or theft of other personal and financial information, larceny, or even industrial espionage and sabotage. Indeed, some companies engaged in advanced manufacturing currently refrain from making connections outside the immediate premises of their factories for fear of data breaches, potentially nullifying the benefits from data sharing and pooling across the larger organization and supply base (Deloitte, 2016). Finding adequate measures to protect against such cyber threats requires shared responsibility among all stakeholders.

Meanwhile, winner-takes-all dynamics seen in platform-based industries (e.g. Google, Uber, Facebook, WeChat), where network effects accrue to first movers and standard setters (Parker et al., 2016), can accentuate polarization in the industrial base. Moreover, a greater ability to exploit new technologies (e.g. collecting and analysing data and turning them into business opportunities) relative to others with access to the same resources and technologies will increasingly drive competitiveness and the benefits accruing from the digital economy (chapter IV).

# D. ROADMAP TO THE REMAINDER OF THE REPORT

The remainder of this report analyses the implications for trade and development in developing countries of the drive towards digitalization of economic activities. From an economic perspective, a number of key policy issues arise, which will influence how different countries, enterprises and people are affected.

Chapter II is devoted to the measurement of the digital economy. It reviews available statistics to shed light on that economy's size and composition. The analysis is constrained by the lack of official statistics in key areas from developing countries, which also represents a major disadvantage for policymakers in these countries. A lack of statistics seriously hampers their ability to design and monitor evidence-based policymaking. The chapter also documents some of the key digital divides that affect the ability of countries and enterprises to engage in and benefit from the evolving digital economy.

Chapter III considers how MSMEs in developing countries may seize opportunities to improve productivity, boost exports and participate in international value chains by leveraging digital technologies. The chapter considers how the use of the Internet and digital solutions can facilitate trade and help to make it more inclusive. It goes on to examine the implications of digital labour platforms that help increase trade in tasks. While this opens up income-generating opportunities for people in developing countries, it also raises concerns of a global race to the bottom.

The chapter also explores a little-researched area: the scope for digitalization to help small enterprises in developing countries participate in global value chains (GVCs) of particular relevance for lower income countries.

Chapter IV focuses on implications for jobs and skills in different countries. It explores what kinds of skills are likely to become more important for individuals and enterprises to enable them to compete in the digital economy. Recent research on the likely impacts of digitalization on the labour market is reviewed.

Chapter V highlights the interface between trade policies and Internet policies. It begins by briefly examining the treatment of e-commerce in international trade agreements. It then turns to the interface between trade policymaking and Internet policymaking in view of the very different cultures characterizing these two domains. It explores possible ways of facilitating more dialogue between trade and internet policy makers in the future.

Chapter VI discusses the cross-cutting policy challenge to reap development gains from trade in a rapidly evolving digital economy. It pays special attention to reducing the divides in the use of digital technologies, to policies that would enable MSMEs to compete better and to trade in the digital economy. The chapter then addresses the policy challenge of ensuring an adequate supply of skills in the digital economy before exploring possible policy responses to an increased reliance on cross-border data flows. The final section looks at the role of capacity-building support from the international community to ensure that no one is left behind in the digital economy.

# NOTES

1   See http://workspace.unpan.org/sites/Internet/Documents/UNPAN96078.pdf .

2   See, for example, Internet Society, 2015a; Sachs et al., 2015; Intel, 2015.

3   See http://unctad.org/meetings/en/Contribution/dtl_eWeek2017c02-G20_en.pdf.

4   See, for example, http://www.itu.int/net/wsis/.

5   See, for example, UNCTAD, 2017a.

6   Source: Neil Sahota, The next frontier is here: 3 key AI capabilities, In: *AI for Social Good: How Artificial Intelligence Can Boost Sustainable Development, ITU News Magazine* (http://www.itu.int/en/itunews/ Documents/2017/2017-01/2017_ITUNews01-en.pdf).

7   See "Here's why some are calling the Internet of Things the next Industrial Revolution, *Business Insider*, 10 February 2016 (http://uk.businessinsider.com/iot-trends-will-shape-the-way-we-interact-2016-1?r=US&IR=T).

8   See http://www.statisticbrain.com/average-cost-of-hard-drive-storage/.

9   The cloud is often used for storage and processing of big data, though not always; many firms run local Hadoop servers to perform analysis.

10  See, for example, "Artificial satellites and helping farmers boost crop yields", *The Economist*, 5 November 2009.

11  See www.bridgeinternationalacademies.com/company/history.

12  See, for example, *Foresight for Digital Development*, Report of the Secretary-General, Economic and Social Council, Commission on Science and Technology for Development, Nineteenth session Geneva, 9–13 May 2016 (E/CN.16/2016/3).

13  See, for example, "The current and future economics of 3D printing and factory production – companies like Zara that leverage new capabilities for new business models", *Next Big Future*, 14 February 2011 (http://www.nextbigfuture.com/2011/02/current-and-future-economics-of-3d.html).

14  See "Hero MotoCorp powers ahead with 3D printing", *ETCIO.com*, 18 February 2015.

15  See "Myanmar farmers reap rewards from 3D printing," *AFP*, 25 December 2015 (http://guardian.ng/technology/ myanmar-farmers-reap-rewards-from-3d-printing/).

16  See "Reflow turns plastic waste into 3D print filament, sends profits back to waste pickers", *Digital Trends*, 4 May 2016 (http://www.digitaltrends.com/cool-tech/reflow-plastic-filament/).

17  See "Kenya based 3D Life Print Project is offering mobile 3D printing of custom prosthetics", *3s Printing Industry. com*, 8 December 2014 (http://3dprintingindustry.com/news/3d-life-print-3d-printing-prosthetics-37698/).

18  See, for example, Azimi et al., 2016, and "US demands removal of 3D printed gun blueprints". *NewEurope*, 10 May 2013 (https://www.neweurope.eu/article/us-demands-removal-3d-printed-gun-blueprints/).

19  UNCTAD field interviews in Cairo.

20  See http://unctad.org/meetings/en/Presentation/dtl_eWeek2017p01_CIGI-IPSOS_en.pdf.

21  It should be noted that the usefulness of distributed ledger technology extends beyond payments. it is a complex technology that developing countries may need to explore further to harness properly. See, for example, https://www.weforum.org/agenda/2017/05/heres-how-blockchain-can-help-the-worlds-poorest-people.

22  See UNCTAD Summary report, E-Commerce Week, Geneva, 24–28 Arpil 2017 (http://unctad.org/meetings/en/ Presentation/dtl_eWeek2017p01_CIGI-IPSOS_en.pdf).

23  See https://cointelegraph.com/news/smart-contracts-separating-ethereum-from-bitcoin.

24  At the most basic "upstream" level in the value chain, calls made from smartphones depend on a set of general interconnection standards (2G, 3G, 4G) that are agreed upon at the industry level and implemented by various consortia and alliances, such as CDMA and GSM (see figure I.3). As mobile handsets have become more complex over time, semiconductor chip sets handle much of the complexity of the system. Handsets depend on these embedded technology standards, just like the providers of retail and mobile services depend on users owning powerful smartphones to access their services.

25  See https://www.pwc.com/gx/en/audit-services/assets/pdf/global-top-100-companies-2017-final.pdf .

26  Digital MNEs include purely digital players that operate in a digital environment, as well as "mixed players" that combine a prominent digital dimension with a physical one (UNCTAD, 2017b: 165).

# MEASURING THE EVOLVING DIGITAL ECONOMY

Reliable measurement of the evolving digital economy is essential for governments to be able to design and implement evidence-based policies. This chapter uses available statistics and data from official and other sources to measure ICT penetration, use, production, employment and trade. The analysis also highlights estimates of more novel features of the digital economy, such as the rise of the sharing economy, 3D printing and robots. It reveals major digital divides and highlights significant gaps in the availability of official statistics, especially in developing countries, indicating a need for a comprehensive effort to help them collect internationally comparable statistics in key areas.[1]

Various metrics confirm that the role of the digital economy is continuing to grow within the global economy. Worldwide, the combined information and communication services and ICT manufacturing sectors is responsible for an estimated 6.5 per cent of global GDP. About 100 million people worldwide are employed in ICT services. ICT services provide relatively well-remunerated employment for women, but the share of women in ICT specialist occupations

remains very low, especially in developing countries. Global e-commerce was estimated at $25 trillion in 2015, up from $16 trillion in 2013. The evolving digital economy is influencing international trade. For example, exports of telecommunications, computer and information services grew by 40 per cent between 2010 and 2015, and amounted to $467 billion, and trade in ICT goods stood at over $2 trillion in 2015. Sales of robots and 3D printers are at their highest level ever and the volume of Internet traffic is expected to be 66 times higher in 2019 that it was in 2005.

At the same time, digital gaps remain and new ones are emerging. For example, more than half of the world's population remains offline and the broadband divide is ever wider. In the case of e-commerce, while more than 70 per cent of people in several developed countries buy goods or services from the Internet, less than 5 per cent do it in most developing countries. Enterprises in developing countries, especially small ones, are not as well positioned as those in developed countries to take advantage of the digital economy, thus missing out of growth opportunities.

# MEASURING THE EVOLVING DIGITAL ECONOMY

**The digital economy is evolving fast....**

**Production of ICT goods and services** **6.5%** of global DGP

**Trade in ICT goods** in 2015 exceeded **$2 trillion**

**100 million** people **are employed in the ICT services sector**

**ICT services exports** rose by **40%** between 2010 and 2015

**Global e-commerce sales:** **$25 trillion** in 2015

**Cross-border B2C e-commerce:** **$7 billion** in 2015

**Global Internet traffic** **66 times higher** in 2019 than in 2015

**Sales of robots** are at the **highest level ever**

Shipments of **3D printers** ×2 in 2016

**380 million** consumers make purchases on overseas websites

**...but at very different speeds**

**Global connectivity gap**

**50%** remains **offline**

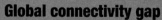

only **1 in 6 in LDCs** is connected

**The gender gap** in Internet use is most pronounced in developing countries

**MSMEs are less prepared** to take advantage of the digital economy

only **16%** of the world's adult population **use the Internet to pay bills**

only **4%** of 3D printers are used in **Africa and Latin America**

# A. ICT ACCESS AND USE BY ENTERPRISES AND INDIVIDUALS

Fundamental indicators of the evolving digital economy are the extent to which enterprises and people have affordable access to relevant ICTs and digital solutions, and whether they make productive use of them. While ICT uptake is improving, the wide variations in the extent to which businesses and individuals are making effective use of ICTs need to be addressed.

## 1. Digital divides remain in several areas

Affordable access to different ICTs is essential for people and enterprises to take active part in the evolving digital economy and reap development gains from it. ICTs are a major means of helping to achieve most of the SDG targets. For many people in developing countries, mobile networks are their only channel of access to the Internet, and mobile phones are key tools for entrepreneurship, empowerment and even financial inclusion (UNCTAD, 2011). Internet use in LDCs is primarily conducted on mobile devices, influencing the scope for and nature of e-commerce (UNCTAD, 2015b). In the context of international trade and development, broadband Internet through third generation (3G) and fourth generation (4G) mobile systems, in particular, is important, because it allows access to more sophisticated and value-added content for the business sector.

Although connectivity has in some respects improved greatly over the past 5–10 years, major gaps still remain: developing countries and LDCs lag behind in terms of fixed-broadband penetration, household access to ICTs and Internet use (figure II.1). In developing countries, while penetration rates of mobile cellular phones reached over 90 per cent, those of mobile broadband were only slightly higher than 40 per cent and those of fixed broadband were still lower than 10 per cent. Moreover, on average, only 40 per cent of people in these countries use the Internet, compared with more than 80 per cent in developed countries.

**Figure II.1.  ICT penetration by level of development, 2016**

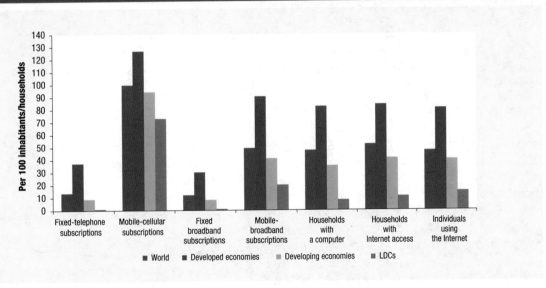

*Source:* ITU, 2016.

*Note:* Data are estimates.

In the LDCs, connectivity has continuously improved over the past decade. Mobile cellular subscriptions, in particular, soared, from an average of only 5 per 100 people in 2005, to as much as 73 in 2016. A number of international initiatives have set targets in relation to connecting the unconnected, particularly in the LDCs. With an estimated 16 per cent of individuals in LDCs using the Internet in 2016, these countries are on track to meet the ITU Connect 2020 Agenda goal of 20 per cent using it by 2020.[2] This is, however, still far from the target of universal access to the Internet set in Goal 9 of the SDGs.[3] In terms of broadband access, LDCs rely almost entirely on mobile networks.

The share of LDCs in global mobile-cellular subscriptions rose from 2 per cent in 2005 to 9 per cent in 2015, but this was still below their 13-per cent share of the world population (figure II.2). Among world Internet users, the LDCs also saw growth, from 0.6 per cent in 2005 to 3.7 per cent in 2015. These positive trends can be contrasted with other socioeconomic areas, such access to electricity and water, where LDCs have continued to fall behind (UNCTAD, 2016b). Indeed, in 2014, their share of people without access to electricity was twice as high as in 1990.

**Figure II.2.    LDCs' shares of world population, of mobile cellular connections and of Internet users, 2005–2015**

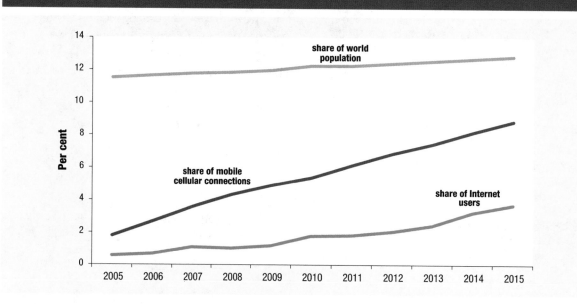

*Source:* UNCTAD based on data from GSMA Intelligence 2017, United Nations Population Fund and ITU *World Telecommunication/ ICT Indicators* databases.

*Note:* Mobile cellular connections refer to SIM cards or phone numbers where SIMs are not used but are registered on a mobile network (GSMA Intelligence, 2017).

Progress in connectivity has been uneven among the LDCs. Between 2012 and 2015, mobile connectivity improved the most in Myanmar, Timor-Leste and Sierra Leone, while other LDCs, including the Central African Republic, Eritrea and South Sudan, have not increased as much. Mobile cellular services in the latter group reach less than a third of the population, and the telecommunications markets are yet to be liberalized. In terms of active mobile broadband subscriptions per 100 people in 2015, the top three LDC performers were Bhutan (56), Cambodia (43) and Vanuatu (41), according to ITU data.

In 2015, developing and transition economies accounted for 70 per cent of the world's Internet users, with the largest number in China and India (figure II.3). Only four developed economies feature among the top ten Internet users. Meanwhile, in Brazil,

India, Mexico and Nigeria, the annual growth rates of Internet use were between 4 and 6 per cent from 2012 to 2015, whereas the growth rates have been much slower in developed economies, except for Japan, as the markets have already reached near saturation.

Nearly 90 per cent of the 750 million people that went online for the first time between 2012 and 2015 were from developing economies, with the largest numbers from India (178 million) and China (122 million) (figure II.4). In many developing countries, nearly half or more of the Internet users went online for the first time in the last three years, as in Bangladesh, India, the Islamic Republic of Iran and Pakistan. In Brazil and China, more than 50 per cent of the population uses the Internet, whereas in India only slightly more than a quarter use it. The next billion Internet users will also be primarily from developing economies.

**Figure II.3. Top 10 economies by number of Internet users in 2015, and growth rates in number of users, 2012–2015**

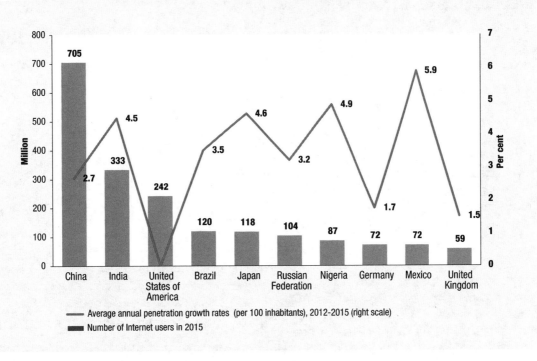

*Source:* UNCTAD based on data from ITU *World Telecommunication/ICT Indicators* database.

**Figure II.4. Top 10 economies by number of people that went online for the first time between 2012 and 2015 (number and percentage share of new users)**

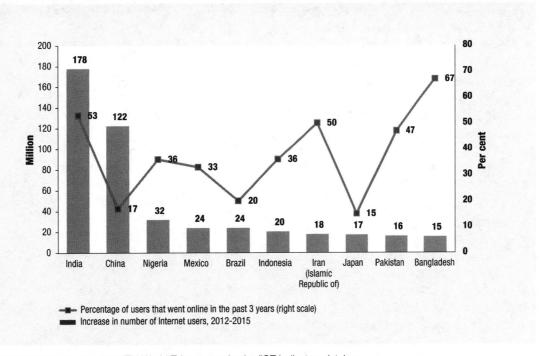

*Source:* UNCTAD based on data from ITU *World Telecommunication/ICT Indicators* database.

Broadband access and use are critical enablers of the digital economy. Despite increased connectivity, broadband use is still very limited in LDCs, where it remains unaffordable for most people. Fixed broadband prices can be three times higher in developing countries than in developed countries, and mobile broadband twice as high (ITU, 2016). In landlocked developing countries, high speed international Internet bandwidth access costs and fixed broadband monthly subscription charges are much higher than in coastal countries located closer to submarine communication cables.[4] In recent years, growth of subscriptions in fixed-broadband has been slower than in mobile broadband in all regions, which raises some concerns with regard to the long-term development of high-capacity networks and services in less developed regions.

The quality of broadband service varies considerably. Download speed, upload speed and latency are quality aspects that affect the use of certain cloud-based applications. For example, small enterprises and other Internet users can make use of basic cloud services, such as webmail and Voice over Internet Protocol (VoIP), which can be used even at relatively low speeds and high latency. By contrast, more advanced services, such as cloud storage, high-definition video streaming and video conferencing, require a higher quality of service provision (UNCTAD, 2013a). Recent research suggests that bandwidth is particularly important for developing countries to boost their trade (Abeliansky and Hilbert, 2017).

In 2015, 69 per cent of the global population was estimated to be covered by 3G mobile broadband, up from 45 per cent in 2011 (ITU, 2015).[5] However, a large divide remains between urban and rural access: 3G networks covered 89 per cent of urban areas, but only 29 per cent of rural areas, and the gap was the most pronounced in low-income countries. Africa is the region with the lowest mobile broadband penetration, but also boasts the highest growth rate of such penetration.

There is a significant gender divide, with an estimated 250 million more men going online than women, and, with few exceptions, the proportion of men using the Internet tends to be higher throughout the world (ITU, 2016). At the global level, the ITU reports an Internet user gender gap of 12 per cent for 2016, the gap being more pronounced in developing countries and especially in the LDCs. Differences in the level of education and school enrolment are important

explanatory factors. Regions with the largest gender gaps in Internet usage are Africa and Asia and the Pacific.

Thus, despite considerable improvements in access to ICTs, significant disparities persist in the use of such technologies, notably broadband. Developing countries, and especially the LDCs, are at a disadvantage in more ways than one. First, broadband penetration is low. Second, even those who have broadband access tend to experience relatively low download and upload speeds, which limit the kind of activities that can be used productively over the Internet. Third, after discounting the differences in gross national income per capita, the use of broadband services tends to be more costly in LDCs and other developing countries than in the more advanced economies. To achieve a more inclusive digital economy, renewed efforts are needed to bridge these divides.

## 2. Business use of ICTs: Small enterprises are lagging behind

There is a growing body of literature on how ICTs can help firms become more efficient and better connected.[6] One important potential impact is increased productivity (UNCTAD, 2015b; Clarke et al., 2015; Pilat, 2005). The operation of markets, including product development, production, business administration and marketing functions can also be impacted. As more and more buyers search the Internet for items they wish to purchase, enterprises increasingly need an online presence to be visible in the market. In Europe, online sales were found to boost enterprises' productivity (UNCTAD, 2015b), and a study for Viet Nam concluded that total factor productivity growth of enterprises that sold online was 1.7 percentage points higher than those that used the Internet but did not sell online (World Bank, 2016a).

Technology use can be measured by indicators such as the availability of computers, Internet and other ICTs in enterprises, as well as by indicators related to the kinds of activities that are performed online. Official data are available for European Union (EU) and OECD countries, and for a small number of developing countries. By contrast, very few low-income countries measure enterprises' use of ICT.

To what extent and for what purpose enterprises are using ICTs vary greatly. In most countries for which data are available, a lower proportion of small enterprises make use of the Internet than large companies. In general, fewer enterprises engage in complex tasks online. For example, enterprises are more likely to use the Internet to obtain information about goods and services, than to deliver products online, which requires adapting their business model to the online world. In countries where ICTs are widely available, more enterprises are likely to perform more complex online tasks. Enterprise size adds to the complexity. A number of countries collect data on enterprises that buy or sell goods and services online (figure II.5). The data show that the share of small firms receiving orders online is consistently lower than that of large firms. Thus, data showing an increase in the overall proportion of businesses that receive orders online does not guarantee that small and medium-sized enterprises (SMEs) are benefiting as much as larger firms.

**Figure II.5.  Proportion of small and large enterprises receiving orders over the Internet, selected countries, latest year**

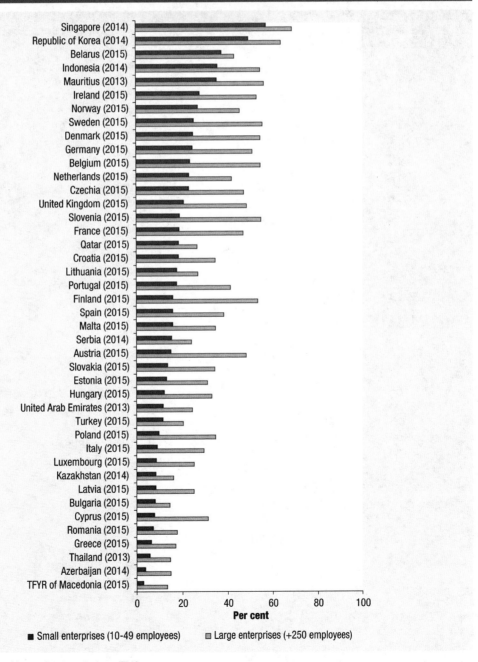

*Source:* UNCTADstat (http://unctadstat.unctad.org/EN/).

### 3. Lack of trust deters household use of ICTs for e-commerce

Surveys of households, individuals and consumers can provide information on Internet and e-commerce use. Eurostat data show that two thirds of Internet users in Europe shopped online in 2016, and the usage rate has been rising steadily, especially among young people.[7] In Denmark, Germany and the United Kingdom more than 80 per cent of Internet users are already buying online. Similar data from some developing countries suggest that the proportion of Internet users that purchase online ranged from below 3 per cent in many LDCs, to 60 per cent in Singapore in 2015.[8]

In developing countries, Internet users have a lower propensity for online shopping than for participation in social networks (figure II.6). This may reflect a combination of a lack of trust in the online environment, limited awareness of e-commerce as well as cultural preferences.

**Figure II.6. Proportion of Internet users purchasing online and participating in social networks, selected countries, 2015**

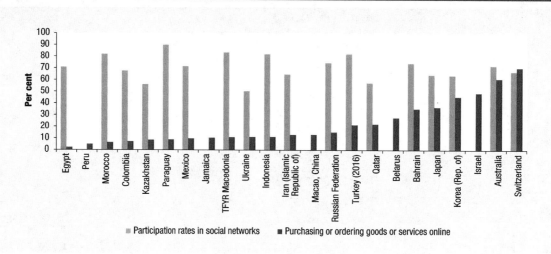

*Source:* Information provided by the ITU.

## B. THE ICT SECTOR

The ICT producing sector is a core element in the digital economy (figure I.1).[9] This section reviews available data to quantify the production side of the digital economy in terms of the measurable monetary value generated by the production of ICT goods and services. It also reports data on employment related to the digital economy. Again, the analysis is constrained by the paucity of data from developing countries.

### 1. Production of ICT goods and services

#### a. Production of ICT services

Data on value added of ICT services (defined as information and communication services) are available for about 65 economies in the United Nations National Accounts database. Based on information for the 10 economies with the largest ICT services production (table II.1), the value added of ICT services is estimated to have been about $3.2 trillion in 2015 (figure II.7). The share of these services in global GDP was relatively stable during the period 2010–2015, at an estimated 4.3 per cent.[10] Table II.1 confirms the prominence of the United States in the production of such services.[11]

#### b. Production of ICT goods

Data on the value added of ICT goods manufacturing[12] are available for certain economic or regional groups, such as the EU[13] and the OECD,[14] as well as for some developing and emerging economies. Table II.2 presents estimates based on official data relating to sales and revenues for the major economies making computer, electronic and optical products in 2014. It suggests that the value added of global production of such ICT goods was about $1.7 trillion,

**Table II.1. Top 10 economies by value added of ICT services, 2015**

|  | Economy | Value added ($ billion) | Share in top 10 (per cent) | Share in GDP (per cent) |
|---|---|---|---|---|
| 1 | United States | 1 106 | 42 | 6.2 |
| 2 | European Union | 697 | 26 | 4.3 |
| 3 | China | 284 | 11 | 2.6 |
| 4 | Japan | 223 | 8 | 5.4 |
| 5 | India | 92 | 3 | 4.5 |
| 6 | Canada | 65 | 2 | 4.2 |
| 7 | Brazil | 54 | 2 | 3.0 |
| 8 | Republic of Korea | 48 | 2 | 3.5 |
| 9 | Australia | 32 | 1 | 2.4 |
| 10 | Indonesia | 30 | 1 | 3.5 |
| **Total for top 10** | | **2 657** | **100** | **4.5** |

*Source:* UNCTAD, based on data from United Nations Statistics division and national statistics.

*Note:* Data refer to International Standard Industrial Classification of All Economic Activities (ISIC) Rev.4 section J, Information and Communication Services. Data are in current prices and converted to United States dollars using annual average exchange rates from mostly national sources.

**Figure II.7. Value added of global ICT services and share in GDP, 2010-2015**

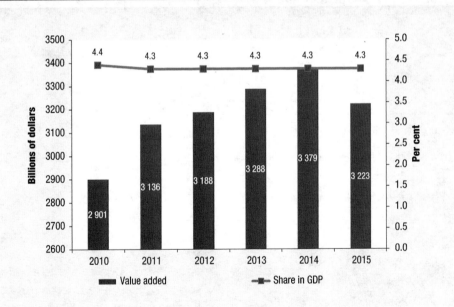

*Source:* UNCTAD, estimated on the basis of the share of global GDP of the economies for which data are available by size of their ICT services.

*Note:* Data refer to ISIC Rev.4 section J, Information and Communication Services. Converted to dollars using annual average exchange rates.

while the revenue generated amounted to about $4 trillion. China was the largest manufacturer by far, its revenues being twice as high as those of the United States. The EU was in third position, followed by five Asian economies. Mexico and Brazil are the only non-Asian developing economies on the list.

Taken together, the value added of computer, electronic and optical products and of ICT services amounted to about $5.1 trillion in 2014, which would be equivalent to about 6.4 per cent of global GDP that year. This is somewhat higher than other recent estimates (Bukht and Heeks, 2017).

| | Economy | Value added ($ billion) | Share in GDP (per cent) | Revenue ($ billion) | Ratio of revenue to value added | Industrial classification (ISIC Rev. 4) |
|---|---|---|---|---|---|---|
| 1 | China | 558* | 5.4 | 1 372 | .. | Communication equipment, computers and other electronic equipment |
| 2 | United States | 267 | 1.5 | 619 | 2.3 | Computer and electronic products |
| 3 | European Union (EU 28) | 135 | 0.7 | 386 | 2.9 | Computer, electronic and optical products |
| 4 | Republic of Korea | 107 | 7.6 | 233 | 2.2 | Manufacture of electronic components, computer, radio, television and communication equipment and apparatuses |
| 5 | Japan | 21 | 0.4 | 82 | 4.0 | Information and communication electronics equipment |
| 6 | Taiwan Province of China | 17 | 3.4 | 25 | 1.4 | Computers, electronic and optical products manufacturing |
| 7 | Malaysia | 17 | 5.0 | 10 | 0.6 | ICT equipment |
| 8 | Singapore | 16 | 5.1 | 66 | 4.2 | Computer, electronic and optical products |
| 9 | Mexico | 9 | 0.7 | 9 | 1.0 | Computer, communication, measurement and other equipment, components and electronic accessories |
| 10 | Brazil | 7 | 0.3 | 37 | 5.3 | Computer, electronic and optical products |
| | **Total for top 10 economies** | **1 154** | **2.2** | **2 691** | **2.5** | |
| | **WORLD** | **1 725** | | **4 024** | **2.3** | |

Table II.2. Top 10 manufacturers of computer, electronic and optical products, 2014

*Source:* UNCTAD, based on national statistics.

*Note:* *Value added for China is estimated based on the average ratio of revenue to value added. World estimates were derived from the share of the leading 10 producers of ICT goods in global GDP.

## 2. ICT-related employment and occupations

Increased use of digital technologies should be reflected in an expansion of ICT-related employment in the economy. Employment in the ICT sector should be distinguished from employment in ICT specialist occupations. The former refers to any employment in enterprises whose main economic activity is to provide ICT services, while the latter relates to specialized jobs that require skills in the production of ICT goods and services (UNCTAD and ILO, 2015). Having a pool of specialized ICT workers is a critical factor in ensuring a country's comparative advantage in the development, installation and servicing of ICTs.[15]

The ILO provides global statistics on employment by industry. However, data availability is limited, including for some large economies. Aggregate data are available only for the transport, storage and communications sector (which includes activities additional to the ICT sector, such as transportation services), which show that total employment in this wider sector has been growing increasingly fast over the past two decades and is expected to continue its upward trend (figure II.8). While it took 16 years (1991–2007) for the sector to grow its share in total employment, from 4 per cent to 5 per cent, it took only 8 years (2007–2015) – half as long – for the share to reach 6 per cent, and forecasts suggest that this new growth pace could be sustained over the next 8 years.

**Figure II.8.  Employment in transport, storage and communications as a share of total employment, 1991–2020**

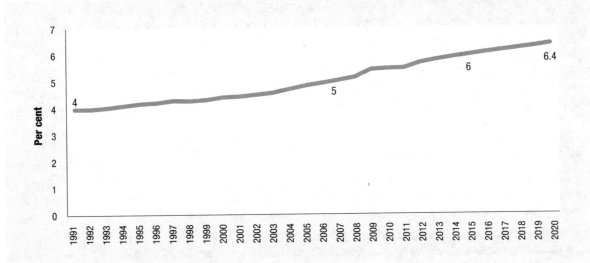

*Source:* UNCTAD, based on data from ILO, *Trends Econometric Models*, November 2016.

*Note:* Data from 2016 to 2020 are ILO forecasts.

**Table II.3.  Employment in information and communication services, selected economies, 2015 or latest year available**

| | Information and communication services | | | | | |
|---|---|---|---|---|---|---|
| | **Total employment in information and communication services** | **Share in total employment** | **of which:** | | | |
| | **(thousands)** | **(per cent)** | **Telecommunication (thousands)** | **Computer software and services (thousands)** | **Telecom and computer services (thousands)** | **Share in total employment** |
| European Union (EU 28) | 6 614 | 3.0 | 1 119 | 3 505 | 4 624 | 2.0 |
| United States | 4 701 | 3.3 | 807 | 2 497 | 3 304 | 2.3 |
| China | .. | .. | .. | .. | 3 366 | 1.8 |
| India | 3 201 | 0.8 | 298 | 1 740 | 2 038 | .. |
| Japan | 2 090 | 3.3 | 200 | .. | .. | .. |
| Brazil | 1 237 | 1.3 | 187 | 588 | 775 | 0.8 |
| Republic of Korea | 772 | 3.0 | .. | .. | .. | .. |
| Indonesia | 541 | 0.5 | 328 | .. | .. | .. |
| Russian Federation | .. | .. | 534 | .. | .. | .. |
| Nigeria | 470 | 1.0 | .. | .. | .. | .. |
| **World (estimate)** | **100 000** | **1.5** | .. | .. | .. | .. |

*Source:* UNCTAD, based on data from ILO, Eurostat and national sources.

*Note:* Available statistics for China cover number of employed persons in urban units, information transmission, computer services and software. Data for India are for 2012 and those for Nigeria are for 2010. Data for telecommunications in Brazil and China are for 2014. The estimates are based on ILO data, as well as on national data for 116 countries that together account for 29 per cent of global employment.

UNCTAD estimates that, globally, employment in *ICT services* accounted for approximately one quarter of the bigger aggregate (i.e. of the transport, storage and communications sector) or 100 million in 2015 (table II.3), and for 1.5 per cent, on average, of global employment, with up to 3 per cent in some developed countries. In some developing countries, such as Brazil, India, Indonesia and Nigeria, employment in this sector accounted for about 1 per cent or less of their total employment.[16] Comprehensive data by industry sub-sector are available only for the United States and the EU. Similar data are not available for the ICT manufacturing sector.

Regarding occupations, many ICT specialists work within the ICT sector itself, while an estimated 50 per cent work in other sectors. This illustrates the economy-wide importance of ICT skills (ILO, 2014). ILO data cover only "ICT professionals", disaggregated by gender, for 65 countries, excluding some major economies such as China, India and the United States. In the EU, ICT specialists accounted for 3.5 per cent of total employment in 2015.[17] As shown in figure II.9, the proportion of women in the total number of ICT specialists in the EU has remained very low, at around 16 per cent since 2011. In the United States, too, women's share in computer-related occupations was low, at less than 25 per cent in 2015, compared with their share in total employment of 47 per cent (figure II.10).[18] Further efforts are needed to address these gender occupational divides in ICT.[19]

**Figure II.9.  EU: Number of ICT specialists and share of women specialists, 2010–2015**

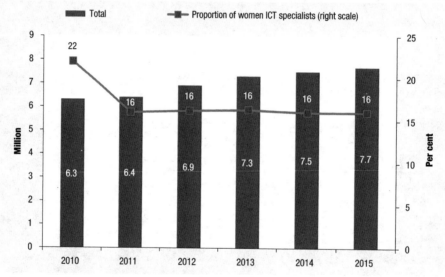

*Source:* UNCTAD, based on data from Eurostat.

**Figure II.10. United States: Share of women in total employment and in computer occupations, 2015 (per cent)**

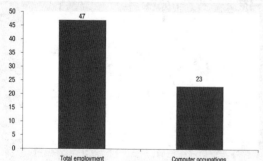

*Source:* UNCTAD, based on data from United States Bureau of Labor Statistics.

Employment data broken down by both industry and occupation offer a more detailed view of the digital economy and where ICT occupations are found. The United States Bureau of Labor Statistics forecasts employment in computer occupations will grow by 13 per cent between 2014 and 2024, adding almost 500,000 new jobs of this kind.[20] Almost seven million people worked either in information and communication services or as computer specialists in other sectors of the United States in 2014. More than 60 per cent of the computer occupations were outside information and communication services. Such detailed information would be valuable for developing countries as well.

# C. THE GROWING ROLE OF E-COMMERCE

E-commerce is a prominent feature of the evolving digital economy, although it remains hard to measure (box II.1). This section looks at trends in business-to-business (B2B) and business-to-consumer (B2C) e-commerce.[21]

Despite the lack of detailed official data, it is possible to estimate the total value of global e-commerce sales (table II.4). UNCTAD estimates that global e-commerce sales amounted to $25.3 trillion in 2015 ($22.4 trillion for B2B plus $2.9 trillion for B2C). Global B2B sales were estimated based on official data for China, Japan, the United States and the EU, which accounted for 67 per cent of world GDP in 2015. Their annual share in total world GDP is used as the basis for deriving a global estimate.

The United States was by far the largest e-commerce market in 2015, with combined sales of over $7 trillion, followed by Japan and China. While the United States was ahead by some margin in B2B e-commerce sales, it was just behind China in the B2C segment. Overall,

B2B dominated, accounting for about 90 per cent of the total among this group of economies. The total value of e-commerce was equivalent to 34 per cent of the total GDP of these economies; in Japan and the Republic of Korea it exceeded 60 per cent. Based on non-official data for the B2C market only, the Russian Federation would rank 12th and India 13th. Given the highly uncertain figures for B2B, it is not possible to estimate where other countries fit in.

The absence of e-commerce data and statistics for most developing countries remains a concern. Without it, their governments are handicapped when formulating and implementing relevant policies. E-commerce statistics are also needed for private enterprises to make informed investments and strategic decisions. A much more concerted effort is needed to strengthen the capacity of developing countries to carry out enterprise and household surveys with a view to generating the statistics needed for analyses of e-commerce trends and development impacts. Particular attention should be given to collecting statistics related to both B2B and B2C e-commerce.

## Box II.1. E-commerce measurement challenges

The availability of official e-commerce statistics varies considerably across countries, and definitions, methodology and scope need to be further harmonized to improve comparability. In the case of the G-20 countries, for example, European e-commerce statistics are generally the most complete and up-to-date. Japan and the Republic of Korea also have relatively recent and complete statistics, although the latter country has stopped compiling B2B data. Data for other developed and developing-country members vary in scope, comparability and timeliness.[a] Official statistics on B2B e-commerce are generally more limited than on B2C e-commerce.

Data on both kinds of e-commerce can be collected through enterprise surveys, although this is not done by most countries in the world. In the case of the United Kingdom, the Office of National Statistics (ONS) carries out an annual e-commerce survey.[b] While data are disaggregated by sales to private customers (B2C), sales to businesses and to public authorities are combined (B2B and B2G). Sectoral coverage is wide, although some sectors (such as agriculture and financial services) are omitted. It should be noted that the retail sector in the United Kingdom accounts for only one quarter of B2C sales, making it a poor proxy for overall B2C. Wholesale trade, transport and storage, and information and communications together account for as much as 45 per cent of total B2C sales. In addition, the size of an enterprise has an impact on the data. Before 2014, ONS had only compiled data covering enterprises with 10 or more employees. When micro enterprises were included in 2014, they accounted for 10 per cent of all web sales to consumers.

*Source:* UNCTAD, based on data from the United Kingdom's Office of National Statistics.

[a]    In Australia and Canada, data are available for retail e-commerce only and for "Internet sales". In the United States, data are available for the broad category of e-commerce, and only for certain industries. Among developing and transition economy G-20 members, only China publishes official statistics on B2B and B2C e-commerce. In some of the others (i.e. Argentina, Brazil, India, Mexico, the Russian Federation and Turkey) data on the B2C market are compiled by industry associations. Indonesia, Saudi Arabia and South Africa have neither official nor regular ongoing industry surveys related to e-commerce.

[b]    See http://webarchive.nationalarchives.gov.uk/20160105160709/http://www.ons.gov.uk/ons/dcp171778_425690.pdf

### Table II.4. Top 10 economies by total, B2B and B2C e-commerce, 2015, unless otherwise indicated

| | Economy | Total | | B2B | | B2C |
|---|---|---|---|---|---|---|
| | | $ billion | Share in GDP (per cent) | $ billion | Share in total e-commerce (per cent) | $ billion |
| 1 | United States | 7 055 | 39 | 6 443 | 91 | 612 |
| 2 | Japan | 2 495 | 60 | 2 382 | 96 | 114 |
| 3 | China | 1 991 | 18 | 1 374 | 69 | 617 |
| 4 | Republic of Korea | 1 161 | 84 | 1 113 | 96 | 48 |
| 5 | Germany (2014) | 1 037 | 27 | 944 | 91 | 93 |
| 6 | United Kingdom | 845 | 30 | 645 | 76 | 200 |
| 7 | France (2014) | 661 | 23 | 588 | 89 | 73 |
| 8 | Canada (2014) | 470 | 26 | 422 | 90 | 48 |
| 9 | Spain | 242 | 20 | 217 | 90 | 25 |
| 10 | Australia | 216 | 16 | 188 | 87 | 28 |
| | Total for top 10 | 16 174 | 34 | 14 317 | 89 | 1 857 |
| | World | 25 293 | .. | 22 389 | .. | 2 904 |

*Source:* UNCTAD, based on data from the United States Census Bureau; Japan Ministry of Economy, Trade and Industry; China Bureau of Statistics; KOSTAT (Republic of Korea); Eurostat (for Germany); United Kingdom Office of National Statistics; National Institute of Statistics and Economic Studies (INSEE, France); Statistics Canada; Australian Bureau of Statistics and National Statistics Institute (INE, Spain).

*Note:* Figures in italics are estimates. Missing data were estimated based on average ratios, converted to dollars using annual average exchange rates.

# D. TRADE ASPECTS OF THE DIGITAL ECONOMY

The external sector of the economy is greatly affected by digitalization. Products and services are increasingly purchased and delivered across borders using electronic networks. This section examines the trade dimension from four perspectives: trade in ICT services; trade in electronically delivered services (ICT-enabled services); trade in ICT goods; and cross-border e-commerce resulting from orders received electronically from abroad.

## 1. Trade in ICT services

The expansion of ICT services in world trade reflects how much the digital economy has grown. World exports of telecommunications and computer services stood at $467 billion in 2016. Exports of ICT services rose at an average annual rate of 8 per cent between 2005 and 2016, increasing their share in all commercial services from 7.8 per cent to 10.3 per cent (figure II.11).[22] Exports of information services, including online content provision, thrived thanks to improved connectivity,

reaching $26 billion in 2016 – nearly three times their 2005 value.

Tables II.5 and II.6 show estimates for the top 10 exporters and importers of ICT services from 2014 to 2016.[23] At $353 billion, world exports of computer services were more than three times higher than world telecommunications services exports in 2016. The EU and the United States topped the list of major exporters of telecommunications services in 2015, with $44 billion and $13 billion worth of exports, respectively, together accounting for over 80 per cent of the top 10 economies. This partly reflects their roles as hubs for much of the world's Internet traffic. Other regional hubs that feature prominently include Hong Kong (China), India, Kuwait and the Russian Federation. In many developing countries, especially those with low incomes, telecommunications were the only or main component of ICT services exports. For example, telecommunications accounted for more than 85 per cent of ICT services exports from Cambodia, Guatemala, Honduras, Myanmar, Senegal, Thailand, Turkey and the United Republic of Tanzania.

The value of computer services exports of the top 10 exporters of such services amounted to $315 billion in 2016. The EU and India together accounted for 86 per cent of the total computer services exports

**Figure II.11. Global exports of telecommunications, computer and information services, 2005–2016**

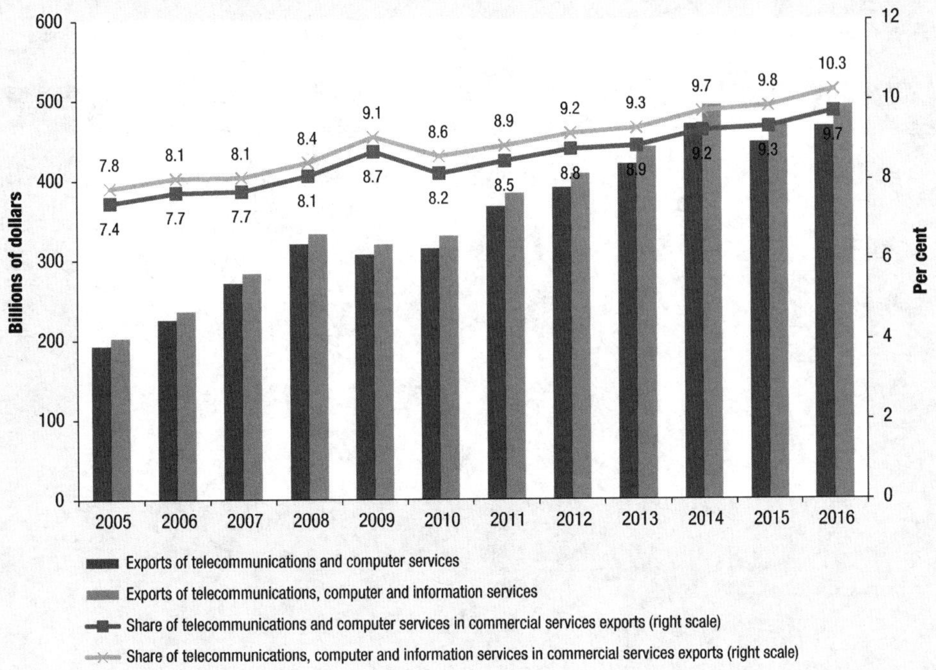

Legend:
- Exports of telecommunications and computer services
- Exports of telecommunications, computer and information services
- Share of telecommunications and computer services in commercial services exports (right scale)
- Share of telecommunications, computer and information services in commercial services exports (right scale)

*Source:* Data and estimates were compiled jointly by UNCTAD, WTO and ITC, and are available online at UNCTADstat.

*Note:* International trade in ICT services is defined as including telecommunications and computer services. This definition was approved by the United Nations Statistical Commission at its 47th session in March 2016 based on a proposal by UNCTAD, 2015c.

**Table II.5. Estimates of telecommunications services exports and their share in world exports, top 10 exporters, 2014–2016**

| Economy | 2014 ($ million) | 2015 ($ million) | 2016 ($ million) | Share in world exports, 2016 (per cent) |
|---|---|---|---|---|
| EU-28 | 52 002 | 43 558 | 45 828 | 40 |
| United States | 13 736 | 12 645 | 12 968 | 11 |
| Kuwait | 3 064 | 2 708 | 2 553 | 2 |
| India | 2 163 | 2 088 | 2 315 | 2 |
| Hong Kong (China) | 1 775 | 1 828 | .. | .. |
| Canada | 1 737 | 1 561 | 1 609 | 1 |
| Russian Federation | 1 732 | 1 418 | 1 179 | 1 |
| United Arab Emirates | 1 116 | 1144 | 1 171 | 1 |
| Israel | 813 | 1 068 | 1 247 | 1 |
| Japan | 1 382 | 1 001 | 1 275 | 1 |
| **Total for top 10 exporters** | **66 293** | **58 517** | **70 146** | **62** |
| **World** | **123 020** | **112 980** | **113 530** | **100** |

*Source:* Data and estimates were compiled jointly by UNCTAD, WTO and ITC, and are avaixlable online at UNCTADstat. EU-28 estimates were provided by Eurostat.

*Note:* Data for the EU-28 include intra-EU trade. EU-28 data were estimated by UNCTAD. Disaggregated data were not available for China, which exported $25 billion worth of telecommunications, computer and information services in 2016. The totals do not necessarily correspond to the sum of all the figures in the column due to rounding.

of the 10 major exporters. If reported separately, Ireland would rank as the largest exporter of computer services, which amounted to $64 billion in 2015. In relative terms, computer services accounted for more than 80 per cent of exports of ICT services of developing and transition economies, such as Argentina, Costa Rica, the Philippines, the Republic of Korea, Sri Lanka, Uruguay and Ukraine.

**Table II.6. Exports of computer services and their share in world exports, top 10 exporters, 2014–2016**

| Economy | 2014 | 2015 | 2016 | Share in world exports, 2016 (Per cent) |
|---|---|---|---|---|
| EU-28 | 219 286 | 202 742 | 213 308 | 60 |
| India | 52 130 | 52 761 | 52 680 | 15 |
| United States | 14 152 | 15 951 | 17 251 | 5 |
| Israel | 8 534 | 8 362 | 10 612 | 3 |
| United Arab Emirates | 4 248 | 4 357 | 4 466 | 1 |
| Canada | 5 603 | 4 289 | 4 420 | 1 |
| Philippines | 3 121 | 3 163 | 5 174 | 1 |
| Russian Federation | 2 651 | 2 455 | 2 664 | 1 |
| Republic of Korea | 1 880 | 2 341 | 2 345 | 1 |
| Japan | 1 653 | 2 088 | 2 318 | 1 |
| **Total for top 10 exporters** | **313 256** | **298 509** | **315 238** | **89** |
| **World** | **346 030** | **333 700** | **353 100** | **100** |

*Source:* Data and estimates were compiled jointly by UNCTAD, WTO and ITC, and are available online at UNCTADstat. EU-28 estimates were provided by Eurostat.

*Note:* Data for the EU include intra-EU trade. EU-28 data were estimated by UNCTAD. Disaggregated data were not available for China which exported $25 billion worth of telecommunications, computer and information services, for Switzerland which exported $13.6 billion and for Singapore which exported $6.4 billion of those services in 2016. The totals do not necessarily correspond to the sum of all the figures in the column due to rounding.

## 2. Trade in ICT-enabled services

The evolving digital economy is not only creating more trade in ICT services; many other services that feature within the "narrow scope" of the digital economy (figure I.1) have also become tradable thanks to improved Internet connectivity. Trade in these ICT-enabled services is believed to have grown very rapidly over the past decade, now constituting a significant proportion of all services exports. Such trade includes various business and knowledge processes. For example, India earned $23 billion from ICT-enabled exports in accounting, customer care, medical transcription, engineering and other services in 2014–2015.[24] As a strategic component of the digital economy, such services are of interest to both developing and developed countries. However, there is a lack of official statistics on the amount and composition of the services trade that is delivered digitally, which is a disadvantage for policymaking in this area, at both national and international levels.

With a view to remedying this situation, UNCTAD has developed a definition of ICT-enabled services as "services products delivered remotely over ICT networks" (UNCTAD, 2015b). It identifies services that are potentially ICT-enabled, and groups them into nine categories. The United States has used these groupings to estimate the volume of such trade in that country. In 2014, 54 per cent ($385 billion) of all services exported from the United States were found to be potentially ICT-enabled (or "digitally deliverable") (Grimm, 2016). The next step is to conduct enterprise surveys to find out how much is *actually* delivered remotely using ICT networks. To this end, in 2016 UNCTAD developed a survey questionnaire in collaboration with the Inter-Agency Task Force on International Trade Statistics, along with experts from Costa Rica, Egypt, India and Thailand. The survey will be pilot tested in these four countries during the course of 2017.

## 3. Trade in ICT goods[25]

Trade in ICT goods has grown dramatically over the past decade, driven by a number of factors, such as the WTO Information Technology Agreement (ITA), various regional and bilateral trade arrangements, rapid technological change and the emergence of new business models. For the first time since 2009, global imports of ICT goods declined in 2015 by 3.6 per cent in current prices, to just over $2 trillion.[26] Most of this decline was due to lower imports from developed economies in Asia and Europe, which fell by 11 per cent and 7 per cent, respectively (figure II.12, right), and also to the decline in imports of computers and peripherals as well as consumer electronic equipment (figure II.12, left). Global exports of ICT services also declined·over the period 2014–2015 by 4 per cent, to $472 billion.

Imports of ICT goods accounted for 13 per cent of global merchandise imports in 2015. There were considerable variations by region, from 27 per cent in East Asia, to only 5 per cent in Africa, and an estimated 4 per cent in both Oceania and the LDCs (figure II.13). Most of the trade in ICT goods, which includes both finished and intermediate goods, was between Asia, Europe and the United States. Developing economies in Asia, many of which host large manufacturing facilities, accounted for nearly half (49 per cent) of global ICT goods imports in 2015, the latest year for which data are available. China alone accounted for one fifth of those imports.

**Figure II.12. Global imports of ICT goods by region (right) and by product category (left), 2000–2015**

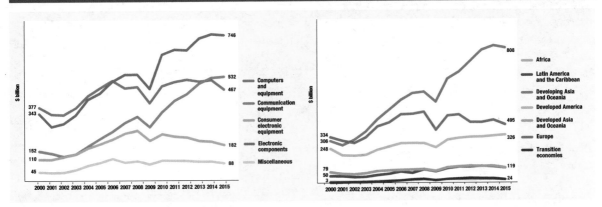

*Source:* UNCTAD, based on data from UNCTADstat.

**Figure II.13. Share of ICT goods in global merchandise imports, by region, 2000–2015**

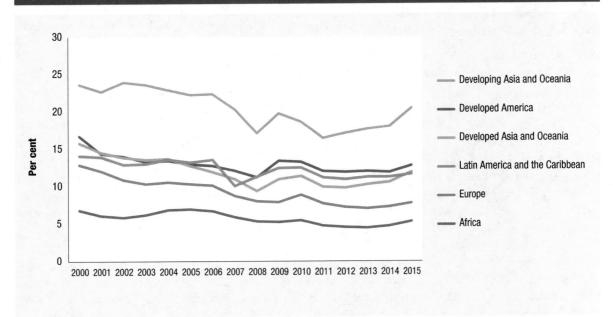

*Source:* UNCTAD, based on data from UNCTADstat.

## Figure II.14. Imports of communications equipment and mobile cellular subscriptions in Zambia (left) and Rwanda (right), 2000–2015

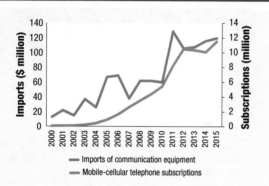
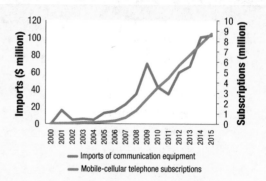

*Source:* UNCTAD, based on data from UNCTADstat and ITU *World Telecommunication/ICT Indicators database.*

LDC imports of ICT goods comprise mainly communications equipment, such as mobile telecommunications equipment and handsets, to which they have gained greater access as a result of lower import prices. As illustrated with data from Rwanda and Zambia, the rise in mobile subscriptions occurred simultaneously as the rise in imports of communications equipment (figure II.14).

China remains the world's leading exporter of ICT goods, which were worth a total of $608 billion in 2015, considerably higher than its exports of telecommunication, computer and information services at $25 billion. India, by contrast, exported ICT services worth $55 billion and ICT goods worth only about $2.3 billion.

## 4. Cross-border e-commerce

Individuals and enterprises ordering or selling goods and services online across borders contribute to international trade and cross-border e-commerce. However, despite growing interest in this mode of trade, there are virtually no official statistics on its value, as few countries publish official estimates of such transactions. Based on the limited information that does exist from official statistics and market research, UNCTAD estimates that cross-border B2C e-commerce in 2015 amounted to $189 billion, with some 380 million consumers making purchases on overseas websites. Table II.7 shows estimated results for the 10 countries with the highest values of cross-border online B2C purchases in 2015.[27] Such purchases accounted for 1.4 per cent of total merchandise imports, and were equivalent to around 7 per cent of domestic B2C e-commerce.

Some regions and countries collect data on at least some aspects of cross-border e-commerce. Eurostat reports data for every other year since 2011 on the proportion of businesses based in the EU that purchased or sold abroad (table II.8). However the data are not disaggregated by type (e.g. electronic data interchange (EDI) or web sale), counterpart (e.g. business or consumer) or value.[28] The proportion of enterprises purchasing from suppliers in their own country has been declining while that of enterprises purchasing from other EU countries has been increasing. Moreover, some 83 million EU residents made cross-border B2C purchases in 2015, corresponding to almost a quarter of all Internet users (figure II.15).

A few European countries provide some details. The United Kingdom breaks down the proportion of electronic sales by EDI and web sales.[29] The proportion of firms making overseas EDI sales is small and on the decline, whereas for overseas web sales it is increasing. Spain reports the distribution of web sales (by value), which shows that almost one fifth were made to clients outside Spain.[30] Since data on the type of client (i.e. consumer or business) are not available, it is not possible to distinguish between B2B and B2C sales.

A few non-European countries publish statistics on cross-border online purchases. Japan reported the value of its cross-border B2C transactions in 2015 with China and the United States (figure II.16, left).[31] They show that Chinese consumers spent more than 30 times more on purchases from Japan than Japanese consumer spent on purchases from China. Meanwhile, United States consumers bought less than half as much from China than what Chinese consumers

**Table II.7. Estimates of cross-border online B2C purchases, top 10 importers, 2015**

| | Cross-border online purchases (B2C) | | | Total B2C ($ billion) | Cross-border online shoppers |
|---|---|---|---|---|---|
| | Total value ($ billion) | Share of B2C in merchandise imports, by value (per cent) | Share of total B2C (per cent) | | Number of shoppers (million) |
| United States | 40 | 1.7 | 7 | 612 | 34 |
| China | 39 | 2.3 | 6 | 617 | 70 |
| Germany | 9 | 0.8 | 10 | 93 | 12 |
| Japan | 2 | 0.3 | 2 | 114 | 9 |
| United Kingdom | 12 | 1.9 | 7 | 200 | 14 |
| France | 4 | 0.7 | 6 | 73 | 12 |
| Netherlands | 0.4 | 0.1 | 2 | 19 | 4 |
| Republic of Korea | 3 | 0.6 | 5 | 48 | 10 |
| Canada | 7 | 1.7 | 16 | 48 | 11 |
| Italy | 3 | 0.8 | 19 | 17 | 6 |
| **Top 10 countries** | **120** | **1.4** | **7** | **1 839** | **181** |
| **WORLD** | **189** | **1.1** | **7** | **2 904** | **380** |

*Source:* UNCTAD estimates, based on official and market research information; trade data are from the WTO; data on cross-border online shoppers are estimated based on information from Eurostat (for France, Germany, Italy, the Netherlands and the United Kingdom), PayPal (for China, Japan and the United States); Statistics Canada and the Korea Internet & Security Agency.

*Note:* While enterprise surveys on B2C sales do not include overseas purchases by domestic consumers, they are shown to reflect the relative size of international purchases.

**Table II.8. Proportion of EU-based enterprises buying and selling online 2011, 2013 and 2015 (per cent)**

| | Proportion of enterprises having made electronic sales | | | Proportion of enterprises having purchased via computer networks from suppliers | | |
|---|---|---|---|---|---|---|
| | 2011 | 2013 | 2015 | 2011 | 2013 | 2015 |
| Own country | 14 | 16 | 18 | 32 | 30 | 28 |
| Other EU countries | 6 | 7 | 8 | 10 | 11 | 13 |
| **Rest of the world** | **4** | **4** | **5** | **5** | **5** | **5** |

*Source:* Eurostat.

*Note:* All enterprises (excluding the financial sector) employing 10 persons or more.

**Figure II.15. Cross-border shopping in the EU: Proportion of EU online shoppers among Internet users (left) and EU online shoppers buying from local and overseas sellers (right), 2015**

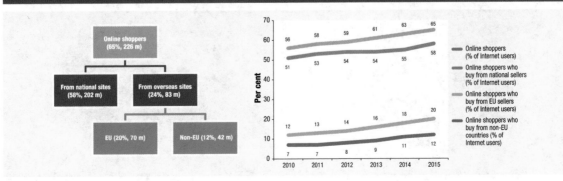

*Source:* UNCTAD, based on data from Eurostat.

*Note:* Percentages in the left chart refer to the proportion of online shoppers among Internet users.

bought from the United States. Statistics Canada reported that in 2013 the United States accounted for 15 per cent of Canadian enterprises' Internet sales (by value) compared with 6 per cent of their sales to the rest of the world, roughly equivalent to the figures reported for Spain above.[32] In the Republic of Korea, overseas B2C online purchases increased 5.5 times between 2010 and 2014, exceeding $1.5 billion in 2014 (figure II.16, right).[33]

Mexico is one of few developing countries that provide data on the number of Internet users shopping only from overseas websites, as well as from both Mexican and overseas sites.[34] In 2015, over 2.5 million Mexicans purchased a product from an overseas website, including almost 1 million who purchased only from abroad (figure II.17, left). In the same year, about 44 per cent of online shoppers in the Republic of Korea

made a purchase abroad, spending 867,000 Korean won ($767) on average per shopper (figure II.17, right).[35] However, some of the leading trading economies, such as China, Japan and the United States, lack *official* data on the proportion of individuals making purchases online from overseas websites.

Data from the Universal Postal Union (UPU) on the volume of international postal traffic offer additional insights. They show that developing countries, especially in Asia and Oceania, are becoming increasingly important participants in cross-border trade. Their share in postal deliveries sent abroad rose from 26 per cent to 43 per cent between 2011 and 2016. During this period, global deliveries of small packets, parcels and packages more than doubled, most likely due largely to e-commerce transactions (OECD and WTO, 2017).

**Figure II.16. Cross-border online B2C sales between China, Japan and the United States, 2015 (left) and cross-border online purchases in the Republic of Korea, various years (right)**

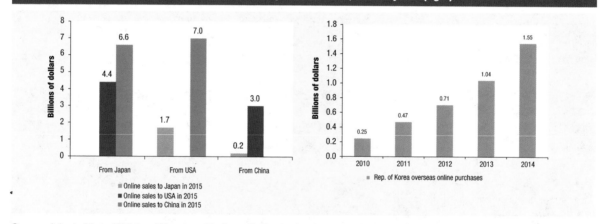

*Source:* Adapted from Ministry of Economy, Trade and Industry, Japan, and Korean Customs Service.

**Figure II.17. Mexican Internet shoppers buying from local and overseas websites (per cent) (left); Republic of Korea B2C overseas online purchases by amount spent per year (right), 2015**

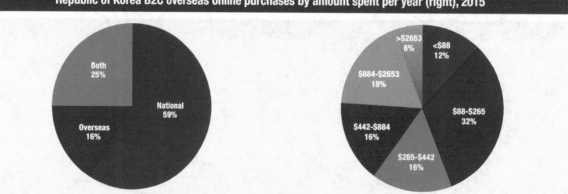

*Source:* UNCTAD, based on data from Instituto Nacional de Estadística y Geografía of Mexico (INEGI) and Korea Internet & Security Agency (KISA).
*Note:* Figures for the Republic of Korea are converted to dollars using the annual average exchange rate.

# E.  MEASURING NOVEL ASPECTS OF THE EVOLVING DIGITAL ECONOMY

As the digital economy evolves, its new dimensions need to be captured. In figure I.1, reference was made to such features as the sharing economy, the gig economy, automation and the algorithmic economy (which is linked to the increased reliance on data). Digital services, including peer-to-peer (P2P) links, applications and tools generate innovation and disruption across many industries. They affect transport (e.g. car hailing services such as Uber), hospitality (e.g. accommodation portals such as Airbnb) and finance (e.g. mobile money services such as M-Pesa), to name just a few examples. Although transactions generated by these applications may be included in data on e-commerce, they need to be complemented by other statistics such as their scope and use in order to highlight their spread and impact. Official statistics of this kind are particularly hard to find, but most estimates point to rapid growth. The following are some major areas of projected growth

- It has been estimated that the "sharing economy" will surge from $14 billion in 2014 to $335 billion by 2025.[36]
- Emerging elements of the digital economy, such as machine-to-machine (M2M) links, 3D printers and robots, signal a shift from personal connectivity to device connectivity. So-called M2Ms (e.g. ATMs, GPS in vehicles, security monitors and wearables) are forecast to grow to 12.2 billion connections by 2020 (figure II.18).[37]
- Global Internet Protocol (IP) traffic, a proxy for data flows, is estimated to grow at a compound annual rate of 23 per cent over the period 2014–2019 – equivalent to a projected 142 million people streaming Internet HD videos simultaneously, all day, every day, by 2019. By then, global Internet traffic will be 66 times the volume of the entire global Internet traffic in 2005.[38]
- Worldwide shipments of 3D printers more than doubled in 2016, to over 450,000, and are expected to reach 6.7 million in 2020.[39]
- Regarding 3D printing, in 2012 40 per cent of such systems were installed in North America, 30 per cent in Europe, 26 per cent in the Asia-Pacific region and only 4 per cent in the rest of the world (Wohlers, 2014).

## Figure II.18.  Projected growth of M2M connections and M2M traffic, 2015–2020

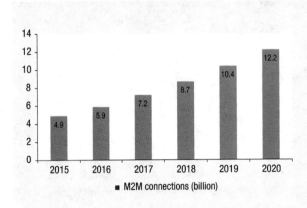
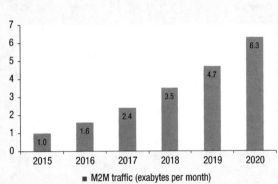

*Source:* Cisco.

According to the International Federation of Robotics, sales of over 250,000 robots were at their highest level ever in 2015.[40] Country data show that there are big differences between countries in terms of the density of robot use in manufacturing (figure II.19), indicating another dimension of the digital economy divide. Many

developing countries, including certain Asian economies, used significantly fewer robots in manufacturing, but emerging economies, such as Mexico, have a higher expansion rate of automation than developed countries (UNCTAD, 2017f).

The challenge in accurately displaying the evolving digital economy and its impacts on society is to move

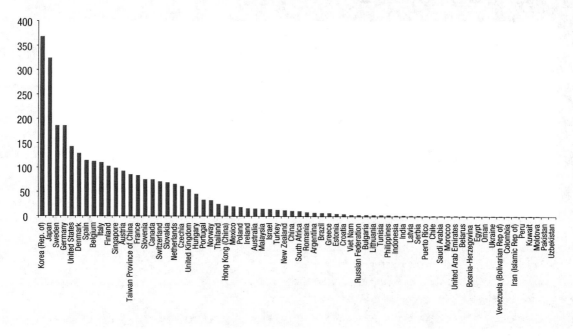

**Figure II.19. Estimated robot density in manufacturing, 2014 (units of robots per 10,000 employees)**

*Source:* UNCTAD (2017f), based on International Federation of Robotics database and Wood, 2017.

*Note:* The chart shows data for all those 67 economies for which data were available.

beyond anecdotal examples to aggregated statistics. New technology may in itself help overcome some of the measurement barriers. There is a debate among data producers of how far big data from private and novel sources can be considered "official" statistics for use by policymakers. The vast amounts of digital information collected by service providers could theoretically be aggregated and the source kept confidential to generate measures of different aspects of the digital economy.[41] Crowd-sourcing is another area with considerable potential for data collection.[42]

# F. CONCLUSIONS

In order to ensure that everybody can benefit from the digital economy, and that no one is left behind, collecting and compiling policy-relevant data and statistics on the multiple facets of the digital divide have become essential. Some official statistics that are available require a painstaking process to assemble and compile. It is possible to make global estimates on the size and certain trade aspects of the digital economy, as well as on the role of electronic communications in triggering orders for e-commerce, and on the global value of M2M and B2C sales that this generates.

However, it is not possible to measure the indirect impacts of the use of electronic communication networks by sectors such as the public sector, health and education on firms' productivity and on social well-being. Also, despite global classifications for employment that would support analysis by industry and occupation, sufficient data are not available to make global estimates. When reporting data on key indicators of the digital economy, many countries do not adhere to international classifications, or they do not provide the necessary level of detail. Worse still, most developing countries do not compile relevant data at all. As a result, the implications of the evolving digital economy for low- and middle-income developing economies generally are not adequately researched (Bukht and Heeks, 2017).

Apart from trade data, international data sets for other aspects of the digital economy are either limited to particular groups of countries (i.e. EU or OECD members) or are not comprehensive, up-to-date or detailed enough (United Nations *National Accounts Main Aggregates Database*). Available statistics are scattered across regional and national databases. In addition, while the digital economy raises new issues in terms of measurement, another question is how new digital forms of consumption should be accounted for in economic statistics such as GDP (Bean, 2016). Currently, the statistics in existing frameworks are not sufficiently exploited.

The crude and highly aggregated way of reporting statistics makes it difficult to derive accurate measures of the evolving digital economy. It will be important to find better means of measuring the size of the market, for example in terms of sales revenues and employment of the largest providers of cloud computing services (UNCTAD, 2013a), AI-enabled design software, as well as more specialized platforms and platform users. Finally, there is a need to further explore how the digital economy itself can support the production of better measurement, including by analysing big data.

# NOTES

1.  The analysis of the value of the digital economy is affected by the value of the United States dollar against major currencies. Consequently, as much of the data in this chapter are in United States dollars, which rose sharply in 2015, that value showed a sharp decline in many countries in 2015. This is somewhat corrected by also showing values as a proportion of GDP or a similar indicator.

2.  See http://www.itu.int/en/connect2020/Pages/default.aspx.

3.  See http://www.un.org/sustainabledevelopment/infrastructure-industrialization/.

4.  See, for example, http://www.lldc2conference.org/custom-content/uploads/2014/07/ITC-June-31.pdf.

5.  See https://www.itu.int/en/ITU-D/Statistics/Documents/facts/ICTFactsFigures2015.pdf.

6.  For example, studies on the use of mobile broadband in firms in lower-income developing economies highlight how ICT supports firm linkages and information availability (Aker, 2010; Donner, 2004; Donner and Escobari, 2010; Esselaar et al., 2007). See also UNCTAD, 2011; World Bank, 2016a.

7.  http://ec.europa.eu/eurostat/statistics-explained/index.php/E-commerce_statistics_for_individuals.

8.  http://www.todayonline.com/business/more-singaporeans-turning-online-shopping-better-bargains.

9.  The most recently agreed definition of the ICT sector covers activities where the production of ICT goods and services is the main activity, and excludes retail (OECD, 2007).

10. The sector had been growing until 2015, when it dropped by 4.6 per cent, mainly due to exchange rate fluctuations.

11. Among countries for which data were available, Ireland has the highest contribution of InfoComm to GDP, at 9 per cent.

12. As per ISIC Rev. 4 "Manufacture of computer electronic and optical products (26), see http://unstats.un.org/unsd/cr/registry/regcs.asp?Cl=27&Lg=1&Co=26.

13. See national accounts aggregates by industry at: http://appsso.Eurostat.ec.europa.eu/nui/submitViewTableAction.do.

14. OECD data do not cover all member States; see "6A. Value added and its components by activity, ISIC rev4" at: http://stats.oecd.org.

15. See http://ec.europa.eu/eurostat/statistics-explained/index.php/ICT_specialists_in_employment. A full list of ICT occupations is available from the International Labour Organization (ILO, 2014).

16. Other studies have estimated that the ICT sector accounts for about 2.5 per cent of global employment, ranging from about 1 per cent in developing countries to 4 per cent in developed countries (OECD, 2014b; World Bank, 2016a).

17. See http://ec.europa.eu/Eurostat/statistics-explained/index.php/EU_labour_force_survey_-_methodology#Occupation and http://ec.europa.eu/Eurostat/statistics-explained/index.php/ICT_specialists_in_employment.

18. See https://www.bls.gov/cps/tables.htm.

19. In Czechia, for example, efforts to increase the proportion of women in tertiary education in computing have helped to raise their share in the total number of ICT specialist occupations from 14 per cent in 2005 to 17 per cent in 2015 (Czech National Statistical Office, *Information Economy in Figures*, 2016).

20. See Industry-occupation matrix data, by industry, at: https://www.bls.gov/emp/ep_table_109.htm.

21. This Report uses the OECD definition of e-commerce (OECD, 2011): purchases and sales conducted over computer networks, using multiple formats and devices, including the web and electronic data interchange (EDI), using personal computers, laptops, tablets and mobile phones of varying levels of sophistication. E-commerce may involve physical goods as well as intangible (digital) products and services that can be delivered digitally (UNCTAD, 2015a). These concepts lead to a framework defined by the mode (i.e. EDI or web sales) and the parties involved (i.e. B2B, B2C, business to government (B2G) and consumer to consumer (C2C)).

22. UNCTAD, WTO and ITC compile data on international trade in services. In the case of telecommunications, computer and information services, some data are available for 190 economies, and data for 2016 are available for most of them (see http://unctadstat.unctad.org/wds/TableViewer/summary.aspx).

23 The transition from the IMF *Balance of Payments Manual* (BPM) 5 to BPM6 data reporting has resulted in aggregate data reporting for telecommunications, computer and information services as a whole. However, the *Manual on Statistics of International Trade in Services 2010* (MSITS, 2010) highlights the importance of publishing more disaggregated data to obtain a more detailed picture of international trade in services. Likewise, UNCTAD (2015b) highlights the importance of publishing disaggregated data to obtain a complete picture of international trade in ICT services, especially in developing countries.

24 Reserve Bank of India press release at: https://rbi.org.in/scripts/BS_PressReleaseDisplay.aspx?prid=35669.

25 ICT goods correspond to a list of 95 products defined at the six-digit level of the Harmonized System Classification version 2007 (HS2007). The selection principle is that ICT goods "must be intended to fulfil the function of information processing and communication by electronic means, including transmission and display" (OECD, 2011).

26 See http://unctad.org/en/pages/newsdetails.aspx?OriginalVersionID=1439.

27 B2C cross-border sales include both goods and services. However due to copyright and other restrictions, it is believed that the value of goods is significantly higher than for services. For example, Apple's iTunes store requires users to purchase from the store of the country they are located in, and provides local addresses and billing options (https://support.apple.com/en-au/HT201389). Data for the world's leading merchandise importers are from the WTO, "Table A6: Leading exporters and importers in world merchandise trade, 2015" (https://www.wto.org/english/res_e/statis_e/wts2016_e/wts16_chap9_e.htm).

28 EUROSTAT, "E-Commerce Statistics," *Statistics Explained*, December 2016 (http://ec.europa.eu/Eurostat/statistics-explained/index.php/E-commerce_statistics – Cross_border_e-commerce_sales_not_fully_exploited_by_enterprises_selling_electronically).

29 ONS, "E-commerce and ICT activity," *Statistical Bulletin*, 2015, (https://www.ons.gov.uk/businessindustryandtrade/itandinternetindustry/bulletins/ecommerceandictactivity/2014).

30 INE, "Survey on the use of ICT and electronic commerce (EC) in enterprises 2014-2015," June 2015 (http://www.ine.es/dynt3/inebase/index.htm?type=pcaxis&file=pcaxis&path=%2Ft09%2Fe02%2F%2Fa2014-2015&L=1).

31 METI, "Results compiled of the E-Commerce Market Survey." *News Release*, June 14 2016 (http://www.meti.go.jp/english/press/2016/0614_02.html).

32 Statistics Canada, "CANSIM - 358-0230 - Survey of Digital Technology and Internet Use, Characteristics of Online Sales by North American Industry Classification System (NAICS) and Size of Enterprise," 11 June 2014 (http://www5.statcan.gc.ca/cansim/a26?lang=eng&id=3580230).

33 United States Department of Commerce, "Korea: New Korean wave - Surging Korean consumers on overseas online retailers," 2015 (http://2016.export.gov/southkorea/industries/ecommerce/ecommmarketresearch/index.asp).

34 INEGI, "Usuarios de Internet Que Han Realizado Compras Vía Internet, Según Origen Del Sitio de Compra, 2002 a 2015," 17 May 2016. (http://www3.inegi.org.mx/sistemas/sisept/default.aspx?t=tinf224&s=est&c=19439).

35 KISA, 2015 Survey on the Internet Economic Activities, Executive summary, 2016 (http://www.kisa.or.kr/eng/usefulreport/surveyReport_View.jsp?cPage=1&p_No=262&b_No=262&d_No=72&ST=&SV= ).

36 See https://www.brookings.edu/research/the-current-and-future-state-of-the-sharing-economy/.

37 http://www.cisco.com/c/en/us/solutions/collateral/service-provider/visual-networking-index-vni/vni-hyperconnectivity-wp.html.

38 See *Cisco*, "The zettabyte era – trends and analysis," 2 June 2016 (http://www.cisco.com/c/en/us/solutions/collateral/service-provider/visual-networking-index-vni/vni-hyperconnectivity-wp.html).

39 See http://www.gartner.com/newsroom/id/3476317.

40 http://www.ifr.org/fileadmin/user_upload/downloads/World_Robotics/2016/Executive_Summary_WR_Industrial_Robots_2016.pdf.

41 For example, Statistics Netherlands has used big data to generate traffic and tourism statistics (see: http://www.riksbank.se/Documents/Forskning/Konferenser_seminarier/2015/Big%20data%20the%20future%20of%20statistics%20Experience%20from%20Statistics%20Netherlands.pdf).

42 Statistics Canada is using crowd-sourcing in a pilot project to map construction across the country (see: http://www.statcan.gc.ca/eng/crowdsourcing).

# DIGITALIZATION, TRADE AND VALUE CHAINS

Digital technologies are improving the prospects for small businesses in developing countries to participate in global trade. They enable enterprises to cut costs, streamline supply chains, and market products and services worldwide with greater ease than before. Increased trade and reduced trade costs can have positive spillover effects on the economy as a whole, for example through enhanced competition, productivity, innovation, a more dynamic business environment and improved access to talents and skills. But benefits from digitalization are not automatic; MSMEs still need to overcome various barriers to successfully exploit the new opportunities.

This chapter highlights three particular aspects related to the interface of digitalization and trade. Section A looks at the scope for the Internet to facilitate more inclusive trade by enabling more enterprises and entrepreneurs to sell to foreign markets. Section B discusses trade in tasks or "cloud work" – a relatively novel form of trade in services that is enabled through digitalization. It opens up new work opportunities for people and small businesses in developing countries, but also raises various concerns. Section C turns attention to a little-studied area: the impact of digitalization on the participation of MSMEs in export-oriented value chains in low- and lower middle-income countries. The final section concludes.

# DIGITALIZATION, TRADE AND VALUE CHAINS

**Opportunities**

**Barriers**

## Better access to global trade for MSMEs / optimized supply chain

 Digital technologies enable to **cut costs**

 **Streamline supply chains,** market products and services with greater ease

**More gains** if SMEs:
▸ Obtain capacity-building, training and other technical assistance
▸ Serve a well-defined niche market rather than competing in mass markets

**Internet & inclusive trade**

## MSMEs in low-income economies struggle to benefit from the digitalization due to:

 inadequate connectivity

 limited awareness

 skills gap

## Global online platforms

 **Global GDP** may increase by 2025 — **$2.7 trillion**

 Creating **new full-time jobs** — **72 million**

 Improving **work outcomes** for — **540 million** people

In 2016, the market of **«online outsourcing»** surpassed

 **$4 billion**

**Cloud work** allows entrepreneurs to outsource jobs to other individual workers or entrepreneurs on the other side of the planet

**Digitalization & cloud work**

## More research is needed

to determinate the **success factors for MSMEs** to break into international trade, at the interface of:

- Global Value Chains
- Platforms
- Relevant policies
- Small exporters
- Digitalization

## Digital work vacancies

in 2016
**51%**
posted by **United States**

almost
**0%**
posted in most countries in **Africa**

**Working conditions**

**Benefits of cloud**

**Risks of cloud**

## Independence and flexibility

 on where, how much and when to work

## People in remote locations

 are offered new labour market opportunities

## People with disabilities

 are offered possibility to perform digital tasks

## Race to the bottom of working conditions and more precarity

 Oversupply of jobseekers

 **No** maternity and paternity leave

 Lack of overtime compensation

 **No** paid sick leave

 **No** minimum age protection

 **No** ability to engage in collective action

 Absence of health insurance

# A. THE INTERNET AS A FACILITATOR OF MORE INCLUSIVE TRADE

Relatively few businesses in developing countries trade across borders. Judging from the World Bank's Enterprise Surveys, the average export participation rates of firms in East Asia and the Pacific are about 10 per cent, in Latin America 12 per cent, and in sub-Saharan Africa 10 per cent (Gordon and Suominen, 2014). Moreover, exports are often driven by a handful of firms, with the top 5 per cent of exporters accounting for over 80 per cent of total exports (ibid.). In addition, at least 70 per cent of the firms generally do not last more than a year as exporters (Volpe Martincus and Carballo, 2008). This low survival rate can be the result of limited geographical diversification of offline sellers' exports. Digitalization has the potential to change some of these commonly observed patterns of international trade.

Various studies have explored issues relating to developing countries, trade and digitalization, which show measurable impacts of the Internet that are influenced by the economic and institutional context (Galperin and Viecens, 2014; Minges, 2016; UNCTAD, 2015b). Some of them look at how the Internet can enhance trade flows (Clarke and Wallsten, 2006; Meijers, 2014; Osnago and Tan, 2016). Others have found a positive correlation between Internet use and the export performance of firms, without, however, determining the causality (Paunov and Rollo, 2016). They show that improved Internet access is of particular importance for single-product and non-exporting firms.

New digital solutions can help overcome challenges to exporting, such as small domestic markets, remoteness from global markets and other geographical disadvantages. By reducing information asymmetries and costs related to communication and information, transactions, search and matching, they can lower overall trade costs. Traditionally, only large and productive firms were able to carry the costs associated with export entry, such as identifying and marketing to distant customers (Melitz, 2003). Moreover, such costs can be significant with each successive export market entry. The Internet can lower some of the fixed costs of exporting, enabling more enterprises to engage in cross-border trade.

Digital technologies also create opportunities for new types of trade (in digitally traded products, services and tasks), as well as for more "traditional" trade using e-commerce and other online platforms to match buyers and sellers. Such platforms can help enhance the visibility of products. Many of them provide access to either free or paid services via the Internet to connect buyers and sellers, such as services related to logistics, payments, market research, trade compliance, data for market intelligence, advertising, refunds and dispute resolution (UNCTAD, 2015b). Star ratings systems and customer reviews on e-commerce platforms can give buyers a sense of trust, which, in the offline economy, would require many transactions between buyer and seller before it is established. In many developing countries, global e-commerce platforms are increasingly complemented by national or regional ones (box III.1).

---

**Box III.1. Selected e-commerce platforms in developing countries**

The development of a local e-commerce industry can provide convenience for residents through shorter shipping times, flexible payment options, relevant products and local language interface. A growing number of e-commerce platforms have emerged in developing countries, many with foreign venture capital, and several are offering a range of complementary services to facilitate e-commerce. However, those with a regional presence often face challenges in terms of cross-border sales, and have had to establish local websites for each market. Local platforms have often been able to grow in the absence of global competitors. The following provides snapshots of some of the most well-known platforms in developing countries.

*Alibaba*, a Chinese company launched in 1999, has quickly grown to become the biggest e-retailer in the world (in terms of gross merchandise value, or GMV).[a] In addition to providing different platforms for C2C, B2C and B2B e-commerce, the Alibaba Group has developed various other services to facilitate e-commerce. For example, its Cainiao logistics service handles more than 70 per cent of the country's express packages, and features a huge network of vehicles, warehouses and distribution centres. By May 2015, it was delivering more than 30 million packages per day, offering same-day delivery in 7 cities and next-day delivery in another 90 cities (Stanford Graduate School of Business, 2016). Its Alipay payment solution was used by over 450 million people, corresponding to 75 per cent of Alibaba's GMV in 2016.

The company's growth has been facilitated partly by government restrictions on foreign investment in e-commerce, which were only recently lifted,[b] and the need for an appropriate Chinese language user interface, as well as for goods adapted to local demands.

Indian B2C retailer, *Flipkart*, was launched in 2007. It has raised over $3 billion from venture capitalists in Hong Kong (China), South Africa and the United States, and is incorporated in Singapore to bypass Indian rules on foreign direct investment (FDI) in retail.[c] It claims 100 million users, 80 million products and 100,000 sellers, and it ships 8 million items a month through 21 warehouses. It is facing increasing competition from Amazon, which launched operations in India in 2013. Amazon is the fifth most popular website in India compared to Flipkart, which ranks ninth.[d]

The *Jumia Group* (formally Africa Internet Group) founded in 2012, has a presence throughout Africa. With several companies as investors, it has raised over $200 million.[e] Offering both retail sales and a marketplace for other sellers, it claims that half a million local African companies are conducting business on its portals every day. It offers retail sales in 7 African countries (Cameroon, Côte d'Ivoire, Egypt, Ghana, Kenya, Morocco and Nigeria), whereas its marketplace is available in 14 countries.[f] Its travel site lists 25,000 hotels in Africa, and the company offers food delivery in 10 countries. Jumia House, an Airbnb-type service, is available in 21 countries. Jumia also offers logistics services in a dozen countries, including cash on delivery, warehousing and logistics solutions. Despite its range of services, it has posted relatively weak results, reflecting the region's limited Internet access, low purchasing power and weak logistics. Nevertheless, its growth has been impressive, with just over 1 million active customers and an increase in its GMV from only €35 million in 2013 to about €289 million in 2015.

*Souq* is a regional online retailer headquartered in the United Arab Emirates with operations in the Gulf States and Egypt. Since its launch in 2005, Souq has grown to host 70,000 vendors offering over a million products and employing over 2,000 people in 2015.[g] It has managed to raise millions of dollars from venture capitalists in several fund-raising rounds.[h] Most of its users are from Egypt and Saudi Arabia. Its success can be attributed to local contextualization (being an Arabic language portal and offering goods that are in demand in the region), its switch from an auction site to a third-party site in 2011, and to good logistics throughout the region.

*MercadoLibre* is an e-commerce marketplace with headquarters in Argentina and operations in 18 Latin American countries. Launched in 1999, its strategic shareholder was eBay between 2001 and 2016.i It offers a range of services to support e-commerce, including logistics and payments. It is the market leader in the major countries in which it operates. Given that most of the region speaks Spanish, it has been relatively easy to develop common platforms. Nevertheless, each country has its own website with no interaction with websites in the other countries.

*Lazada*, headquartered in Singapore, was launched in 2012 as an online retailer and marketplace. By June 2017, it was operating in 6 South-East Asian countries: Indonesia, Malaysia, the Philippines, Singapore, Thailand and Viet Nam. Originally backed by Rocket Internet (Germany), China's e-commerce giant, Alibaba, acquired a controlling stake for $1 billion in 2016.[j] Lazada ranks first in e-commerce website visits in 5 of the 6 countries in which it operates. It has benefited from entering the ASEAN market before large global e-commerce companies, and its portals have been adapted to the region's different languages and consumer preferences. Lazada has its own transportation fleet, which delivers around a third of its orders to more than 80 cities throughout the region.[k] It is flexible with payments and accepts cash on delivery.

*Source:* UNCTAD.

[a]   "Global 1000 spotlight: The top 10 e-retail players dominate," *Internet Retailer*, 5 August 2016, (https://www.internetretailer.com/2016/08/05/global-1000-spotlight-top-10-e-retail-players-dominate).

[b]   See http://www.usito.org/news/china-lifts-restrictions-e-commerce-foreign-investment .

[c]   See https://www.crunchbase.com/organization/flipkart#/entity and http://www.myonlineca.in/startup-blog/flipkart-companies-financial-report.

[d]   See http://www.alexa.com/topsites/countries/IN .

[e]   See https://www.crunchbase.com/organization/jumia-nigeria#/entity .

[f]   The information in this paragraph comes from various Jumia websites, such as http://market.jumia.com, https://food.jumia.com/index.html, http://house.jumia.com, and https://services.jumia.com .

[g]   See "Souq.com chief explains one of Dubai's biggest online success stories", *The National*, 7 October 2015 (http://www.thenational.ae/business/the-life/souqcom-chief-explains-one-of-dubais-biggest-online-success-stories) .

[h]   See "Souq.com raises more than AED 1 Billion (USD 275 Million), the largest e-commerce funding in the Middle East history." Souq press release, 29 February 2016 (http://pr.souq.com/123241-souq-com-raises-more-than-aed-1-billion-usd-275-million-the-largest-e-commerce-funding-in-the-middle-east-history).

i   See "eBay to sell a majority of its stake in MercadoLibre, Inc. - eBay Inc.," Announcement, 12 October 2016 (https://www.ebayinc.com/stories/news/ebay-to-sell-a-majority-of-its-stake-in-mercadolibre-inc/).

j   See "Alibaba expands in Southeast Asia with $1 Billion Lazada deal", Bloomberg, 12 April 2016 (https://www.bloomberg.com/news/articles/2016-04-12/alibaba-to-pay-1-billion-for-control-of-lazada-e-commerce-site).

k   See http://www.economist.com/news/business/21645763-global-online-shopping-giants-may-not-find-it-easy-conquer-region-home-field.

By leveraging the Internet, companies of all sizes can become more visible to prospective customers abroad. In Europe, nearly half of all online sellers export to other EU countries.[1] While there are few official statistics in developing countries to gauge the impact of online selling on firms' export performance, private sector sources suggest that ICT use by enterprises, especially small ones, is correlated with higher exports. SMEs that are heavy Internet users have been found to be almost 50 per cent more likely to export various products and services than those that use the Internet less (Zwillenberg et al., 2014). Data from some global e-commerce platforms support this observation. In Chile, for example, all companies that were commercially selling on eBay in 2013 were exporting, on average, to as many as 28 different markets (eBay, 2013). Similar patterns have also been observed in other countries, such as Brazil, China, Mexico, the Republic of Korea and South Africa (eBay, 2016).

In smaller economies, such as those in the Pacific islands, social media platforms, such as Facebook, are emerging as a marketing tool for many companies. Anecdotal evidence abounds of SMEs that are harnessing various platforms to boost sales, including across borders (box III.2).

Women entrepreneurs in developing economies are often at a disadvantage compared with men in terms of access to finance, time constraints, mobility, and access to skills and training. E-commerce and digital solutions can help them overcome some of these barriers (UNCTAD 2011 and 2014). A 2015 survey of Pacific island exporters found that firms that were active online had a greater concentration of women executives under 45 years of age (Asian Development Bank, 2015). These women were able to run their online businesses while also performing household work, and they recognized the great potential of ICT to expand their market reach and support earnings. In Central Asia, half of the women-led companies reported using the Internet, and many gave priority to market expansion as well as better integration of ICT in order to increase production efficiency (51 per cent in Uzbekistan, 42 per cent in Kyrgyzstan, 36 per cent in Kazakhstan, and 16 per cent in Azerbaijan) (Asian

---

**Box III.2. Harnessing e-commerce platforms for exports: The cases of Urmex (Mexico) and Skin Outfit (India)**

Once a dusty storefront serving passersby in Toluca, Mexico, the USB drive manufacturer, Urmex, used to promote its products with flyers and cold calls. To test traction online, the company invested less than $10 in online advertising to reach customers in Mexico City. Realizing an immediate return on investment, it invested in further online campaigns across Mexico and later in other parts of Latin America using Google AdWords, YouTube and Twitter. It also started selling on Mercado Libre and Alibaba. As a result, by 2012, 60 per cent of Urmex's profits were being generated by exports to Latin America.

Around the same time in Mumbai, India, Taushif Ansari worked for a merchant, making leather jackets. In 2012, he started his own business – Skin Outfit – and registered with e-commerce marketplace eBay.[a] For the first six months he sold only two or three leather jackets. Then sales started to pick up, and in 2014 he employed five craftsmen, selling up to 170 jackets a month to Australia, New Zealand, the United Kingdom and the United States. As a result, he was able to earn over $12,000 per year in a country where per capita income is less than $1,500.

*Source:* Gordon and Suominen, 2014.

a   "Window to the world," *Businesstoday*, 7 December 2014 (www.businesstoday.in/magazine/features/ebay-india-website-helps-small-business-expand-global-reach/story/212398.html).

---

Development Bank, 2014). In addition, the proportion of women workers on some digital labour platforms (see section III.B) is considerably higher than in non-agricultural employment (World Bank, 2016b).

However, although digitalization can help make trade more inclusive, gains are not automatic. Companies still need to ensure that their goods and services meet the quality standards and prices expected by the potential clients. Challenges include ensuring that entrepreneurs have the required capabilities to engage in e-commerce, let alone cross-border trade, such as capabilities in digital marketing and the ability to comply with various trade rules (box III.3). An enabling environment with affordable Internet access, access to finance and affordable shipping services is also essential.

## Box III.3. Critical barriers for SMEs to engage in cross-border e-commerce

A number of critical barriers prevent SMEs in developing countries and LDCs from effectively engaging in e-commerce. The major barriers listed below derive from an assessment undertaken by the International Trade Centre (ITC).

**Lack of awareness, understanding or motivation** among policymakers, trade and investment support institutions and SMEs about opportunities for increased trade online and how to overcome related barriers.

**Lack of access, affordability and skills** with respect to relevant technologies. Many SMEs do not master technology or they lack relevant skills. Even those able to access online marketplaces may lack competence in using complementary technologies such as inventory control and order handling. Solutions involve acquiring the requisite technical knowledge and often this costs more than smaller enterprises can afford.

**Poor availability of international and local payment solutions**. Merchants may lack online payment solutions. Restrictions may result from a variety of factors, including foreign exchange controls, policies on the part of international payment providers and inadequate information about various merchants to permit effective due diligence with counterparts. Available solutions for small local businesses (e.g. bank transfers or cheques) may encounter trust problems with international customers, or may be costly to use.

**Lack of access to cost-effective logistics**. Often, the international services provided by local postal monopolies are of low-quality, and express delivery may be costly. Without collaboration, the volumes of international transport needs of SMEs remain low, leaving them in a weak position for negotiating better rates. SMEs also face the administrative burden of understanding and managing export and import duties and regulations. Without proper consideration for the handling of returned shipments, the advantages of international e-commerce can quickly disappear.

**Limited capability to manage requests and relationships with international customers.** Cultural and language barriers can hamper the ability of small companies to handle customer enquiries. Moreover, reputation takes time to build, but can be damaged quickly on the Internet.

**Low visibility, lack of a reputation and poor trust in target markets.** Potential customers need to know about the exporting firm and its products, and have trust in the marketing channel. Raising awareness of a firm's products and services is hard: promotional activities may be prohibitively costly and require a certain understanding of the end market. Building trust may require cultural awareness as well as technological solutions, such as access to verified standard security certification and, for B2B transactions, verified digital signatures.

**Lack of conformity with legal and fiscal requirements in target markets.** Failure to account for value added tax and import duties can result in the consumer having to cover unanticipated extra costs on delivery. This may lead to costly returns of goods, a loss of reputation, and the eventual barring of the merchant from e-commerce sites. More fundamentally, correct export and import licences must be obtained and retained.

*Source:* International Trade Centre (http://www.intracen.org/itc/sectors/services/e-commerce/).

Access to online cross-border payment services, supported by relevant laws and regulations, is important for local firms to engage in exports. Private payment systems, such as PayPal and Visa, are less likely to invest in locations where regulations are poor or unclear, which in turn deters major e-commerce platforms from providing their services to such locations (UNCTAD, 2015b). As the importance of online and mobile payments grows, more firms will require access to digital payment systems that can handle relatively small amounts at reasonable cost. Thus, online payments-related regulations adapted to smaller businesses are vital (ITC, 2015). With the proliferation of different payment solutions on the market, interoperability becomes increasingly important as well.

The need for compliance with customs requirements is another challenge for SMEs (box III.3). Small businesses are disproportionately affected by complex customs procedures, given their smaller shipments and, as a result, relatively higher fixed costs of compliance. Compliance is particularly challenging for smaller e-commerce sellers that export to multiple markets, each with their own regulations. Indeed, customs regimes, trusted trader and other programmes that help fast-track trade through customs tend to be tailored to the needs of relatively large traders shipping sizeable trade volumes on a regular basis. The criteria stipulated by such programmes are often difficult to meet, especially by small businesses.

Making effective use of ICTs in transport and trade facilitation – key components of international trade logistics – as well as in relevant business processes, requires particular skills, effective standardization and conversion of trade documents into electronic format, as well as the development of single windows.[2] Meanwhile, digitalization can help to promote sustainability in transport and trade logistics. This can be achieved partly by enhancing the efficiency, visibility, security and safety of shipments, strengthening quality control, improving resource allocation and reducing externalities in the form of waste, environmental damage and carbon emissions.[3]

# B. ONLINE WORK AND TRADE IN TASKS

## 1. The rise of digital labour platforms

A core feature of online platforms is their ability to aggregate demand and supply in ways that were not possible before (faster, cheaper and more easily coordinated), creating new ways of organizing production and work. These platforms have, in effect, become new "marketplaces" for both location-bound services (transportation and personal services) and location-independent services (e.g. various ICT and business services). Digitally intermediated services can create new jobs and tasks across the entire skills spectrum, with important effects on the labour market (Drahokoupil and Fabo, 2016). The following are some of the major effects:

- They permit the reorganization of activities that traditionally relied on an employment relationship into self-employment activities (e.g. freelancers, independent contractors).

- They facilitate the remote provision of tradable services, including internationally, potentially leading to the offshoring of work from local labour markets.

- They increase competition by lowering barriers to entry, even if they only reorganize self-employment, leading potentially to greater pressure on pay and working conditions. Thus, while they can create new work opportunities, they may also lead to a race to the bottom in terms of working conditions.

- They often rely on reviews and ratings. The system requires significant trust not only in the platforms (which may match people who have never met before and are based in remote locations), but also in the functioning of the review systems: can they be faked, are people paid to write reviews, who

has control of the content of the reviews, is there a possibility of censorship?

- Finally, they may contribute to increased breakdown (fragmentation) of work activities into individual, small tasks (or micro-work).[4] The tasks cover a large spectrum, from requiring low to high skills, and from low to high value added activities.

Following the categorization of "digital labour" (figure III.1), a distinction can be made between "cloud work" and "gig work". A task that can be performed from anywhere via the Internet is considered to be "cloud work". This includes work done via freelance marketplaces (e.g. Upwork and Freelancer), micro-task platforms (e.g. Amazon Mechanical Turk, Crowdflower) and contest-based platforms (e.g. 99designs). "Gig work", on the other hand, refers to location-based work facilitated by digital platforms, such as in transportation (e.g. Uber), accommodation (e.g. Airbnb) and household services (e.g. Taskrabbit). The remainder of this section focuses mainly on trade related to cloud work.

The market for "online outsourcing" surpassed $4 billion in 2016 (Kuek et al., 2015), and is estimated to be growing at an annual rate of 25 per cent (Kässi and Lehdonvirta, 2016).[5] The so-called Online Labour Index (an index of the largest English-language online work platforms that represent 60 per cent of the global market) shows that the biggest category of work performed via digital labour platforms is related to software development and technology (Kässi and Lehdonvirta, 2016). Thus, digital labour markets are doing more than just facilitating the lower, "click-worker", end of the market (figure III.2).

International competition for cloud work is expected to increase, for several reasons. Of the 3.5 billion people that already have access to the Internet, most live in low-income countries, and many seek new earning opportunities. As the next billion people go online, the average income of Internet users will progressively decline. Moreover, standardization, modularization and commodification will facilitate trade in more tasks.[6]

## 2. Cloud work and trade in tasks

Some cloud work has its roots in business process outsourcing (BPO). But whereas traditional BPOs involve large and medium-sized firms outsourcing business processes to (usually offshore) firms, cloud work allows even single entrepreneurs to outsource jobs to other individual workers or entrepreneurs on

## Figure III.1. Categorization of commercial digital labour markets

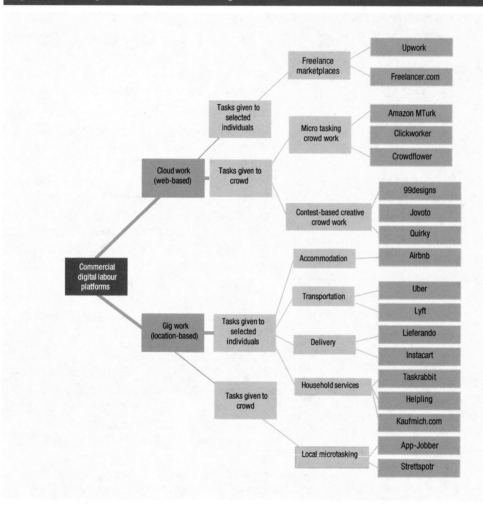

*Source:* Reproduced from Schmidt, 2017.

## Figure III.2. Task breakdown in digital labour platforms, 2016

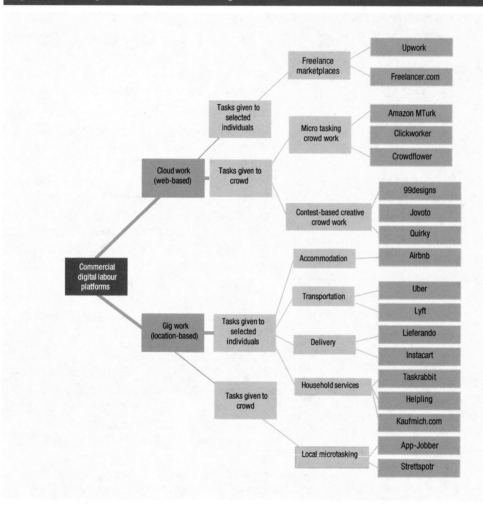

*Source:* Oxford Internet Institute Online Labour Index.

the other side of the planet. Most occupations consist of a number of tasks many of which can potentially be carried out remotely (chapter IV).[7] The provision of such tasks using online platforms can involve people anywhere in the world as long as they have access to the required ICT infrastructure and relevant skills. As digital technologies advance (for example with increased storage and file transfer possibilities, collaborative and document-sharing capabilities, audio and video facilities to conduct meetings and private networks), the scope for international trade in tasks will expand further.

The geography of cloud work is skewed. In 2016, the United States alone accounted for 51 per cent of all digital work vacancies posted (figure III.3), followed by a handful of countries (e.g. India, Australia, the United Kingdom and Canada, in that order), which together posted 24 per cent of such vacancies. In Latin America, Brazil accounts for the largest number of posted vacancies. In Africa, by contrast, most countries have not yet posted a single one. Even relative tech hubs, such as Egypt and South Africa, accounted for only 0.5 per cent each of the announced vacancies (Ojanpera, 2016).

While recruiters of cloud work are geographically highly concentrated, the jobseekers are more dispersed, originating from both rich and poor countries, according to data from one of the world's largest cloud work platforms (Graham et al., 2017). The largest numbers of online jobseekers are located in India and the Philippines, indicating possible spillover effects of BPOs.

Most digital labour platforms do not directly employ the people performing the tasks traded. Instead, they often describe the relationships between a client and a worker as a form of contracting to a freelancer or an independent contractor. This allows platforms and clients to access a global pool of workers without having to comply with local regulations and the costs and risks (to the client or platform side) associated with traditional employment contracts. Risks that would otherwise be shouldered by firms are therefore borne by those performing the tasks.

Although some national regulations try to distinguish between characteristics of employees versus freelancers (usually based on how much control workers have over their work), the nature of online platforms and the diversity of work practices that they mediate can mean that both types of workers end up earning a wage through the platforms. Some workers embrace the "freelancer" classification, while others prefer to be classified as employees (IG Metall, 2016). In some developed countries with relatively strong regulatory frameworks, these relationships are being tested.[8] In low-income developing economies, there is less clarity concerning the classification of various cloud and gig workers.

**Figure III.3. Availability of online work vacancies, share of global open vacancies, September 2016 (per cent)**

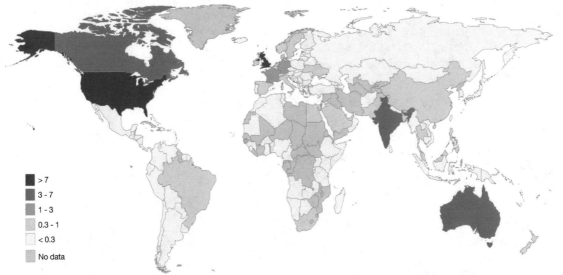

> 7
3 - 7
1 - 3
0.3 - 1
< 0.3
No data

*Source:* Oxford Internet Institute, Mapping the Availability of Online Labour, available at https://www.oii.ox.ac.uk/blog/mapping-the-availability-of-online-labour/

### a. Opportunities presented by cloud work

Online talent platforms may have a substantial economic impact. According to some studies, they could increase global GDP by $2.7 trillion by 2025, creating 72 million new full-time jobs and improving work outcomes for 540 million people (Manyika et al., 2015). Digital labour platforms can also offer solutions to challenges such as skills mismatches, informal employment, youth unemployment and underutilization of skills of the workforce. These platforms are expanding opportunities for web designers, coders, search engine optimizers, designers, translators, marketers, accountants and thousands of other types of professionals to sell their services to clients in foreign countries. Annually, some 40 million users search these platforms for jobs or talent.

Domestic platforms have emerged in some developing countries. In Nigeria, for example, Asuqu connects small businesses to creative people and professionals that offer their services, such as photographers, animators, short film creators, creative directors, web designers, architects, engineers, consultants, make-up artists and interior designers.[9] And Argentina's Workana enables 400,000 Latin American freelancers to connect with SMEs looking for part-time remote staff (Suominen, 2017a).

For workers, the ability to perform tasks digitally and remotely offers flexibility, and expands their opportunities to participate in the labour market, choose the location from which to work (e.g. from home, a library, café or an office), how many hours to work and when. For companies, it presents additional ways of improving agility and responsiveness, productivity and efficiency, taking advantage of lower costs and/or wages as well as particular skills niches, using specific services on an "on-demand and as-needed" basis, or using time differences for continued "relayed" working shifts.

There can be an inclusion aspect to digitally traded work. For example, digital platforms for tasks and talent may enable more people in remote locations or with disabilities to participate in the labour market. Those physically unable to leave their home, or those with speech, hearing and vision impairments, may be able to communicate, work, learn and train using online platforms.[10] In some contexts, online workers may be able to circumvent exclusionary barriers to work in their own country of residence. This may apply to migrants lacking the appropriate visas to work in their country of residence, people lacking required certificates or diplomas for work in a particular market, or those who fall on the wrong side of affirmative action laws (Graham, Hjorth and Lehdonvirta, 2017).

Many workers and freelancers value the opportunities of digitally traded work to earn an income or to supplement it. Almost 50 per cent of workers on Elance (now Upwork) reported that online freelancing was their sole source of income and 63 per cent that such work provided at least half of their family's total income (Kuek et al., 2015).[11] Full-time online workers were found to earn salaries comparable to, or higher than, their peers in traditional work settings (Kuek et al., 2015). For example, they can expect to be paid more than $1 per hour for tasks such as transcription, data entry and basic administrative services, some $20 per hour for software development and website design, and up to $40 per hour for consulting on patents or venture capital.

According to some studies in Kenya, Nigeria, the Philippines, Ukraine and the United States, cloud workers did not see this work as a primary source of income (Kuek et al., 2015). This is partly because the number of jobs posted on online platforms decline significantly during holiday periods, and partly because the amount of income generated is less predictable than in more traditional, fixed employment. In some cases, online freelancers (as opposed to other forms of online work) report online work as their sole source of income. A study of online freelancers in India reported that workers benefit from new employment opportunities, income, skills enhancement, career progression and flexibility afforded by such work (D'Cruz and Noronha, 2016).

The ability of people to engage in cloud work depends on various factors. Different tasks require varying levels of skills and experience. Meanwhile, basic, low-skilled tasks may serve as a stepping stone to other, more complicated tasks. In general, countries with a strong supply of workers experienced in BPOs and knowledge process outsourcing may find it easier to seize opportunities from cloud work.

### b. Challenges relating to cloud work

The rise of cloud work has raised questions related to working conditions and the longer term consequences for the bargaining power of workers (see, for example, De Stefano, 2016). While platform-enabled work offers the opportunity to generate an income along with greater flexibility, workers may find themselves in what might be considered more "precarious working arrangements" than in a traditional employer-employee relationship. Some raise concerns about the power of the various platforms, describing online labour as "platform-regulated markets", where there is insufficient protection of workers' rights (Berg, 2016). The benefit of increased flexibility may need to be weighed against the cost of foregoing assurances and protections, such as overtime compensation, minimum wage protection, health insurance, maternity and paternity leave, employer-sponsored retirement plans, paid sick leave and the ability to engage in collective action. Some experts caution against the risk of cloud work and gig work leading to a commodification of work as online platforms give access to "humans-as-a-service" (De Stefano, 2016; Irani and Silberman, 2015).

Digital platforms greatly expand the pool of workers that employers can access (Beerepoot and Lambregts, 2015). However, a large oversupply of jobseekers on online platforms weakens the bargaining power of the workers, and may lead to a tendency of a race to the bottom in terms of wages and other working conditions such as long hours of work (see, for example, Graham et al., 2017). Some online workers spend up to 80 hours a week freelancing, and are often expected to work unsociable hours to meet the demands of clients in other time zones (Graham et al., 2017b). The German trade union, IG Metall, warns that many online workers (both cloud workers and gig workers) earn below the minimum wage in their jurisdictions (IG Metall, 2016).

There may also be instances of exclusionary practices. Some job listings rule out applicants from certain countries. Furthermore, there are reports of implicit exclusion, where jobseekers have encountered preconceived notions that clients in high-income countries have about their countries (Kassi et al., 2016). Other studies note that overseas online workers are frequently paid less for similar tasks than domestic workers (Lehdonvirta et al., 2014; Graham et al., 2017).

There is a risk that the present system will create good and well-paying jobs only for a few, while for the majority, there will be little security and persistent concerns over job quality and level of compensation. This means that strategies beyond cheap, unskilled labour need to be developed if cloud work is to provide workers with sustainable livelihoods. As a result, a balance needs to be sought between the opportunities for innovation and better matching of job opportunities created by online labour platforms, on the one hand, and the risk of a race to the bottom and weaker worker protection on the other.

\*\*\*\*\*

Digital platform-based services offer both opportunities and challenges for trade in tasks and employment. Better data and more research are needed to be able to analyse the costs and benefits of online trade in tasks for both workers and enterprises, and to enable the formulation of appropriate evidence-based policies and regulatory responses. As noted above, online work arrangements are often criticized for being precarious, as they involve more informal types of working relations. On the other hand, in developing countries where other economic opportunities are in short supply, having a phone and an Internet connection can now provide opportunities to generate an income and develop new skills and professional networks.

# C. DIGITALIZATION, VALUE CHAINS AND SMALL BUSINESSES IN DEVELOPING COUNTRIES

## 1. The role of global value chains

There is growing empirical evidence that global value chains (GVCs) represent the principal way in which low-income and lower-middle-income developing economies (together referred to hereafter as "lower-income" developing economies) trade (Gereffi, 2014; Gereffi and Lee, 2012). Globalized, fragmented chains of production have begun to emerge as lead firms have increasingly focused on their core competencies and outsourced activities seen to be non-core or of lesser value (Kaplinsky and Morris, 2002; Porter, 1998). With improved access to digital technologies, services and business processes have become more tradable. This in turn has resulted in outsourcing and offshoring – as firms have taken advantage of labour cost differentials – and in networks of production that expand across global boundaries (Dicken, 2011; Murphy, 2013).

In these evolving GVCs, export-oriented firms in lower-income developing economies are typically assuming low-value roles, from which they may, over time, be able to upgrade through technological learning and knowledge absorption. Upgrading can take different forms: product, process, functional (firms taking on new functions in chains) or chain (firms moving to new value chains) upgrading, all of which can allow firms that are able to innovate or exploit their knowledge to capture more value (Kaplinsky and Morris, 2002). The ability to upgrade in a value chain depends on a firm's absorptive capacity and ability to learn how to transform, but also on the way in which the fragmented production networks are managed and coordinated (governed) by the lead firm (Gereffi et al., 2005; Gereffi, 1999).

While governance of value-chains varies, trends towards greater fragmentation have been observed in many sectors.[12] Lead firms and retailers are increasingly focusing on the high-value marketing and innovation of products and services segments (Sturgeon, 2002), leading to the outsourcing and globalization of a wider range of more complex production activities – but also of low-value activities – chain coordination and control aspects (Fold, 2001; Gereffi et al., 2005). In this process, lead firms governing such value chains pay great attention to standards and quality (Ponte and Gibbon, 2005).

For MSMEs in lower-income developing economies, GVC participation offers both opportunities and challenges. In particular, standards and quality requirements can be demanding. Achieving them may require external support and close cooperation with other actors along the value chain, which may only be available for certain preferred suppliers (Lee et al., 2012). In addition, MSMEs with weak absorptive capacity and limited financial means may get stuck in low-value activities with slim opportunities for upgrading. Profits typically accrue at places where products are invented, developed and branded, and this is unlikely to shift any time soon towards lower-income developing economies (Fold, 2001).

## 2. Impact of different kinds of digitalization of GVCs

Despite its growing relevance, few studies on digitalization have examined the underlying context of firm activity and the main forms of GVCs. With increased ICT use in developing countries, digitalization is enabling new modes of management of and participation in GVCs. It can help smaller firms overcome informational or knowledge deficiencies, such as those related to value chain coordination,

information flows and knowledge about markets (Craviotti, 2012). The analysis in this section examines ways in which improved connectivity can support MSMEs' linkages within GVCs, which is of considerable relevance for trade in lower-income developing economies. These enterprises account for a very significant share of economic activities in these economies, but are typically lagging behind larger firms in terms of ICT use (chapter II). The analysis considers three stylistic modes through which MSMEs are currently using ICTs and other digital resources in support of exports via value chains: "thintegration", "online platforms" and "full digitalization".

### a. Thintegration

The notion of "thin integration" or "thintegration" (Murphy and Carmody, 2015) refers to a minimal level of value chain digitalization, which is common in lower-income developing economies. Digital technologies may in this case help facilitate tighter coordination of the value chains, but they rarely lead to any significant transformation of relations or an increased capture of value by the local firms involved.

Many small firms in the furniture, garments and tourism sectors in lower-income developing economies are beginning to use ICTs. For instance, small furniture producers in South Africa frequently use mobile phones for communicating with employees and coordinating production. They also look at designs online as a way of building market knowledge (ibid.). Subcontractors in Asia involved in garment exports receive orders and details for products by e-mail (McNamara, 2008). Similarly, for tourism in East Africa, small hotels and travel agents use ICTs to do research about tourism sights, coordinate and send e-mail confirmations of bookings (Foster and Graham, 2015a). In these cases, the adoption of digital technologies does not significantly alter the structure of the value chains; firms continue to rely on intermediaries even after the introduction of ICTs. Reluctance to engage in more substantial digitalization sometimes reflects challenges related to the complexity associated with the logistics of exporting and integrating with external payments systems (Moodley, 2002), as well as a lack of channels to build knowledge of trends from consuming countries (Murphy and Carmody, 2015).

In agriculture, thintegration often involves the use of e-mail, mobile phones and spreadsheets by value-chain actors as a way to coordinate activities (Foster and Graham, 2015b). With growing demands related to quality, yields and logistics in agricultural exports, farmers increasingly need to coordinate inputs (such as fertilizers and seeds), the provision of finance (loans, insurance) and logistics (including rapid chain storage or cold chains) (Parikh et al., 2007). As they move away from selling basic commodities to higher value added agricultural production (such as new crop varieties or ethically produced crops), the need for effective coordination is accentuated. However such coordination is often costly to the farmers, and there are potential benefits from using more integrated digital solutions (de Silva and Ratnadiwakara, 2008). Some pilot schemes have therefore sought to provide more systematic support for exporters, including ICT-enabled seed quality testing and mobile finance services, which are burgeoning in East Africa, for example. However, these schemes are ad hoc and rarely institutionalized throughout sectors (Brugger, 2011; CTA, 2015).

Agricultural producers' export performance depends on their ability to meet quality requirements and standards. While digital tools can play a role here, there are few known examples of specific ICT-enabled interventions aimed at helping farmers upgrade their skills and processes with an export focus in particular. Some agricultural cooperatives have used ICTs to share information about improving practices between farming groups, but these have not led to radical changes in services or to improving farmers' ability to meet quality standards (Foster and Graham, 2015b).

In all aspects of agricultural production, gaining new knowledge and skills is key. This applies to the process of choosing crops, exploiting soil and weather information, enhancing farm management and improving harvesting practices. Traditionally, such activities have been supported by extension services, which are often fragmented and underfunded (Brugger, 2011; Poulton and Macartney, 2012). Various ICT systems can help overcome such limitations and provide vital information to farmers by enhancing existing extension services or providing learning or extension services remotely.[13] ICT-enabled solutions range from simple messaging applications that provide basic advice on crops, soils or weather conditions and interactive mobile apps that can support farmers' skills development, to full-fledged decision support systems aimed at helping farmers improve quality and yields (Baumüller, 2015; Brugger, 2011). ICTs can also support the sharing of good practices in areas such as seed selection and smallholder management, which

are of relevance to producers targeting local and/or export markets (Bagazonzya et al., 2011).

There is little knowledge of how ICTs have been leveraged specifically for export-related activities, apart from some pilot schemes related to exporting, standards and traceability (Bagazonzya et al., 2011; Vodafone, 2011). There have been some welcome recent initiatives, such as the Trade for Sustainable Development programme led by the International Trade Centre (ITC, 2016a), and pilot projects in the horticulture sector linked to EU market access (Ihedigbo, 2014). However, given the importance of standards and quality to small agricultural exporters, there is need for more significant interventions. Standards bodies, in particular, could play a more active role in helping to build capacity and supplement existing modes of auditing by ICTs to enable more producers to attain the quality levels needed to succeed in export markets (Foster and Graham, 2015b).

### b. Platform digitalization

The second mode of digitalization observed in value chains involves the use of online platforms. It is used in different ways across sectors, with varying impacts. The following examples from the agriculture and tourism sectors as well as from some global e-commerce platforms are discussed.

### i. Platforms in agriculture

Improved access to markets for agricultural output and for securing fair prices within those markets are key potential benefits of ICT use. Diffusion of ICTs has been found to reduce market price differentials between scattered trading points, with stronger impacts on prices in more isolated markets (Aker, 2010; Muto and Yamano, 2009; Zanello et al., 2014). One way of improving the functioning of markets is to set up systems of ICT-enabled price dissemination. Such systems mainly involve commodities for which transparent market price information is available and for which there are a large number of buyers and sellers.

When selling across borders, greater price transparency may need to be complemented by efforts to enhance the ability of potential exporters to trade. Some market information systems offer producers transparent price information or the possibility to sell their outputs via various platform-based exchanges, such as face-to-face auctions or online e-commerce platforms.

ICT-supported price information and commodity exchanges are now in operation in many developing countries. Examples include the Ethiopia commodity exchange and the Nairobi coffee auction, both of which are supporting coffee exports (EuropeAid, 2012). While some of these exchanges have been successful, many are only partially digitalized.[14] Analog commodity exchanges tend to be slow to adopt ICTs. For example, the Kenyan tea auction has been digitized for some operations, such as for payments and for the provision of limited price information, but it has not been transformed into a fully ICT-enabled online platform, which would facilitate more efficient trading (Foster and Graham, 2015b; Waema and Katua, 2014). Without digitalization, commodity exchanges risk remaining centralized marketplaces that give traders and intermediaries who are able to travel to these centres to trade a greater advantage than producers and processors in more remote locations.

The most successful online platform exchanges tend to be privately run systems or ones that involve combinations of private, public and donor funding. Examples include eChopal (India), Esoko (Ghana), mFarm (Kenya) and Novus Agro (Nigeria). All of them use ICTs to provide price information alongside other services (such as export advice or logistics) for agricultural exporters (Brugger, 2011; GEMS4, 2016; Parikh et al., 2007). Such platforms have been found to be more dynamic and more responsive to market needs, and they can lead to higher export prices (Goyal, 2010).

However, there is a need for more research on the effectiveness of various online platforms (Duncombe, 2016). Price and export platforms can be problematic for marginal producers if they become exposed to exchange rate fluctuations, changes in retailer demand, national policies and prices. This is particularly an issue for sellers using online platforms that cover multiple regions and countries, and when buyers can rapidly shift between exporters when economic and policy conditions change (Kumar, 2014). For producers to make effective use of online platforms, they also need to meet quality, safety and volume requirements. This is especially challenging for smallholder farmers. For example, many small-scale soybean producers prefer to continue to trade through intermediaries rather than via the online market platform eChopal. This is because the intermediaries are willing to accept lower quality goods that they could subsequently sort and improve, a service not offered through eChopal (ibid.). The online

platform may nevertheless be useful in serving as an incentive for more small producers to upgrade their skills over time to be able to avoid intermediaries in the future.

Digitalization of market price information and online platform trading are set to play a growing role by enabling scattered producers to become better organized for exporting activities. Farmers in lower-income developing economies are likely to be successfully integrated when online platforms are available locally and allow farmers to interact more directly, rather than having to trade through intermediaries. Platforms in agriculture also tend to be more successful when they provide a range of agriculture support services and systems (such as logistics, finance, insurance and provision of seeds and fertilizers) in addition to price information (Burrell and Oreglia, 2013).

### ii. Platforms in tourism

Digitalization has become central to all processes in the tourism industry. The tourism product itself, inasmuch as it consists of an experience, comprises information that is produced and consumed even before the trip itself has begun. Online platforms, such as online travel agents (OTAs), can allow MSMEs to reach more potential international tourists. However, as discussed below, making effective use of OTA systems can be challenging for many small tourist firms (Foster and Graham, 2015a). Even when hotels are able to participate in online platforms, the business they generate can sometimes be unpredictable (see box III.4).

There are some cases of small firms in tourism successfully using online platforms to support their growth. Some local platforms and systems provide specific solutions for MSMEs. For example, in South Africa, the online hotel booking software solution, NightsBridge, offers customized systems for MSMEs through an easy-to-use hotel reservation and booking management system (which then automatically links up with other OTA providers) (Foster and Graham, 2015a; Murphy et al., 2014). There are particular opportunities for small hotels in niche areas, such as ecotourism and environmental travel, where an online presence can give MSMEs access to international markets. When firms offer attractive products, online visibility provides marketing credentials and facilities to both customers and international tourism firms (Foster and Graham, 2015a; Lai and Shafer, 2005).

---

**Box III.4. Small hotels and online travel agents in East Africa**

High-end tourism in East Africa typically involves "packaged" trips, with tour operators in the home country of the travellers arranging a package of hotels and logistics. They tend to use hotels and lodges that are well-known to them. Small hotels that lack good connections and sufficiently good-quality accommodation find it difficult to reach such travellers. These hotels may see opportunities from participating in online platforms that offer new ways of reaching international tourists or business travellers.

However, integration into OTAs is not always straightforward. It can involve complex requirements, such as integrating a hotel's booking systems with an application programming interface or using specialist "channel management" software, for which many small hotels lack the necessary skills and infrastructure. They may still be managing bookings via a paper-based ledger or a customized medium, such as an excel spreadsheet, which is not sufficient to be able to integrate with the OTAs.

One large OTA that was keen to include more Rwandan hotels in its system sought to find a solution to this problem. It contracted a local firm to act as intermediary to process and deal with bookings received via the OTA. The firm liaised with small hotels to confirm the booking details. Ironically, the smaller hotels' use of an online platform in this case was made possible only by the reintroduction of an intermediary.

Small hotels are sometimes sceptical about the benefits of OTA use. The OTA contracts hotels to block a certain number of rooms that can be used exclusively by that OTA. While this is designed to avoid double bookings, hotels often find that they end up with empty rooms. Moreover, many hotels are not sure how to improve their booking arrangements through OTAs: whether they need to pay for search engine optimization, use social media to build a presence, and how to use websites such as TripAdvisor to attract customers.

*Source:* Adapted from Foster and Graham, 2015a.

---

### iii. Use of global platforms

Notwithstanding the limitations in the provision of support to MSME involvement in some value chains, global online platforms are becoming increasingly important. Direct sales of certain types of goods on international markets (such as intermediate products, gifts, retail food) can sometimes be more viable, particularly when they are differentiated or value-added outputs.

Early studies in developing countries found that the use of e-commerce platforms for exports by some firms encountered problems due to difficulties in evaluating the trustworthiness and quality of firms, production processes and products, or because payment solutions were poorly integrated or inflexible (Molla and Heeks, 2007; Paré, 2002). Newer generations of such platforms offer more export opportunities for small firms. They include more sophisticated ratings, more viable payment options and guarantees that can provide stronger protection for both buyers and sellers, thereby helping to overcome the "trust deficit" (Parker et al., 2016).

It is becoming easier for firms in lower-income developing economies to integrate, for example, with e-commerce sites like Amazon Marketplace and eBay, as well as B2B sites like Alibaba and TradeKey. E-commerce platforms are extending their protections and coverage to support traders in a growing number of countries (eBay, 2013). This enables SMEs to trade using a convenient payment system and platforms in their own language. With more widespread Internet access, such platforms are becoming increasingly important export facilitation channels for intermediate or final goods (UNCTAD, 2015b; World Bank, 2016b). However, access to them remains uneven across the developing world (Kende, 2015; UNCTAD, 2015b).

### c. Full digitalization

Improved connectivity is gradually enabling more complete digital systems integration of value chains. Activities affected by digitalization in this case go beyond online trading and chain coordination, to using ICTs for the integration of a wider range of activities into single systems, thus making value chains increasingly data-driven. This trend is fast emerging, particularly in GVCs that are governed by large enterprises and MNEs.

### i. Full digitalization in agriculture

In agriculture, fully digitally integrated systems often start with the collection of agricultural data (e.g. on the weight or quality of crops). Data-integrated devices include mobile data collection apps (Brugger, 2011), tracking based on bar codes and radio frequency identification (RFID) (Bagazonzya et al., 2011), as well as field collection devices (e.g. scales and weighbridges)

(Foster and Graham, 2015b). Such devices seamlessly integrate with computerized information systems that can enable tracking of information on every transaction in great detail. As goods move along the value chain, additional segments of the information system rely on digital solutions for different purposes: tracking and facilitating payments (including with mobile money), tracking goods in processing factories, enabling agribusinesses to manage exporting by smallholders, improving data management in value chains (Armstrong et al., 2011), and sending specific information messages to farmers through short message service (SMS) (Technoserve, 2016).

Digitally integrated value chains are context-specific and vary, depending on the kinds of products involved. Examples include pilot projects to digitize the value chains of nuts using SAP software in Ghana, and the enterprise resource planning (ERP) software, SAGE, in Kenya (Franz et al., 2014; Rammohan, 2010). Non-governmental organizations (NGOs) and development partners have created similar digitized value chain pilot schemes in partnership with agribusinesses in Kenya and Ghana, providing fully integrated solutions for farmers, intermediaries and agribusinesses (Ashraf et al., 2009; Bagazonzya et al., 2011; IFDC, 2015; Technoserve, 2016).

The use of digitally integrated systems in agriculture is still limited, though there are indications that they can boost overall value chain efficiency by helping to improve the management and tracking of goods and payments in complex value chains, reduce costs and open up export opportunities for more farmers. Farmers appreciate the possibility for easy tracking of payments and lower risk of being cheated (for example, through losses resulting from false weighing or during transportation). More research is needed on potential barriers to inclusion in such systems. When activities are digitalized, they replace activities previously coordinated by farmer groups, cooperatives and unions. Such transformation may pose a challenge to those producers that lack the ability to adapt and meet the necessary requirements to participate in the digitalized system (Foster and Graham, 2015b), which again calls for the need for capacity-building and skills development.

### ii. Full digitalization in garments production

In the garments sector, value chains are increasingly aligned with "fast fashion" models, which revolve around strategies of retailers maintaining low stocks, rapidly evolving customized designs and just-in-time production (Tokatli, 2008). The dominant model for exporters is based on customized made-to-order production, where export relationships between producers and retailers derive from a level of mutual trust (Moodley et al., 2003). For MSMEs involved as subcontractors in such export value chains, connections are typically made through intermediaries (such as buying agents) and often require the movement of samples for inspection (Ahsan and Azeem, 2010; Thanh et al., 2009).

In such contexts, the potential for more open platforms is limited. Instead, retailers require the close integration of supplier firms through formal linkages. Trusted contractors are often given access to the internal information systems of the retailers so that they can track stock levels and record their production (Humphrey et al., 2003; Nayak et al., 2015). More advanced firms may further integrate production through the use of RFID and bar codes to track goods and enterprise resource planning (ERP) tools to monitor stocks and payments (McNamara, 2008).

Thus, there is a split in the garment value chains between preferred suppliers that are digitally integrated and subcontractors that are only "thintegrated". This split may have implications for subcontractors and their potential to upgrade due to the distant contact they have with retailers. All firms, however, feel the impacts of the "fast fashion" models. Facilitated by digitally integrated value chains, these models can create new risks for firms that are transferred to contractors and subcontractors in terms of stock requirements, unpredictable orders and demand for a rapid turnaround (Tokatli, 2008).

## 3. Who gains from the digitalization of GVCs?

What are the possible implications of the different models of value-chain digitalization? In the case of thintegration, ICT use is typically ad hoc and minimal. ICTs may be used to improve coordination and activities in GVCs, but without significantly changing the overarching relationships in them. Slow progress towards more sophisticated forms of digitalization often reflects well-known barriers: lack of skills, motivation, resources and appropriate systems (Van Dijk, 2005). In tourism, for example, skills gaps often limit the extent to which small hotels are able to technically link into global systems, even if they enjoy good connectivity. In some sectors of agriculture, the use of online platforms is feasible mainly if firms can obtain complementary support in the form of capacity-building, training or other technical assistance that can enable them to obtain finance or meet quality standards.

In buyer-driven GVCs controlled by a few lead firms, such as in garments and agricultural commodities (Gereffi, 1999), various forms of more open online platforms allow sellers from lower-income developing economies to reach buyers. Examples include the use of agricultural price platforms by exporters in Africa and the use of e-commerce platforms by agricultural firms. However, where large buyers are dominant, they are likely to exercise control over access to markets and to their trusted brands, in which case the transformational impact of digital platforms will be limited. Moreover, the quality of goods and services in some value chains (such as in garments) can be difficult to assess remotely, making digital platforms less suitable for managing the exchanges.

Platforms are the most useful in markets characterized by a diversity of buyers rather than by the dominance of a single market or set of firms. They also offer scope for functional upgrading in value chains where producers build trust and potentially move to sell higher value-added exports. For instance, cases have been noted of producers using platforms to upgrade from commodities to beer-making, or from basic goods to food products that could be regionally exported (Hinson, 2010; Tiamiyu et al., 2012).

Participation in online platforms may be more useful for smaller firms that compete in specific, well-defined market segments, such as niche trading in tourism and in value-added food products (e.g. ethical goods) as well as in regional and emerging market value chains. While such segments and markets may seem relatively small, these kinds of online platforms can help producers reach more clients and achieve sufficient scale and income generation.

## D. CONCLUSIONS

This chapter has shown how the use of digital solutions is creating new opportunities for companies of all sizes to engage in international trade, notably by increasing market access for customers, supply chains and competitors, and by reducing trade costs. It is affecting MSMEs in countries at all levels of development, but in different ways. Potential economic benefits for developing-country companies and consumers range

from greater efficiencies to deeper specialization and division of labour, gains from variety and greater predictability for all players, as well as lower costs and prices of inputs and final products. Digital technologies can also be used to empower women entrepreneurs. However, in order to harness digitalization in support of trade, investments in ICT infrastructure need to be complemented by an appropriate set of regulations and institutions, and support for skills development.

The rise of trade in tasks mediated by online labour platforms is creating new income-generating opportunities for people in developing countries who have adequate connectivity and relevant skills. However, an oversupply of jobseekers on online platforms can weaken the bargaining power of the workers, and may provoke a race to the bottom in terms of wages and other working conditions. Some experts caution against the risk of cloud work and gig work leading to the commodification of work. Further research and policy dialogue will be important to ensure that this expanding area of the economy will provide decent and quality jobs (Berg, 2016). The focus needs to be on policy areas such as labour market and social security policies, taxation and skills development. Some policy developments will be best undertaken at the national level, though international initiatives may help to develop relevant guidelines and share good practices.

When considering adequate responses to the drawbacks of cloud work, constructive approaches should be explored to protecting the workers involved without stifling the growth and innovation opportunities that such work may offer. As emphasized in the ILO Fundamental Principles and Rights at Work, no worker should be denied access to basic human rights such as freedom of association and the right to collective bargaining (De Stefano, 2016).

The *Crowdworking Code of Conduct*, which was compiled by eight German work platforms, is one example of how unions and platforms can work together to ensure that fair payment mechanisms are set up for workers. There are also proposals to make workers' existing ratings portable from one platform to another in order to reduce the dependence on specific platforms (De Stefano, 2016). Websites such as Turkopticon (https://turkopticon.ucsd.edu/) and FairCrowdwork Watch (www.faircrowdwork.org) have been established to raise awareness among workers about bad clients and jobs. There is a growing international movement to support cooperatives, but so far mainly for gig work (see, for example, Scholz and Schneider, 2017). Instead of allowing intermediaries to extract rents, worker-owned labour platforms may help ensure that workers are paid fair wages and are not subject to unreasonable working conditions. Some cooperatives already exist in the case of "gig work",[15] but examples in the cloud work sector are still lacking.

Digitalization in sectors of particular importance for developing countries is evolving at different speeds, with diverse implications for the enterprises concerned. Many small firms in developing countries continue to have limited participation in the digital economy, often reflecting inadequate connectivity, a low level of awareness of the benefits of digitalization,

skills gaps and other barriers. In order to enable and foster favourable development outcomes from the digitalization of GVCs, a number of policy challenges need to be addressed (as discussed in chapter VI).

More research is needed at the interface of digitalization, GVCs, platforms, small exporters and relevant policies, examining how different factors may enable firms to succeed in international trade. Countries need to work towards creating an enabling environment for trade in the digital economy. In this context, there should be close collaboration between the public and private sectors, as well as with civil society, to address challenges and shape solutions effectively and in a timely manner.

# NOTES

1. Eurostat data from 2014 (http://ec.europa.eu/eurostat/statistics-explained/index.php/E-commerce_statistics).

2. The single window concept refers to a facility that allows parties involved in trade and transport to lodge standardized information and documents with a single entry point to fulfil all import, export, and transit-related regulatory requirements (see http://tfig.unece.org/contents/single-window-for-trade.htm).

3. For further information, see *UNCTAD Sustainable Freight Transport* portal (https://unctadsftportal.org/) and *UNCTAD Review of Maritime Transport*, various issues (http://unctad.org/RMT) .

4. For example, Amazon Mechanical Turk (MTurk) refers to these as "HITs – Human Intelligence Tasks – individual tasks that you work on" (see https://www.mturk.com/mturk/welcome, accessed 10 March 2017).

5. These authors define online outsourcing as "the contracting of third-party workers and providers (often overseas) to supply services or perform tasks via Internet-based marketplaces or platforms. These technology-mediated channels allow clients to outsource their paid work to a large, distributed, global labor pool of remote workers, to enable performance, coordination, quality control, delivery, and payment of such services online" (Kuek et al., 2015: page 1).

6. In much the same way as the development of standardized container sizes spurred economic globalization, the development of standardized chunks of work also facilitates cross-border trade.

7. Some of the smaller tasks can be provided by some form of remotely located AI system. In this way, the trend towards cloud work may also accelerate the move towards the automation of tasks.

8. For example, in a case brought by GMB, a British trade union, a tribunal ruled that Uber could not classify its drivers in the United Kingdom as self-employed workers (see Employment Tribunal: "Mr Y Aslam, Mr J Farrar and Others -V- Uber", Case Numbers: 2202551/2015 & Others, 28 October 2016, at: https://www.judiciary.gov.uk/wp-content/uploads/2016/10/aslam-and-farrar-v-uber-reasons-20161028.pdf).

9. See Asuqu, at: https://www.asuqu.com/.

10. This is in addition to audio and video communication technologies, and technologies such as speech recognition, speech to text, big pointer utilities, screen magnifiers, screen readers and electronic Braille (see, for example, http://www.hongkiat.com/blog/assistive-apps-gadgets/).

11. In a more recent survey of crowd workers on Amazon Mechanical Turk and Crowdflower, 40 per cent of the workers said they relied on crowd work as their main source of income (Berg, 2016).

12. This may change in the future, especially if protectionist sentiments translate into barriers to trade. Moreover, automation and robotization may reduce fragmentation tendencies, although there is still little evidence of their impact on outsourcing and offshoring.

13. For a recent review, see http://www.e-agriculture.org/blog/icts-and-agricultural-extension-services .

14. More research is needed into why the exchanges are not fully digitalized and the possible implications for the users and for policies.

15. For instance, Stocksy.com is a stock photo site where photographers are co-owners, and Fairmondo.de is a cooperative version of eBay.

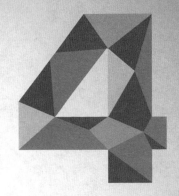

# THE DIGITAL ECONOMY, JOBS AND SKILLS

Increased digitalization is expected to have disruptive effects on jobs and skills. It will lead to new types of jobs and employment, change the nature and conditions of work, alter skills requirements and affect the functioning of the labour markets as well as the international division of labour. As countries and locations benefit from improved access to similar digital infrastructure, being able to exploit these resources better than others becomes an increasingly important determinant of the competitiveness of enterprises and locations.

This chapter explores possible implications of digitalization on jobs and skills in the short to medium term. Section A looks at the nature and conditions of work. Section B discusses possible effects on net job creation and section C examines the implications for skills requirements. Section D considers various policy implications and section E concludes.

# THE DIGITAL ECONOMY, JOBS AND SKILLS

## The 4 key changes
### due to **increased digitalization**

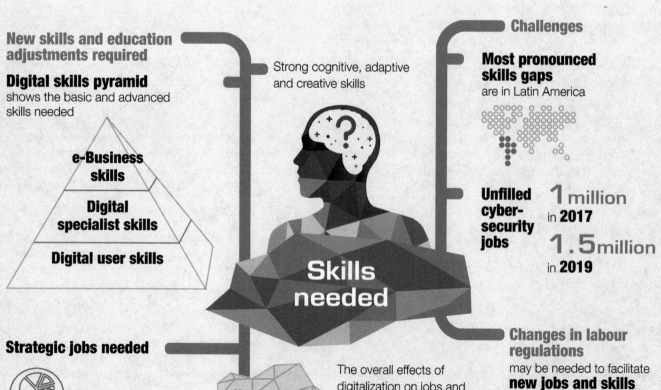

**New jobs and occupations created**

Production of **new goods and services** (e-commerce, 3D printing, software, apps development, AI)

Production of **existing products** responding to increased demand

**Some jobs will dissapear** as a result of **automation**

more than **85%** of retail workers in **Indonesia and the Philippines** are at high risk of automation

**The conditions of work will be affected**

**Benefits:** to people in remote locations and people with disabilities, bringing flexibility and independence

**Risks:** increased competition via online labour platforms; race to the bottom of working conditions with an increasing precarity

**Labour market**

**More work will involve digital skills**

---

**New skills and education adjustments required**

**Digital skills pyramid** shows the basic and advanced skills needed

- e-Business skills
- Digital specialist skills
- Digital user skills

Strong cognitive, adaptive and creative skills

**Skills needed**

**Strategic jobs needed**

Data scientists & analysts

**Uncertainty**

The overall effects of digitalization on jobs and skills remain uncertain; they will be context-specific and differ among countries and sectors.

**Challenges**

**Most pronounced skills gaps** are in Latin America

**Unfilled cyber-security jobs**

**1** million in **2017**

**1.5** million in **2019**

**Changes in labour regulations** may be needed to facilitate **new jobs and skills transitions**

# A. HOW WILL DIGITALIZATION TRANSFORM JOBS?

Four sets of changes to the labour market can be expected with increased digitalization (Degryse, 2016): job creation, job destruction, job changes and job shifts.

Greater reliance on digital technologies will lead to the creation of new jobs and occupations in various sectors, including for the production of new goods and services or existing products that respond to increased demand. The demand for work can be expected to grow in areas such as data analysis, software and applications (apps) development, networking and artificial intelligence (AI), as well as designing and production of new intelligent machines, robots and 3D printers. For example, with the greater use of IoT, firms will need to hire more product managers, software developers (including for smart phones), hardware designers, data scientists, user experience designers and sales managers.[1] Similarly, there is likely to be job growth in "pure" digital firms. For example, in the United States, the number of employees in e-commerce firms that do not have a physical retail shop rose by 66 per cent between 2010 and 2014, from 130,000 to 210,000.[2] And in Viet Nam, by August 2015, some 29,000 people were engaged in developing mobile apps (Mandel, 2015). As the digital economy grows, enterprises across sectors are likely to hire more people with skills related to cyber security. Estimates suggest that there are one million unfilled cyber-security jobs worldwide, and that by 2019 the number will have risen to 1.5 million.[3]

Other areas where the demand for more workers can be expected to increase include the production of new infrastructure, transport equipment, ICT products and complex software (Nübler, 2016). While the implementation of labour-saving technologies may help increase productivity, there is also likely to be scope for expanding work in new ways. For example, reduced health-care costs may boost the demand for more sophisticated medical services, and the automation of some banking services may lead to more customized "relationship banking" (ibid.).

Secondly, digitalization will make some jobs obsolete. Advances in computerization, software, automation, robots and AI enhance the scope for disruptions to traditional industries, with smart machines taking over functions currently performed by people. For example, according to a 2016 study, 89 per cent of all salaried workers in the Philippines' BPO sector are at high risk of losing their jobs to automation (ILO, 2016). On-site security guards may similarly be replaced by sensors monitored remotely in centres that provide surveillance for multiple sites.

Thirdly, the nature of work will be affected. Digitalization may automate some tasks or activities but not others. An increasing number of tasks that are components of even highly skilled jobs risk becoming automated and/or outsourced. For example, secretarial work was first disrupted when computers reduced the need for assistants. The next disruption may be the shift to digital assistants, further reducing the need for secretarial assistance. The use of digital devices will grow in different jobs, requiring different kinds of skills. Car mechanics routinely run diagnostics on laptops, and truck drivers use GPS devices, including for route optimization, fuel efficiency and fuel prices. The next technology, which is already being rolled out, is connected devices that transmit usage and maintenance data (e.g. of car engines and tyres) directly to the factory and service facilities.

Routine tasks that follow explicit and codifiable procedures, whether they are manually intensive (such as typing) or cognitive intensive (e.g. book-keeping), are more likely to be automated with software (Autor et al., 2003). A profound – and yet unanswered – question is what percentage of tasks in various jobs will ultimately yield to automation, and how much labour will be needed to perform the remaining tasks. Whether a job will continue to exist in a transformed form or disappear altogether, automation will change the traditional division of labour and tasks, affecting all sectors and all levels of skills.

Finally, digitalization will change the conditions of work. Online platforms are matching tasks across the whole skills spectrum (from "counting clicks" to writing articles or coding). As noted in chapter III, these platforms are transforming labour markets by favouring certain types of contracts (freelance and contract work over regular employment) and enabling the entry of new competitors. As a result, workers with high levels of social protection find themselves in competition with other workers (in the domestic market or abroad) with low levels of social protection (Degryse, 2016). This has implications for how benefits, health care and pensions are organized, and for the provision of training and continuing education.

# B. WHAT WILL BE THE OVERALL JOB IMPACT OF DIGITALIZATION?

Opinions differ widely on what will be the likely overall impact of digitalization on aggregate employment, and whether job creation will outweigh job destruction.[4] A particular concern is that those losing their job may find it hard to fill the new vacancies created by digitalization, at least not without reskilling or retraining. The rapid pace of technological change and disruption accentuates the risk of mismatching of skills and highlights the urgent need for adjustment measures. All sectors will experience changes from digitalization, although the implications will vary considerably among countries, depending on their level of digitalization and the structure of the economy.

Is there reason to expect that this wave of technological change will differ from previous technological revolutions, which did not result in mass unemployment?[5] Aggregate unemployment numbers of the past suggest that displaced workers ultimately found employment.[6] While there may be initial negative employment impacts when technologies lead to labour-saving efficiency gains, new jobs are created, including through multiplier effects when the technology contributes to accelerating growth. However, such "second round effects" take time to materialize. The question is how long the transition will last and how the human costs involved can be mitigated. Even though the agricultural and industrial revolutions did not lead to long-term mass unemployment, they were accompanied by social dislocations and painful adjustment processes (e.g. Murray and van Welsum, 2014). The International Labour Organization (ILO) will be looking closely at the effect of digitalization on the future of work as it celebrates its 100 year anniversary in 2019.[7]

Contrary to previous industrial revolutions, this time new technologies will have (indeed are already starting to have) a significant impact not only on labour-intensive manufacturing, clerical, retail and customer services occupations, but also on what

have traditionally been considered high-skilled service sector occupations, such as in law, financial services, education and health care. The fact that multiple economic sectors will be affected makes it all the more challenging for the economy to absorb those losing their jobs.

It is premature to estimate how many jobs created will ultimately compare with how many are lost. The impact will differ by technology, country and over time, and will also depend on policy decisions (see Qiang, 2009). Assessments range from negative or small positive impacts, to substantially positive multiplier effects (see, for example, van Welsum et al., 2013). Other studies have estimated the number of jobs that would potentially be affected by digital technologies and/or automation (e.g. Frey and Osborne, 2017) and by robots (Acemoglu and Restrepo, 2017).

Many reports envisage a bleak future for jobs. A study for the United States estimated that 47 per cent of jobs will be potentially exposed to automation (Frey and Osborne, 2017).[8] In South-East Asia, more than 85 per cent of salaried retail workers in Indonesia and the Philippines are at high risk of automation, as are an equally high share of salaried workers in the textiles, clothing and footwear sectors in Cambodia and Viet Nam (ILO, 2016). At the same time, while many jobs will change as some tasks are automated, they may not necessarily be displaced (Arntz et al., 2016).

Although there is not much evidence to confirm that this technological wave will be different from earlier cycles, labour markets in some developed countries appear to have become increasingly polarized, especially in the United States since the 1990s (Autor et al., 2001; Goos et al., 2014; Michaels et al., 2010). Meanwhile, another study has found that while increased use of ICTs may lead to polarization, this has not been the case for the use of industrial robots (Graetz and Michaels, 2015). In most developing countries for which detailed statistics are available, the share of employment in low- and high-skilled occupations is rising, while its share in medium-skilled occupations intensive in routine tasks is falling (World Bank, 2016a).

The extent and pace of automation will depend not only on technical feasibility, but also on factors such as the cost of automation and the relative scarcity, skills and costs of workers who would otherwise perform the tasks (Chui et al., 2016). Decisions to introduce automation will be determined by its benefits (e.g. cost reduction, improved efficiency and productivity), but they will also be influenced by regulatory issues and social acceptance.

The share of routine versus non-routine tasks and jobs, as well as the degree of digital technology penetration in an economy will determine the time lag in the disruption caused by digitalization in countries (World Bank, 2016a). The short-term impact in low- and middle-income developing economies may be moderated by less pressure to introduce automation due to relatively lower labour costs and limited technology adoption. Thus, transformation may take longer where the rate of technology adoption is starting from a lower level and at a slower pace. At the same time, as more activities become automated, there is a greater probability of reshoring back to developed countries, of production that had previously been offshored to lower cost locations in developing countries. This could affect workers in the textiles and clothing sectors in countries such as Cambodia and Viet Nam, for example (ILO, 2016).

Focusing specifically on the use of robots in the manufacturing sector, UNCTAD's *Trade and Development Report 2017* suggests that existing evidence on the potential adverse effects of automation on employment and income may be focusing too much on what is technically feasible and too little on what is economically profitable (UNCTAD, 2017f). It predicts that further automation is likely to reinforce the tendency of concentration of manufacturing output and employment in those developed and developing countries that are already competitive. Indeed, in countries like China, Germany, Mexico and the Republic Korea, the increased use of robots has been accompanied by increases or very small declines in manufacturing employment. This may, however, make it more difficult for other developing countries to follow the traditional path of industrialization.

## C. NEED FOR NEW SKILLS

Whatever the rate of change or ultimate outcome of the process of digitalization, the workers of tomorrow will need skills that enable them to create economic value in a world where many jobs are likely to be replaced by automation, software, AI and robots (Levy and Murnane, 2013). Workers will need to be "racing with the machines" rather than "against them", finding ways in which their skills complement the tasks that machines can carry out and enable them to use and/or augment AI.[9]

People displaced by automation do not necessarily have the skills to perform the tasks that are required in the newly created jobs and tasks.[10] Skills gaps are already visible in the world. A study of emerging economies found that they are particularly significant in Latin America (Melguizo and Perea, 2016). Firms in that region were three times more likely than firms in South Asia, and 13 times more likely than those in the Asia-Pacific region, to experience operational problems due to a shortage of human capital. And in a 2016 survey of 42,000 employers, 40 per cent of the respondents reported difficulties filling vacancies, especially those requiring skilled "trade workers", IT personnel, sales representatives, engineers and technicians.[11]

The absence of interventions to address skills shortages may result in significant mismatches, aggravated by the rapid pace of change in the demand for skills (Cornell ILR School, 2013, 2014; Stewart, 2014). Mismatches and shortages hinder firms' efforts to innovate and adopt new technologies. They reduce labour productivity and make firms less competitive vis-à-vis those that have access to the required skills. At the individual level, a lack of required skills makes it difficult to find a job.

Many different types of skills will be needed in the digital economy. The relationship between three distinct – but complementary – groups of digital skills can be represented in the shape of a "skills pyramid" (figure IV.1). Each group spans from basic to advanced skills. A broad and basic level of digital literacy and competency among citizens and firms constitutes the foundation of the digital economy. Building on this, more specialized and technical skills are required by the producers of digital/ICT tools. Finally, a third set of skills is required by those who apply/create/invent innovative business models and by users of digital/ICT tools and their applications. Developed and developing countries alike will need an adequate supply of these distinct types of skills to be able to take advantage of digital technologies.

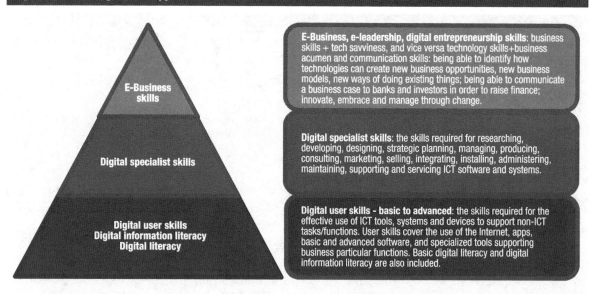

**Figure IV.1. The digital skills pyramid**

E-Business skills

**E-Business, e-leadership, digital entrepreneurship skills**: business skills + tech savviness, and vice versa technology skills+business acumen and communication skills: being able to identify how technologies can create new business opportunities, new business models, new ways of doing existing things; being able to communicate a business case to banks and investors in order to raise finance; innovate, embrace and manage through change.

Digital specialist skills

**Digital specialist skills**: the skills required for researching, developing, designing, strategic planning, managing, producing, consulting, marketing, selling, integrating, installing, administering, maintaining, supporting and servicing ICT software and systems.

Digital user skills
Digital information literacy
Digital literacy

**Digital user skills - basic to advanced**: the skills required for the effective use of ICT tools, systems and devices to support non-ICT tasks/functions. User skills cover the use of the Internet, apps, basic and advanced software, and specialized tools supporting business particular functions. Basic digital literacy and digital information literacy are also included.

*Source:* European Commission, 2014; van Welsum and Lanvin, 2012.

At the bottom of the pyramid, a broad base of *foundational digital skills* is required by all consumers and users of digital services and ICT tools, including:

- *Digital literacy skills*, for example to use ICT devices and to be able to go online and navigate the Internet.

- *Digital information literacy skills* to find information online and distinguish between reliable and non-reliable sources and information.

- *Basic digital/ICT user skills* to use basic software to perform tasks such as sending and receiving e-mails, word processing and using spreadsheets in many different occupations.

- *More advanced digital/ICT user skills* for more complex operations using basic software packages and more advanced packages (e.g. sector-specific packages for data treatment and analysis, design, architecture or accounting). Analysts of all kinds of data need to learn about new data sources, new ways of collecting data, how regulations concerning data affect what can be collected and analysed, and what technologies to adopt for secure data storage and use.

Beyond the foundational skills, a higher level of skills is required to build, supply, deploy and manage digital tools and services. Such *specialist skills* range from those required to roll out, upgrade and repair physical ICT infrastructure (e.g. cables, hardware such as computers, routers and servers) to those possessed by software engineers, apps developers, systems architects and data scientists.

New technological developments give rise to new skill requirements or to a different emphasis on certain skills. The growth of IoT, for example, increases the demand for people with skills related to data analytics, business management, hardware and systems design, and security.[12] As IoT and big data become more widely used, data scientists and analysts become more central and strategic in the operations of many firms. Being able to figure out what to do with increasing amounts of data, and identifying what is valuable and what creates new business opportunities will be key. Such roles in turn will require broader skill sets, combining analytical, software and architecture skills with business acumen and communications skills (evolving towards the next layer in the pyramid).

Skills such as those related to design, user experience, material science, energy efficiency and batteries become more important for many specialists as technologies, devices and applications diffuse further. There is also some evidence that the labour market increasingly rewards social skills, especially since these cannot easily be automated or artificially replicated (Deming, 2015).

*E-business, e-leadership, digital entrepreneurship* represents the most sophisticated group of skills in the pyramid. These are required in order to leverage digital tools and services for reconfiguring business models, creating new businesses and deploying technology tools and services to transform various aspects of the digital economy. Introducing technology in a business/

organization will require people with these skills at all levels: (i) more advanced and/or savvy users who see ways for technology use to improve various tasks, (ii) those working in or leading the technology units in larger businesses, and (iii) chief executive officers (CEOs) with the insight and courage to introduce technology to transform (part(s) of) the business.

E-leadership skills combine business skills with technical skills, and are necessary for being able to: (i) identify how technologies can create new business opportunities, new business models and new ways of doing things, and (ii) communicate these opportunities to decision-makers in the company and its board, as well as to banks and investors to raise finance.

Beyond the growing need for digital skills, the evolving digital economy is expected to reward complementary, non-cognitive skills (Frey and Osborne, 2013; Deming, 2015). Non-cognitive skills are often referred to as "soft skills", and include social, emotional and behavioural skills such as perseverance, conscientiousness, self-control and leadership ability (Duckworth and Yeager, 2015). Evidence from developed countries suggests that the payoffs are strong for individuals who possess both cognitive and non-cognitive skills (e.g. Deming, 2015). As more and more tasks can be automated, people have to become good at tasks that computers/robots/AI cannot do, or cannot do as well. As pointed out by Levy and Murnane (2013: 4), "In order to prepare young people to do the jobs computers cannot do we must re-focus our education system around one objective: giving students the foundational skills in problem solving and communication that computers don't have".

# D. CONCLUSIONS

Digitalization is transforming jobs across all sectors and economies, and will create opportunities as well as challenges in developing countries. However, its overall effects remain uncertain, being context-specific and differing between countries and sectors. The main risk of digitalization is unlikely to be joblessness, but rather increased polarization and widening income inequality. This is because most of the gains from productivity growth may not be widely shared; rather, they will likely benefit capital owners and a few highly skilled workers with strong cognitive, adaptive and creative skills, who are the best equipped to work with the machines.

While challenging, the impacts of digitalization on skills requirements, jobs and employment raise issues that are necessary to address. Countries that lack people with the relevant skills will be at a disadvantage. A range of policy measures on both the demand and supply side, including in the areas of education and skills development and in the labour market, may have to be considered. Measures will need to be adapted to each country, taking into account the current state and level of education, training and skills as well as the degree of digital connectivity and use. Irrespective of the situation in countries today, they should start preparing for future transformations. Activities and discussions related to the ILO's Future of Work Centenary Initiative could support such preparations.[13] The policy challenge is discussed further in chapter VI.

# NOTES

1   See e.g. https://www.weforum.org/agenda/2014/10/internet-of-things-will-affect-our-jobs/.

2   Data refer to electronic shopping (NAICS 454111); source: United States Census Bureau, County Business Patterns.

3   See http://blog.indeed.com/2017/01/17/cybersecurity-skills-gap-report/.

4   See, for example, the materials and videos of experts (academics, business leaders, journalists and policy makers) discussing the topics at: https://www.conference-board.org/crossatlanticroundtable/; and https://www.conference-board.org/crossatlanticroundtable/index.cfm?id=25321.

5   See https://www.conference-board.org/crossatlanticroundtable/index.cfm?id=25321.

6   Most developed countries have seen successive shifts of the labour force employed in agriculture, to manufacturing and then to services, but not into permanent unemployment (http://www.economist.com/news/briefing/21594264-previous-technological-innovation-has-always-delivered-more-long-run-employment-not-less ; accessed 10 May 2017).

7   See www.ilo.org/futureofwork.

8   Another study related to the United States for the period 1990–2007 concluded that every new robot per 1,000 workers could reduce the employment-to-population ratio by 0.18–0.34 percentage points, and depress wages (Acemoglu and Restrepo, 2017).

9   See https://www.ted.com/talks/erik_brynjolfsson_the_key_to_growth_race_em_with_em_the_machines?language=en.

10  For example, when robots replace manual workers on an assembly line, someone will need to operate and maintain the robots and the software that controls them, but it is unlikely that this function could be performed by many, or any, of the displaced assembly line workers.

11  See: http://manpowergroup.com/talent-shortage-2016.

12  See, for example, the European e-skills manifesto for different years (http://eskills4jobs.ec.europa.eu/manifesto).

13  See www.ilo.org/futureofwork.

# INTERNATIONAL TRADE AGREEMENTS
# AND INTERNET GOVERNANCE

As trade is increasingly affected by digitalization and conducted over the Internet, it becomes important for policymakers to factor in how the Internet itself is governed and operated. International trade policies are developed in a very different manner than Internet policies. While the former involves State-to-State negotiations behind closed doors, Internet governance is characterized by multi-stakeholder dialogue.

Section A of this chapter looks at the treatment of e-commerce in international trade agreements. Section B then turns to the interface between trade policy making and Internet policy making, highlighting the very different cultures characterizing these two communities. It explores possible ways of facilitating more dialogue between trade and Internet policy makers in the future. Section C concludes.

# INTERNATIONAL TRADE AGREEMENTS AND INTERNET GOVERNANCE

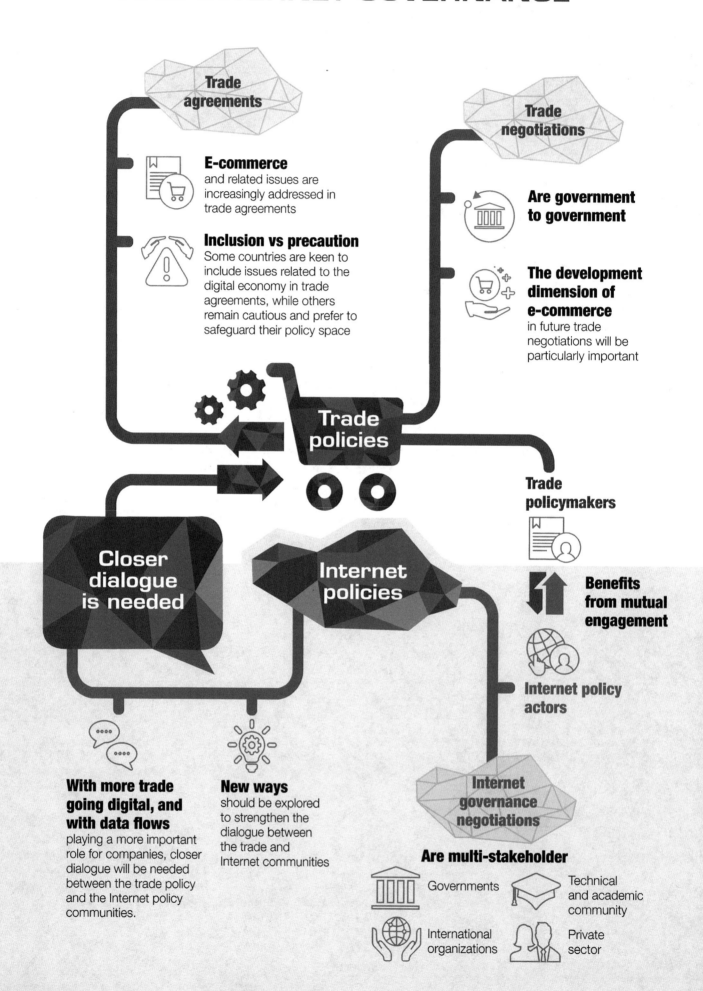

**Trade agreements**

**E-commerce**
and related issues are increasingly addressed in trade agreements

**Inclusion vs precaution**
Some countries are keen to include issues related to the digital economy in trade agreements, while others remain cautious and prefer to safeguard their policy space

**Trade negotiations**

**Are government to government**

**The development dimension of e-commerce**
in future trade negotiations will be particularly important

**Trade policies**

**Trade policymakers**

**Benefits from mutual engagement**

**Internet policy actors**

**Closer dialogue is needed**

**Internet policies**

**With more trade going digital, and with data flows**
playing a more important role for companies, closer dialogue will be needed between the trade policy and the Internet policy communities.

**New ways**
should be explored to strengthen the dialogue between the trade and Internet communities

**Internet governance negotiations**

**Are multi-stakeholder**

Governments

International organizations

Technical and academic community

Private sector

# A. INTERNATIONAL TRADE AGREEMENTS AND E-COMMERCE

There is growing attention to the treatment of e-commerce in international trade agreements at the bilateral, regional, plurilateral and multilateral levels. Given that countries are at very different stages of e-trade readiness (chapter II) and give different priority to various trade policy concerns, their responses to the evolving landscape vary considerably. Some countries are keen to include e-commerce and various issues related to the digital economy in trade agreements, while others remain cautious, preferring to safeguard their policy space in this fast-evolving area.

## 1. Regional and bilateral trade agreements

Several bilateral free trade agreements (FTAs) have adopted provisions of relevance for e-commerce and the digital economy. The 2003 Singapore-Australia FTA was among the first such treaties to include a full chapter on e-commerce. It also covered many of the issues that are still high on the international policy agenda, such as e-certification, data and consumer protection online (Weber, 2015). Many FTAs negotiated by the United States and the EU also include provisions related to e-commerce.

A review of regional trade agreements (RTAs) notified to the WTO found that more than half of those containing e-commerce provisions had provisions on transparency and non-discrimination similar to provisions and principles contained in WTO agreements (WTO Secretariat, 2017). Common issues addressed in these agreements include transparency, customs duties and exceptions. Domestic regulation and cooperation also feature frequently. Other common provisions are concerned with definitions, scope, non-discrimination, consumer protection, unsolicited electronic messages, electronic authentication and data flows.

The coverage and approach of different agreements can vary greatly. For example, a study of FTAs agreed between three Latin American countries (Chile, Colombia and Peru) with the United States, the EU and China, respectively, detected several differences in approach (del Carmen Vásquez Callo Müller, 2014: 37). The author concludes that "US RTAs contain more comprehensive and enforceable

regulations than EU RTAs, with the latter classified as innovative rather than enforceable. Striking is the lack of regulations addressing electronic commerce, IP and data protection in PRC [China] PTAs." However, she goes on to note that the sectoral coverage and levels of commitment in most of these RTAs are more extensive than those in the GATS.

Whereas bilateral agreements can be tailored to the needs of the two parties concerned, widespread reliance on bilateral solutions contributes to a spaghetti bowl fragmentation of rules and regulations. It may also lead to the progressive marginalization of those countries that lack the necessary institutional, legal and technical infrastructure to participate in complex trade negotiations. It is generally difficult for small countries to cope with a diverse and fragmented legal landscape, whereas larger economies are in a better position to insist on relatively consistent treatment among their different partners. Most FTAs encourage broader forms of collaboration in international forums for setting common standards and guidelines to ensure that e-commerce is addressed in a consistent manner (WTO Secretariat, 2017).

## 2. Plurilateral agreements

Trade negotiations of direct relevance for e-commerce have also been undertaken in plurilateral contexts. This applies, for example, to the Trans-Pacific Partnership (TPP) agreement and to the draft Trade in Services Agreement (TISA). Both processes brought together developed and developing economies of different economic size, level of development and cultural backgrounds, and have resulted in proposed rules/disciplines of relevance to e-commerce and the digital economy. However, at the time of preparing this report, the future of both agreements remained uncertain.

The TPP is a mega-regional agreement with 12 original contracting parties,[1] of which seven are developing countries. It dedicates a full chapter to e-commerce, containing 18 articles. Eleven are drafted as strong obligations (using the term "shall"), and seven as soft obligations (best endeavours or subject to its laws and regulations clauses). For example, the TPP requires members to allow full cross-border data transfers, bans forced localization of computing facilities and services, prohibits requirements to transfer technology as a condition for conducting business, and prohibits the imposition of customs duties or taxes on Internet traffic. There are exemptions in sensitive areas such as consumer protection, privacy and national security.

TISA, which is a services-only agreement, is still under negotiation among 23 WTO member States, 13 of which are developing economies.[2] Based on information available by April 2017, most provisions dealing with e-commerce in the draft text are in an annex on electronic commerce and in another on localization. The latter contains an article on local content and other performance requirements, and refers to the use of a certain type of technology or to the inclusion of a certain level of local content for a good or a service (e.g. cloud computing platforms or software). With regard to CBDFs, no agreement had been reached at the last round of negotiations in early December 2016. The draft TISA text includes a provision on source codes along the same lines as in the TPP. It establishes a general prohibition on requiring open source codes which apply only to mass-market software, and includes an exception for software used for critical infrastructure.

## 3. Multilateral discussions

E-commerce touches upon several WTO agreements. Pursuant to the ministerial decision that launched the WTO work programme on e-commerce in 1998,[3] its General Council designated issues to be examined by the WTO councils concerned with trade in goods, services and IPRs, as well as by the Committee on Trade and Development.[4] At the 10th WTO Ministerial in Nairobi in 2015, member States decided to continue the work under the WTO work programme on e-commerce, instruct the General Council to hold periodic reviews, and maintain the current practice of not imposing customs duties on electronic transmissions until the next Ministerial in 2017.

Since then, various groups of States have organized workshops and activities to discuss the interface between e-commerce and trade policies. Examples include MIKTA, which comprises Australia, Indonesia, Mexico, the Republic of Korea, Turkey and the Friends of the E-commerce for Development (FEDs).[5] The FEDs group, which was founded at the UNCTAD 14 Ministerial Conference, has organized several workshops and held a ministerial meeting during the UNCTAD E-Commerce Week 2017. At that meeting, the ministers released a roadmap, mapping *e-Trade for all* (see box VI.7) development objectives into a possible WTO framework for e-commerce.[6]

At the time of preparing this report, there were mixed views among WTO member States on the desirability of launching formal discussions on e-commerce in the WTO. Twelve submissions had been made by some 30 delegations, covering a wide range of issues, such as the definition of e-commerce, transparency, regulatory framework and infrastructure gaps relating to e-commerce.[7] However, in his progress review at the end of 2016, the Chair of the General Council noted:[8] "On the way forward, it is clear that some delegations want to see some progress by the Ministerial Conference in Buenos Aires (MC11). Others do not share this view and want to continue the exploratory nature of the Work Programme." As of June 2017, this divergence of views remained.

Harnessing development gains from trade does not derive from trade agreements alone, but also from coherence in the policy mix to ensure a favourable impact on the most vulnerable constituencies/actors. This involves, among other things, making sure that benefits are shared as widely and as fairly as possible once new markets are opened up to trade. This makes the development dimension of e-commerce in future trade negotiations particularly important. Adequate attention needs to be given to the readiness of countries to engage in e-commerce and in the digital economy more broadly. For most developing countries, this will require additional support from the international community (see chapter VI).

# B. THE NEED FOR BRIDGING TRADE AND INTERNET POLICYMAKING

As more trade is affected by digitalization and conducted over the Internet, it becomes increasingly important for trade policymakers to factor in how the Internet itself is governed and operated. International trade policies are developed in a different manner than Internet policies. While the former typically involves State-to-State negotiations behind closed doors, Internet governance is characterized by multi-stakeholder dialogue. This section explores possible ways of bridging these different cultures with a view to ensuring greater inclusiveness in future policymaking.

## 1. Internet governance and multi-stakeholder involvement

There is a well-organized and globalized Internet community which is deeply invested in approaches to Internet governance and operations that are sharply at odds with the standard procedures and outputs of international trade policymaking. Much of the work in coordinating Internet resources and making the network of networks function efficiently is of a highly technical nature, and takes place in institutional settings that are generally unknown to trade negotiators. Indeed, many in the trade community are unlikely to be familiar with the wide array of organizations and actors that are involved in the governance and operation of the Internet (box V.1).

---

### Box V.1. Key stakeholders in Internet governance

A wide variety of actors are involved in the process of governing and operating the Internet. The following are some of the main actors and stakeholders.

- The Internet Corporation for Assigned Names and Numbers (ICANN) manages an array of Internet identifiers essential to the Internet's operation.

- The Internet Engineering Task Force (IETF) and the related Internet Architecture Board (IAB) establish technical standards and protocols that allow different systems to interoperate.

- The World Wide Web Consortium (W3C) sets technical standards specific to the Web.

- Five regional Internet registries (RIRs) manage the regional allocation of Inernet protocol (IP) numbers.

- Country or regionally based network operators groups provide forums for Internet network operators to discuss matters of mutual interest.

- There are various associations of Internet service providers (ISPs), Internet exchange points (IXPs), domain name system (DNS) and root zone operators.

- The Internet Society, with 96,000 members and 170 chapters around the world, engages in advocacy, capacity development and related activities, and provides the legal home for the IETF and the IAB.

- There are also a variety of capacity-building programmes, professional associations, industry associations, individual companies, technical groups, civil society organizations and individuals involved in discussions on issues of governance and operating of the Internet.

In addition to these organizations that are part of the global Internet community, that community also participates extensively in and supports the United Nations-linked Internet Governance Forum (IGF) and its various national and regional spinoffs.

Governments as well as other stakeholders also participate in the Internet-related discussions of the United Nations Commission on Science and Technology for Development (CSTD),[a] which currently hosts the Working Group on Enhanced Cooperation (WGEC), established in 2016.

The Tunis Agenda for the Information Society, which emerged from the World Summit on the Information Society (WSIS) in 2005, called for enhanced cooperation to enable governments to carry out, on an equal footing, their roles and responsibilities with respect to international public policy issues pertaining to the Internet, but not in day-to-day technical and operational matters that do not affect such issues.[b] The overall review of the WSIS carried out by the General Assembly in 2015 (A/RES/70./125), while noting the progress made towards enhanced cooperation, requested the Chair of the CSTD, through the Economic and Social Council, to establish a working group on enhanced cooperation to develop recommendations on how to further implement enhanced cooperation as envisioned in the Tunis Agenda. The WGEC is to report to the 21st session of the CSTD in 2018.

*Source*: UNCTAD.

[a] More information about the CSTD and its work is available at: www.unctad.org/cstd.

[b] A/71/67-E/2016/51.

---

Two characteristics are notable about the Internet policy discussions. First, participants are drawn from a global community of experts and practitioners with a strong sense of ownership of its respective processes and decisions. In both discourse and actual practice, it is the community, and not any central secretariat, that performs the bulk of the policy or institutional development work. Although the same can be said about intergovernmental processes, Internet stakeholder communities work, at least in part, on a voluntary basis. If they believe that agreed outcomes of their work will be subverted or ignored, their commitment to the processes and the agreements made may quickly wane.

Second, these processes tend to be multi-stakeholder in character. The communities are accustomed to peer-to-peer participation on an equal-footing, and therefore each stakeholder, in principle – and often in practice – has an equal degree of intellectual influence on problem-solving. They are wedded to the notions of full transparency, open and inclusive participation by any interested party, reliance on remote participation technologies, "bottom-up" agenda-setting, iterative, multi-stage consultation processes in which objections to proposals are fully vetted and addressed in order to move forward, and ultimately, decision-making based on "rough consensus", meaning that not every single party must be fully satisfied with every detail for a policy process to move forward. A sort of meta-level "community of communities" has evolved, often simply referred to as the "Internet community."[9]

It should be noted that all governments are not equally supportive of the sort of multi-stakeholder participation that is common in Internet governance processes. For example, while 171 governments participate in ICANN's Governance Advisory Committee, some of these believe that the role of governments under ICANN's bylaws is too limited, and that governments should have the ultimate decision making authority on key issues. Some observers are also concerned about the unequal geographical representation in core Internet governance institutions, such as ICANN, ISOC, IETF and the IAB (Hampson and Jardine, 2016). Although these organizations are officially open to representation from all parts of the world, they do not yet well reflect the shifting demographics of the Internet.

## 2. The Internet community's criticism of trade deals

From a collective standpoint, many stakeholders in Internet governance are suspicious of global governance processes that work in fundamentally different ways but also affect their domain of activity. International trade negotiations affecting the Internet are often also seen in this light. With respect to both procedural mechanics and substantive outcomes that become public, many in the Internet community have expressed concerns about the language that has been

(or may become) included in the trade agreements concerned.

With regard to procedures, two bodies have made observations that typify the kinds of concerns expressed. The Global Commission on Internet Governance (GCIG), which comprises a variety of senior government, private sector, Internet technical community and civil society representatives, as well as academics, noted the following in its report:

> Bilateral and multilateral free trade agreements can significantly affect Internet governance issues. Many, such as the Trans-Pacific Partnership Agreement, specifically address important issues such as data localization, encryption, censorship and transparency, all of which are generally regarded as forming part of the Internet governance landscape. However, they are negotiated exclusively by governments and usually in secret. At the same time, such agreements substantially benefit the Internet in a myriad of ways, such as by agreeing on rules to improve competition and market access. Further agreements such as the US-Europe Transatlantic Trade and Investment Partnership and the Trade in Services Agreement under the World Trade Organization are expected to cover similar territory. The fact that these negotiations are open only to governments has inspired protests by non-governmental actors demanding that they be informed and engaged in negotiations to allay fears that the new rules embedded in these agreements favour the interests of governments or corporations over those of other Internet users. The closed nature of the negotiations also means that the benefits governments hope to achieve may not be evident to the general public (GCIG, 2016: 78).

The comments of a second body, the Open Digital Trade Network (ODTN), are also noteworthy.[10] Initiated by the Electronic Frontier Foundation, a long-time advocate of online civil liberties, the ODTN platform aims at collaboration on joint initiatives designed to address the incorporation of Internet-related public policy issues into trade agreements that are negotiated behind closed doors. While not against international trade agreements, per se, ODTN participants argue that trade negotiations that touch upon the Internet environment should be conducted in a transparent and accountable manner, and should include measures to guard against the capture of trade processes by special interests to the detriment of the global public interest in maintaining an open Internet. One of its main concerns is encapsulated in the following excerpt from its Brussels Declaration: [11]

> We recognize the considerable social and economic benefits that could flow from an international trading system that is fair, sustainable, democratic, and

accountable. These goals can only be achieved through processes that ensure effective public participation. Modern trade agreements are negotiated in closed, opaque and unaccountable fora that lack democratic safeguards and are vulnerable to undue influence. These are not simply issues of principle; the secrecy prevents negotiators from having access to all points of view and excludes many stakeholders with demonstrable expertise that would be valuable to the negotiators. This is particularly notable in relation to issues that have impacts on the online and digital environment, which have been increasingly subsumed into trade agreements over the past two decades.

Stakeholders have also expressed concerns about various substantive aspects of rules governing trade in the digital economy. Contentious issues include the inclusion of provisions concerning intellectual property, encryption, source codes, intermediary liability, network neutrality, spam, authentication and consumer protection.[12] While many Internet experts are interested in ensuring that trade agreements will not be used to challenge privacy protection for commercial purposes, they are wary about the prospect of the proliferation of national and regional restrictions on CBDFs eroding Internet openness. By imposing territorial borders on cyberspace, such restrictions may not only raise costs and impede the efficiency of operations, they may also constrain the ability of willing network endpoints to exchange data, and could contribute to Internet fragmentation (Drake et al., 2016).

## 3. Options for enhancing the trade and Internet policy dialogue

As the role of the Internet in international trade is set to grow further, it may be worthwhile to explore possible ways of strengthening dialogue between the trade and Internet communities. The engagement of stakeholders from the Internet governance realm may constitute an opportunity to advance a dynamic and development-supporting global digital economy. Many Internet community stakeholders have extensive technical and policy expertise and experience navigating the intricacies of Internet-related issues. Trade policymakers could benefit by engaging with these actors in order to ensure that any agreements relevant to those issues are operationally feasible, politically sustainable and less likely to have negative, unintended consequences.

What might such a broadened dialogue entail? One possible starting point for consideration was outlined in a recent white paper published by the World Economic Forum (Drake, 2017). It argues for three coordinated tracks of cooperation that could progressively nudge governments towards shared and widely supported norms for CBDFs and data localization policies. Those three tracks are discussed below.

### a. Non-treaty-making intergovernmental forums

The first track considers the role of non-treaty-making intergovernmental forums. Discussions in such venues, with inputs from stakeholders, could contribute by examining the issues and identifying costs and benefits of different approaches for countries at different stages of development. Collaboratively designing "soft law" declarative statements of mutual intent, free from the immediate pressure of trade negotiations, might advance collective procedural and substantive learning, and prepare the groundwork for the trade community. Related work has begun within certain intergovernmental forums such as the G-7, G-20 and the OECD (see (Drake, 2017), but it could benefit from greater consistency and coordination, as well as stronger involvement by developing countries. UNCTAD offers support to developing countries' efforts to devise privacy and data protection laws that are aligned with international and regional instruments, and it could provide a platform to advance national, regional and global multi-stakeholder dialogue on the matter (UNCTAD, 2016a).

### b. Inclusive dialogue for consensus-building

A second track considers how to advance with an inclusive dialogue towards consensus-building. There are different options for enabling multi-stakeholder participation. In the context of indigenous Internet governance institutions, stakeholders expect to engage fully in peer-to-peer or "equal footing" decision-making. But in the context of inclusive intergovernmental processes, expectations are more limited, for example, to being able to participate in the dialogue, and submit documents to a process in which governments retain final control over decision-making. With respect to CBDFs and related issues, it may be worth considering approaches that are as open, transparent and inclusive as possible in agenda-setting and even in rules design and implementation, while preserving governments' decision-making authority.

This could be done by establishing a two-tier, concentric-circles arrangement. The inner circle would comprise experts drawn from the Internet and trade communities – including key industry associations and firms, technical bodies, civil society, academic and research institutions, governments and international organizations – working on an equal footing. Participants could gather physically or virtually on a platform hosted by one or more organizations to develop a clear picture of the relevant issues, costs and benefits of different policy approaches at the national and global levels.

**Three models may serve as inspiration:**

- *Setting up of a commission with a fixed duration and a mandate to produce recommendations and supporting analyses.* The GCIG has released a broadly framed report and more than 50 papers authored by members of its global Research Advisory Network, which focus on specific issues. The more narrowly focused Global Commission on the Stability of Cyberspace (GCSC) launched in 2017 follows a similar approach.[13]

- *An open-ended mandate.* This approach has been applied by the Fissile Materials Working Group, an independent non-governmental coalition of more than 70 organizations working to prevent nuclear terrorism. It comprises a steering committee, working groups, organizational members, partner organizations and other elements drawn from the scientific and policy communities. It monitors trends, produces reports and issues policy recommendations.[14] A more elaborate, open-ended model is applied by the United Nations Sustainable Development Solutions Network launched in 2012 under the auspices of the United Nations Secretary-General. It has a secretariat, leadership council, executive committee, academic advisory council and member associations that are linked to, but independent of, the United Nations.[15]

- *Link to one or more international organizations.* A third model would be a configuration closely linked to one or more relevant international organizations. For example, one study has proposed the establishment by the WTO of an external group of experts to recommend steps that could be taken to support digital trade (Meltzer, 2016). This would involve the creation of a repository of information and insights about the relationship between the digital economy and the international trade system, rules and agreements. While the proposal is WTO-centric,

its core elements could also interface with other organizations and processes if appropriate.

The outer circle of the multi-stakeholder track could comprise a broadly inclusive range of interested stakeholders. Online platforms could give the public access to documents and progress reports, as well as opportunities to provide inputs into both the intergovernmental and multi-stakeholder settings mentioned above. Face-to-face platforms could be provided in the context of, for example, the UNCTAD E-Commerce Week, the new UNCTAD Intergovernmental Group of Experts on E-Commerce and the Digital Economy or the Internet Governance Forum. Such an approach could provide ideas and perspectives, as well as political legitimacy and support for national and global policy initiatives.

### c. Intergovernmental trade policymaking track

The third track of cooperation relates to work undertaken in intergovernmental trade policy settings. Trade negotiations could be informed by a broader matrix of analysis and dialogue to promote collective learning, international norms development and a baseline of national policy convergence. Such an evolutionary approach could offer developing-country governments the opportunity to present their constraints and express their preferences. At the same time, relevant stakeholders would be able to track the proceedings' broad developments, and contribute perspectives and experiences, which would ultimately increase their buy-in and support for Internet-related trade policies.

This recalibration and alignment might involve several procedural and substantive elements. With respect to existing trade rules, a focused assessment could seek to clarify the applicability of the GATS framework and national commitments with respect to trade in the digital economy. To the extent that the potential linkage between such work and pressures for new negotiations may hamper progress, it might be useful to explore the issues in a non-negotiating setting.

With respect to potential new trade rules, it will be important to consider which issues to address via trade disciplines rather than through other mechanisms. Whether such trade rules should be broad in scope or narrowly tailored is controversial. The sort of analysis and dialogue processes mentioned previously may help improve the prospects for politically acceptable outcomes. Different actors in the governmental and non-governmental sectors will probably advance different lists of dos and don'ts with regard to any potential new rules. These differences and their reasons may need to be discussed in a systematic manner that can enrich and ultimately add legitimacy to trade policymaking processes. Non-negotiating and multi-stakeholder mechanisms could usefully be brought into play in this context.

In addition, there is scope for enhancing the transparency of future trade negotiations pertaining to the Internet. While the exchange of concessions to be inscribed in national schedules may need to be carried out in the traditional manner, the selection of issues to be covered and the design of regime norms and rules could be pursued in a more open manner. Governments could solicit input and share proposed texts, and multi-stakeholder meetings could assess the issues free from the pressures of trade bargaining and then feed any resulting inputs back to trade negotiators for consideration.

Finally, it may be desirable to enhance the participation of Internet stakeholders and other relevant parties in national trade consultation processes. Governments in both developed and developing countries need to reach out more effectively, and non-governmental actors must be prepared to take advantage of the opportunities this presents.

# C. CONCLUSIONS

As international trade becomes increasingly affected by the digitalization of economic activities, there is growing need for countries to consider how best to address the interface between trade policies and Internet policies. At the bilateral level, a number of free trade agreements have included provisions related to e-commerce and cross-border data flows. Some plurilateral agreements have also included similar references, but their future was at the time of drafting this report highly uncertain. At the global level as well, it remains to be seen if and how issues related to e-commerce and the digital economy may be reflected in future work of the WTO.

This may be an opportune time to consider options that could invigorate the relevant discussions without prejudicing any eventual outcomes. It may be worth considering ways to strengthen the trade policy process on Internet issues by opening the process to the relevant stakeholders, especially those with significant Internet expertise. As noted above, trade policymakers could benefit by engaging with these actors with a view to ensuring that any agreements relevant to those issues are operationally feasible, politically sustainable and less likely to have any unintended, undesirable consequences. The discussion in this chapter will hopefully provide useful ideas that may help to bridge future policy discussions of mutual relevance to trade and Internet policymaking.

# NOTES

1   Australia, Brunei Darussalam, Canada, Chile, Malaysia, Japan, Mexico, New Zealand, Peru, Singapore, the United States and Viet Nam. On 23 January 2017, the United States decided to withdraw from the TPP.

2   Australia, Canada, Chile, Taiwan Province of China, Colombia, Costa Rica, the EU, Hong Kong (China), Iceland, Israel, Japan, the Republic of Korea, Liechtenstein, Mauritius, Mexico, New Zealand, Norway, Pakistan, Panama, Peru, Switzerland, Turkey and the United States.

3   WT/MIN(98)/DEC/2.

4   WT/L/274.

5   As on June 2017, FED members were Argentina, Chile, Colombia, Costa Rica, Kazakhstan, Kenya, Mexico, Moldova, Nigeria, Pakistan, Sri Lanka and Uruguay.

6   See, for example, https://www.ip-watch.org/weblog/wp-content/uploads/2017/04/FEDs-mapping-e-Trade-for-All-into-Trade-Policy-April-2017.pdf?ef2610 .

7   See https://www.bmwi-registrierung.de/G20-TIWG-February-2017/pdf/G20%20TIWG%20discussion%20paper%20E-commerce%20WTO%20Rules%20and%20RTAs.pdf.

8   WT/GC/W/728.

9   For different but related graphical representations of the ecosystem, see the diagram from the Internet Society at: http://content.netmundial.br/files/243-1.png, as well as from ICANN at: https://www.icann.org/sites/default/files/assets/governance-2500x1664-21mar13-en.png (accessed 1 June 2017).

10   ODTN is an expert group of stakeholders representing Internet users, consumers, innovative businesses, cultural institutions, and scholars.

11   See "Brussels Declaration on Trade and the Internet", 15 March 2016, available at https://www.eff.org/files/2016/03/15/brussels_declaration.pdf (accessed 1 June 2017).

12   For example, see Bureau Européen des Unions de Consommateurs (BEUC), Analysis of the TiSA e-commerce annex & recommendations to the negotiators, TiSA leaks, September 2016 (http://www.beuc.eu/publications/beuc-x-2016-083_lau_beucs_analysis_e-commerce_tisa_2016.pdf, accessed 1 June 2017); and EDRi's red lines on TTIP, January 2015 (https://edri.org/files/TTIP_redlines_20150112.pdf, accessed 1 June 2017). BEUC and EDRi are coalitions of 43 and 35 civil society organizations, respectively.

13   See: https://cyberstability.org/.

14   See: http://www.fmwg.org/.

15   See: http://unsdsn.org.

# POLICIES FOR TRADE AND DEVELOPMENT IN THE DIGITAL ECONOMY

Policymakers are facing a formidable task in keeping up with the rapid pace of technological change, a general scarcity of relevant data and a high degree of uncertainty over the shape of the future. The challenges in this regard are highly contextual. Countries vary greatly in terms of their readiness to engage in and benefit from the digital economy, with LDCs lagging the furthest behind. Ensuring that no one is left behind in the digital economy therefore requires global efforts in providing adequate support.

This chapter addresses selected policy areas that are of particular relevance at the interface of trade and the digital economy. It starts by highlighting the need for a cross-cutting, multi-stakeholder approach to formulating policies and strategies. Section B then discusses how to reduce various digital divides and boost ICT use. Section C explores selected ways to enhance the ability of MSMEs to export in the digital economy, notably through participation in GVCs, by leveraging the role of trade promotion organizations and by improving trade logistics. Section D focuses on the skills development challenge. Section E is concerned with the governing of cross-border data flows in the digital economy. Section F concludes by calling for a significant increase of financial support and other assistance to scale up capacity-building in relevant areas in developing countries.

# POLICIES FOR TRADE AND DEVELOPMENT IN THE DIGITAL ECONOMY

## Expand ICT Connectivity

**Secure an open, transparent and fair telecommunications market**

**Attract investment** and facilitate infrastructure imports of relevant equipment and services

## Education and skills

**Adjust education and training** systems to deliver the skills required in the digital economy

Expand opportunities for workers and teachers to **retrain and upgrade their skills**

**Make use of redistribution policies** to mitigate the risk of increased polarization and income inequality

## A multifaceted policy challenge

### Trade

**Adapt trade promotion policies to the digital economy**

Trade promotion organizations can **embed digital tools** in their services offered to small businesses

**Trade logistics, digitalization and e-commerce**

Opportunities to embrace **cross-border e-commerce**

**New technologies** to help navigate traffic and reduce the need for long-distance transportation

Conditions, procedures and resources **for MSMEs**

### International support

**Boost international support to developing countries**

Make use of the eTrade for all initiative (**etradeforall.org**)

eTrade for all
Connecting the dots

**Current levels of support are inadequate**

**1.2%** **Share of ICT** in total aid for trade declined from 3% in 2002-2005 to 1.2 % in 2015

Total aid for trade

### Cross-border data flows

**Strike a balance between:**

**The need** for companies to collect and analyse data for innovation and efficiency gains

**The concerns** of various stakeholders with respect to security, privacy, and ownership of data

**Move towards one unifying initiative** or a smaller number of data initiatives that are internationally compatible

# A. COPING WITH THE CROSS-CUTTING NATURE OF THE POLICY CHALLENGE

As shown in preceding chapters, digitalization opens the door to new ways of addressing multiple development challenges, such as financial inclusion, women's economic empowerment, different modes of integration into GVCs and improved trade performance. However, it is also already disrupting many industries and value chains, and will continue to do so. In response, governments face the challenge of responding with new policies and strategies across a wide spectrum of areas, including ICT infrastructure, education and skills development, competition, science, technology and innovation, as well as others.

Digitally induced transformations will vary considerably among countries. Many developing countries, and especially the LDCs, face various barriers to the adoption and effective use of digital technologies. Inadequate human expertise and skills, unstable power supply, poor connectivity and limited bandwidth constrain the effective deployment of e-commerce, cloud computing, big data and IoT. Also, limited resources prevent governments, businesses and households from investing adequately in ICT devices and equipment. Moreover, small domestic ICT sectors in many developing countries hamper their ability to support the adoption of new technological solutions, adapt or develop relevant applications and software, and analyse data that could help them harness the benefits of the digital economy. Most developing countries are lagging behind in productive capacity in areas such as smart sensors, embedded systems, software development, network vendors and telecommunications, and thus are likely to have to source such digital technologies, goods and services from abroad.

Meanwhile, strong network economies can create winner-takes-all industries, giving rise to concerns related to competition policy and consumer protection. Some of the most pressing issues facing both developed and developing countries include the market power of high-tech industry leaders, innovative business models, new markets versus regulation, the roles and responsibilities of platforms, personal data as a commodity, lack of appropriate tools and remedies for enforcement authorities, and the need for international cooperation.[1]

Limited regulatory capacity risks exposing consumers and businesses in developing countries to fraud, cyber crime and privacy abuse as smart devices proliferate with little planning or oversight. In this context, given the increase in cybersecurity threats, developing countries need to build the capacity to counter such threats, as they are particularly vulnerable in this area at present.

While the time will vary until the effects of digitalization become evident in a country or a sector, governments should start assessing the likely effects as a matter of urgency. Such assessments are essential to identify what kinds of policies and measures may be appropriate to seize opportunities and address risks. For many developing countries, formulating relevant policies and implementing adequate measures will be important not least to avoid falling further behind as the digital economy evolves.

Each country needs to define policy responses best suited to its specific characteristics, priorities and national objectives. Moreover, actions need to be taken simultaneously in several areas, as isolated actions in only one area at a time will have limited impact. For example, providing adequate infrastructure does not in itself bring any benefits if people and businesses lack the skills or the enabling environment to exploit it. This implies that effective cross-sectoral collaboration is needed both within the government and with other stakeholders. The main ministries that would need to be involved include those responsible for justice, finance, education, science, technology and innovation, ICT, transportation services, trade and investment, rural development and employment. In addition, it would require the collaboration of relevant government regulatory and promotional agencies, postal services, national IT associations, chambers of commerce, academia and consumer organizations, where they exist (UNCTAD, 2015b). In designing and implementing relevant policy measures, governments can benefit from dialogues with representatives from the private sector, civil society and the technical and academic communities. Such dialogues can be organized in different ways, including through advisory boards or committees, task forces or consultation processes.

Several developed and developing countries have sought to adapt their policies and strategies to the evolving digital economy, and have established various forms of inter-agency collaboration in this context. The following are some significant examples:

- In Rwanda, an LDC, President Kagame is personally committed to the transformation of the country into a digital economy.[2]

- In Pakistan, in 2015 the Government constituted a high-level working group to develop a Strategic E-Commerce Policy Framework for the country. The group, which has the full support of the Prime Minister, is led by the Commerce Ministry, and comprises officials also from the Ministries of Information Technology and Finance, the State Bank of Pakistan and the Pakistan Software Export Board.[3]

- Chile's Digital Agenda 2020 was created following consultations among the Government, private sector, civil society and academia. It lists 63 measures to drive connectivity, the digital economy, and trade and consumer rights, among others, which are to be implemented by three government ministries.[4] The Government has created a portal for citizens to track progress with implementation.

- In Germany, the Federal Ministry for Economic Affairs and Energy and the Federal Ministry for Education and Research have created a coordinating body bringing together stakeholders to assess the long-term strategy for "Industrie 4.0" (OECD, 2017a).

The cross-cutting nature of the effects of digitalization has prompted developed countries to examine the issues involved and the policy implications in a comprehensive manner through the OECD Going Digital project (box VI.1). Developing countries, including the LDCs, will see a growing need to engage in similar discussions at the national, regional and global levels. While seeking to create an economic environment conducive to harnessing the opportunities created by the digital economy, governments should link these efforts to their support of relevant objectives in their country's development agenda, not least in terms of achieving the SDGs. Clearly defined objectives and recognition of possible concerns are a first step towards formulating relevant policies.

The new UNCTAD Intergovernmental Group of Experts on E-Commerce and the Digital Economy provides a useful forum for member States to engage in

---

**Box VI.1. OECD's Going Digital project**

Recognizing that benefits from digitalization go hand in hand with disruptions, in January 2017 the OECD officially launched a project entitled Going Digital: Making the Transformation Work for Growth and Well-being. The project underlines the necessity of a coherent and comprehensive policy approach to harness the benefits of digital transformation. Through the project, it is hoped that policymakers will gain a better understanding of the nature of the digital transformation that is taking place, and develop tools to create a policy environment that will enable their economies and societies to prosper in an increasingly digital and data-driven world.

The composition of the core contributors to the project is indicative of the breadth of the policy issues concerned:

- The Competition Committee
- The Committee on Consumer Policy
- The Committee on Digital Economy Policy
- The Committee on Industry, Innovation and Entrepreneurship
- The Insurance and Private Pensions Committee
- The Committee on Financial Markets
- The Committee on Fiscal Affairs
- The Committee on Scientific and Technological Policy
- The Committee on Statistics and Statistics Policy
- The Economic Policy Committee
- The Education Policy Committee
- The Employment, Labour and Social Affairs Committee
- The Public Governance Committee
- The Trade Committee

*Source:* OECD, 2017b.

---

multilateral discussions on related policy issues. This Intergovernmental Group of Experts could benefit from the creation of a Working Group on Measuring E-commerce and the Digital Economy. This group could discuss ways to support the production of relevant statistics on the digital economy in developing countries and could serve as a forum for national statistical offices and other organizations involved in the collection of relevant data. Given the complexity of the issues at hand, policy discussions will also need to be complemented by adequate international assistance to many developing countries, especially the LDCs (discussed in section F below).

# B. REDUCING THE DIVIDES IN DIGITAL TECHNOLOGY USE

Adequate, affordable and reliable connectivity is a basic requirement for people and enterprises to engage successfully in the digital economy (chapter II). In developing countries, it is therefore necessary to accelerate the building and maintenance of a high-coverage, high-speed, reliable and affordable digital infrastructure as a priority. Narrowing the divides between and within countries in access to and use of digital technologies is important in order to maximize benefits, and combat existing and new inequalities not only in income, but also in individuals' economic, social and political participation and opportunities. Improving the quality and affordability of broadband is essential to enable additional investments in and use of data centres, cloud computing, big data and IoT (Global Connectivity Index, 2017).

The need for connectivity is explicitly specified in the 2030 Agenda for Sustainable Development. More than half of the world's population is still offline, and the pace of growth in Internet access and use is slowing down (Unwin, 2017). And, as mentioned in chapter II, progress has been slow towards achieving the target in SDG 9 of significantly increasing access to ICTs and striving to provide universal and affordable access to the Internet in LDCs by 2020. Ideally, there should be universal coverage of high-speed broadband, with regular upgrading of infrastructure, and a reduction or elimination of unjustified regulatory barriers to service providers wishing to access the network or other services. The current low level of broadband penetration in many developing countries is highly unsatisfactory. It is therefore encouraging that more than 150 countries had adopted national broadband plans by 2016, up from just 31 a decade earlier (Broadband Commission, 2016).

Part of the solution lies in increasing investment in infrastructure. UNCTAD has estimated the investment costs for the provision of near-universal basic 3G coverage to be about $100 billion for developing countries, and less than $40 billion for LDCs – perhaps less daunting than might be expected (UNCTAD, 2017b). The estimate suggests that the investment necessary to ensure universal broadband access is not an insurmountable obstacle in terms of initial capital outlays.

However, work to increase the proportion of people using the Internet will require efforts to boost the demand side as well. In low-income countries, limited uptake of the Internet is partly due to low purchasing power, lack of awareness of the value of using the Internet, skills limitations, a lack of trust in the online environment, and/or the absence of relevant content (e.g. in the local language). According to the Broadband Commission (2017) the following measures have proved successful in getting more people online: (a) provision of direct subsidies to disadvantaged user groups for buying devices and lowering the costs of Internet use; (b) reducing value added tax (VAT) and import duties on ICT equipment; (c) provision of free public Internet access; (d) the creation of relevant online content, apps and services, coupled with public awareness campaigns; and (e) providing ICT skills training to different levels of user groups to improve their capabilities and facilitate greater use, not only in the work or school environment, but also at home. Other studies stress the importance of community networks to reach people in rural or remote areas who are currently unconnected (Rey-Moreno, 2017).

During the UNCTAD E-Commerce Week 2017, participants called for a "new deal" between all key stakeholders to prevent the digital divide from becoming a digital chasm (UNCTAD, 2017g). They encouraged governments to ensure policy frameworks and regulations that create an open, transparent and fair telecoms market to attract more domestic and foreign investments. Measures proposed to make broadband use more affordable included infrastructure-sharing, effective spectrum management and the avoidance of high taxes and import duties on telecoms/ICT equipment and services. Participants also called for more sharing of good practices, including in relevant intergovernmental organizations, and more capacity-building in relevant areas. To harness digitalization fully in support of trade, investments in ICT infrastructure need to be complemented by adequate regulations, skills and institutions (World Bank, 2016b; Bankole et al., 2015; Paunov and Rollo, 2016).

Special attention should be given to addressing the gender divide in the digital economy. As noted in chapter II, the gender gap in ICT use is more pronounced in developing countries, and especially in the LDCs. Similarly, the rate of women's participation in ICT specialist occupations remains low. Based on the discussion during UNCTAD E-Commerce Week 2017, three short-term measures can be proposed to address the gender dimension in e-commerce (UNCTAD, 2017g). First, a network of women entrepreneurs in e-commerce in developing countries should be established in order to give them a stronger voice in policy discussions at the national, regional and international level. The network would also be helpful to showcase women role models in e-commerce in developing countries. Second, good practices among women entrepreneurs should be disseminated more effectively, in particular on how to grow a business and access export markets. Finally, the availability of gender-disaggregated statistics related to the digital economy should be improved.

# C. ENABLING SMALL BUSINESSES TO COMPETE IN THE DIGITAL ECONOMY

## 1. Facilitating MSME participation in value chains

MSMEs in developing economies, and especially in LDCs, will need affordable access to appropriate ICT infrastructure to be able to compete effectively in the digital economy. This includes mobile telephony, as a minimum, but increasingly also broadband connectivity, with access to affordable connectivity extended into rural areas as well. In addition, there is a need to bolster the ability of MSMEs to make effective use of ICTs. The fact that smaller firms generally lag far behind large ones in ICT use (chapter II) represents a barrier to their effective integration into GVCs, which are becoming increasingly reliant on digital solutions.

The analysis in chapter III indicated that digitalization is evolving at very different speeds in value chains of particular importance for low-income and lower middle-income developing economies, with diverse implications for the enterprises concerned. In order to enable and foster favourable development outcomes and avoid the exclusion of smaller businesses from the digital transformation of GVCs, a number of measures need to be taken. The way local value chains are coordinated for the sourcing of inputs and the movement of goods for export, and the way they provide information and management to exporters, affect the ability of MSMEs to participate. Many such value chains are privately led, and involve exporters or agribusinesses, but they lack clear policy directions.

Nevertheless, since they are likely to intersect with activities of public institutions (e.g. agricultural development commissions) there is some potential for government influence.

There is a growing need for helping many small-scale producers to meet standards and quality requirements, and for monitoring their compliance. While support mechanisms exist in developing countries (such as fair trade and environmental standards bodies in African countries), many are privately run and not always financially accessible to small producers (Foster et al., 2017). ICT-based systems should support more efficient diffusion of the required skills and monitoring in this area. Initiatives discussed previously, such as the ITC's Trade for Sustainable Development initiative and pilot projects on horticulture exports to the EU, present opportunities to gain further understanding of best practices in this area.[5]

In the right circumstances, e-commerce platforms can expand the opportunities for small enterprises in developing countries to export both to final consumers (B2C) and to other businesses (B2B). However, access to global e-commerce, payments platforms and apps markets still varies greatly (ITC, 2016; UNCTAD, 2015b; Liyanage, 2015). Policymakers may choose to engage with the platform owners to ensure that their platforms can be fully used, and that existing regulations do not hamper access. They may also support the provision of training for SMEs on how to leverage such platforms. Some tourism platform providers have organized roadshows and training in East Africa, and strategic partnerships and provision of support to SMEs have been undertaken with Alibaba for using its platform in Viet Nam (Mai and Tuan, 2012). In China, partnerships aim to encourage small firms to join platforms as a core goal of firm modernization (Foster and Azmeh, 2016; ITC, 2016).

## 2. Adapting trade promotion to the digital economy

In many developing countries, export promotion, which is a key component of the trade policy toolkit, needs to adapt to the evolving digital economy. Trade promotion organizations (TPOs) are increasingly recognizing the need to incorporate digital tools in their services offered to small businesses.[6] Online platforms can be better leveraged to present businesses internationally and reach desired communities. They can also be used to facilitate data collection and analysis, and to assess customer needs. With the growing importance of online marketing channels, e-market solutions as well as social media platforms should be used in events or trade shows, and in other efforts to facilitate exports.

With increased reliance on online trade, export promotion needs to adapt, especially to help MSMEs take advantage of digital solutions. Online platforms have made it possible even for small businesses to directly reach customers abroad without the support of TPOs as intermediaries (chapter III). This does not mean, however, that TPOs will become irrelevant. In fact, digitalization is creating challenges that TPOs – in collaboration with other stakeholders – could help resolve through the provision of online customized services. In addition, even with online commerce, many traditional challenges remain, such as helping firms to meet standards and quality requirements, customs handling, and dealing with trust issues, asymmetries and gaps in information.

Cross-border e-commerce involves locating foreign customers online, marketing to them via social media and e-commerce platforms, branding, labelling and pricing products geared to particular foreign customers' income levels and tastes, building online advertisement strategies and partnering with e-commerce platforms. While sellers on e-commerce platforms may start to export following their discovery by a foreign buyer, their international growth requires a more systematic and strategic approach.

In most countries, current export promotion and trade capacity-building efforts are insufficiently adapted for helping MSMEs engage in the digital economy. Public sector support tends to be ad hoc, and many TPOs lack up-to-date know-how on cross-border online sales. Public-private partnerships can be useful in such a context. While TPOs can set targets and offer companies e-commerce capacity-building programmes, the trainers need to have the relevant private sector experience. For example, Mexico's export promotion agency, ProMéxico, which organizes seminars and training for SMEs, has also created a B2B platform for SMEs selling to overseas markets. It offers consulting services to help them develop digital marketing strategies, online stores, online payment systems and social media engagement.[7] Each company can request financial support of about $4,000 to help cover these costs. In Costa Rica, Procomer has launched a service that brings together B2C and B2B sales channels and customers of three global platforms – igourmet, Alibaba and Amazon.[8]

Several e-commerce platforms provide capacity-building. For example, the Deauville Partnership, World Bank and ITC teamed up with the B2B e-commerce platform, TradeKey, to help merchants in Jordan, Morocco and Tunisia reach international buyers.[9] And in May 2017, the Government of Pakistan and Alibaba announced a partnership to encourage e-commerce exports by SMEs, with the Alibaba Group providing online and offline training to SMEs on how to make use of the company's platforms and optimize exports.[10] The public sector can offer incentives for private sector involvement, both by recruiting and pre-screening companies for training and funding some of the training. An innovative funding model for e-commerce capacity-building could be the establishment of a social impact bond (Suominen, 2016a). Such a bond would involve private foundations, social impact investors, and/or e-commerce platforms making an initial investment, which would be compensated by governments, and perhaps also by development agencies, only if the project meets certain specified metrics (such as the number of e-commerce-related jobs created or the amount of new online exports achieved).

## 3. Trade logistics in the digital economy

Policymakers need to improve their understanding of the issues at the interface of trade logistics, digitalization and e-commerce. They should explore and tap into relevant opportunities to embrace cross-border e-commerce and create conditions (e.g. alignment of standards), procedures and resources that will enable e-commerce to thrive, while at the same time keeping in mind the interests of MSMEs, in particular (UNCTAD, 2017g).

The digital economy affects the trade logistics that underpin globalized trade and international value chains in many ways. First, an increasing number of products are delivered digitally rather than physically. Second, the expansion of e-commerce in physical products has resulted in rapid growth in small parcel and low-value shipments that are often shipped by small businesses and individuals, many of them ill-equipped to comply with complex trade rules. The shift from large shipments to huge numbers of small parcels and packages has been referred to as a "tsunami of parcels" (UNCTAD, 2017g).

As a result, border regulatory agencies are increasingly expected to process and release shipments very quickly (i.e. in minutes to hours). Consequently, those agencies have limited time to ensure compliance and, due to the fast-paced nature of e-commerce, are under pressure to optimize their performance. Their capacity, business models and resources are constantly challenged to cope with the "tsunami". This heightens the need for them to rethink, realign and reallocate resources to meet the new dynamics of trade. Both national administrations and international organizations are making progress on addressing these issues without compromising on security, safety, revenue leakage and monitoring. Fortunately, there is capacity in trade logistics, including shipping, ports, urban freight/city logistics and air transport channels to deal with the anticipated increase in shipments. International organizations, practitioners and other stakeholders are cognizant of the underlying challenges and are aligning their work accordingly.

The WTO Trade Facilitation Agreement (TFA) includes provisions that aim to modernize border clearance procedures and streamline processes. Such efforts

become even more important in the evolving digital economy. Although a step in the right direction, the TFA is not sufficient on its own; it does not address all issues arising from the proliferation of small parcels in trade, often shipped by small businesses. The new digital landscape calls for new and innovative solutions.

One approach to facilitate trade by MSMEs is the Exporta Fácil programme first implemented by Brazil in 2002.[11] By simplifying the export process, it helped reduce costs from 16 per cent to 1 per cent of the value of exported goods, and helped boost exports from $12 million during the first year of the project, to more than $230 million in 2016 (UPU, 2017). Its approach has since been introduced by the postal systems of several Latin American countries. It has simplified customs clearance for SMEs for shipments typically weighing less than 30 kilograms and with a value of less than $5,000. The postal system has taken over and centralized the tasks of various agencies involved in the export process, such as customs, health and environment, and export agencies. Modelled on Exporta Fácil, the Universal Postal Union (UPU) has launched a

## Box VI.2. Some proposals for facilitating trade by MSMEs

In recent years, several ideas have been floated with a view to adapting trade facilitation to the needs of smaller businesses in the digital economy. This box highlights a few examples.

Trusted eTrader programmes tailored to MSMEs would enable customs authorities to use anonymized big data held by major online platforms for risk-targeting in trade. It is modelled on the Air Cargo Advanced Screening programme that the United States piloted a few years ago with private express carriers (Suominen, 2015). The programmes could also incentivize and simplify MSMEs' compliance with trade rules. For example, customs agencies and other partners could set up a compliance platform on which importers and exporters could access a customized trade compliance form tailored to their products and markets with only a few fields to fill. Consistent and compliant companies could be identified as "Trusted eTraders", and as such, qualify for expedited entry.

Simplified, paperless and one-stop clearance processes could involve a "single-window" approach for one-stop compliance, enabling the collection and remittance of taxes for goods above the de minimis level away from the border, and the use of electronic documents in international trade. To simplify clearance, countries could create harmonized tariff codes for low-value items that qualify for clearance. There could also be a simplified returns policy that exonerates returned goods from the imposition of duties or tariffs. It should be noted, though, that implementing single windows can be hampered by structural and infrastructural deficits, poor data-sharing, inadequate coordination and low standards of administrative practice (World Bank and African Development Bank, 2012).

A proposal put forward by the freight forwarding industry is for countries to expand on the provisions of the WTO TFA to facilitate cross-border e-commerce. This could involve offering simplified entry for low-value shipments, national treatment for transport and logistics services, expanding market access, strengthening online trust and confidence through consumer protection across borders, and introducing electronic payments and other e-commerce-related services (Global Express Association, 2016). Countries that accept these kinds of TFA Plus commitments for low- value shipments could be given preferred access to trade-related capacity-building programmes.

Source: UNCTAD.

programme entitled Easy Exports, and a first pilot scheme was launched in Tunisia in January 2017 (UPU, 2017). Other innovative proposals have also been made in recent years (box VI.2).

For several years, investments in trade facilitation have focused on activities at the border: modernizing customs and upgrading road, air, port and rail infrastructure. Trade facilitation in the evolving digital economy will need to look beyond the border, as e-commerce is resulting in many small parcels being transported through congested megacities. Traffic congestion slows down deliveries and undermines the savings and efficiencies. Rural areas also need trade facilitation. E-commerce has become a means for consumers and companies who are located far away from big retailers to purchase products and inputs, and for rural sellers to reach urban markets.

New technologies may help to overcome some logistical bottlenecks. They can enable navigating traffic more efficiently by calculating the fastest routes or identifying the most fuel-/time-efficient pick-ups. In addition, trade facilitation experts and city planners may encourage greater use of 3D printing, resulting in long-distance sales of designs and local distribution of the final products that are printed on-site.[12] Meanwhile, real-time data and the ability to analyse and exchange such information can make the processing of shipments more efficient. Data analytics can help optimize and predict deliveries, develop intelligent traffic systems and enable shared delivery services.[13] Meanwhile, package delivery by drones is already being tested by some e-commerce companies.[14]

# D. DEVELOPING SKILLS FOR THE DIGITAL ECONOMY

## 1. The changing role of policies

Digitally induced changes in labour markets and skills requirements (chapter IV) have implications for formal education systems, which tend to be slow to adjust, as well as for private and public skills development strategies. This will require an overhaul of education and training systems, as well as individual attitudes, and it may involve crafting appropriate curricula now for skills and jobs that will be required in the future.

Who is responsible for reskilling people and equipping the workforce with the right skills? While governments have a fundamental role to play in providing the educational basis, and firms may provide some training (particularly firm specific), the burden of keeping skills updated and relevant will fall progressively on each individual. At the same time, it is hard for individuals to know what skills they should develop and to shoulder the cost of developing them. It will no longer be sufficient to learn the skills at school on the expectation that these will equip people for lifelong employment. Instead, people will be required increasingly to consider a future of lifelong learning and change, with high degrees of adaptability and flexibility.

As part of SDG 4, the international education community has pledged to achieve inclusive and equitable quality primary and secondary education by 2030, and to "promote lifelong learning opportunities for all". In order to meet this target, some 69 million additional teachers – who are well-trained, motivated and empowered – will be needed worldwide before 2030. At the current pace, it is estimated that the world will achieve universal primary education in 2042, and universal upper secondary education only in 2084 (UNESCO, 2017).

Supplying the economy with the right skills may require a variety of actions (table VI.1). In order to ensure that the supply of skills matches demand, it may also be necessary to forecast digital skill needs of the future, disseminate information on such needs to students, jobseekers and firms, and make education and training systems more responsive to market needs.

To some extent, domestically developed skills may need to be complemented by inflows of talent from abroad. While skills migration may have negative consequences for countries from where local talent moves abroad, geographic mobility of talent, including at the international level, is a key element for developing skills, acquiring knowledge generated abroad, accessing qualified staff and building excellence in research and development. The international acquisition and development of talent (and its loss) therefore require policy attention.

## Table VI.1. Policy instruments to develop relevant skills for the digital economy

### A. General objective: Develop skills for the digital economy

| Specific objectives | Policy instruments | Examples |
|---|---|---|
| Promote complementary non-cognitive skills | • Reform teaching methods to promote non-cognitive skills<br>• Promote learning to learn as a key competency<br>• Encourage other learning activities (work placements, extracurricular activities) that promote non-cognitive skills | • Japan reformed the national curricula in the late 1990s to strengthen students' abilities to think critically and creatively, and to identify and solve problems independently<br>• Intel's Educar training programme includes support for teachers in the use of methodologies that promote the development of critical thinking and research |
| Ensure all citizens have the basic ICT skills required to work | • Integration of ICT curricula in primary and secondary education<br>• Digital literacy programme targeting specific groups (older, women, school dropouts, rural areas, jobseekers) | • Portugal has a National Strategy for Digital Inclusion and Literacy<br>• Mexico provides digital literacy programmes through "digital inclusion centres"<br>• #techmums, an NGO in the United Kingdom, teaches mothers technical skills and builds their confidence, encouraging them into education, entrepreneurship and employment |
| Enhance offer of, and enrolment in, ICT programmes in vocational and higher education, and lifelong training | • Develop (upgrade) ICT curricula<br>• Promote greater industrial collaboration in ICT training<br>• Financially support students/ programmes in ICT-related fields<br>• Facilitate expansion and access to lifelong learning and retraining<br>• Facilitate development of a relevant segment of private education | • In Costa Rica, Intel experts participate in the design of study programmes to train engineers in the fields of information technology, robotics and automation<br>• Turkey adopted a Life-long Learning Strategy in 2011 |
| Improve quality of teaching | • Facilitate access to relevant teacher training<br>• Finance training to upgrade skills and lifelong learning for current teachers<br>• Hire external professionals to collaborate with/ support teachers<br>• Recruit teachers with industry experience<br>• Provide the necessary ICT infrastructure and Internet bandwidth in schools and institutions of higher education | • India offers national awards for teachers' use of ICT in education<br>• Intel's Educar programme in Costa Rica offers courses to teachers to facilitate the use of modern technologies<br>• Solar-powered mobile ICT computer laboratories sponsored by Samsung connect rural sub-Saharan African schools |
| Make ICT skills more attractive to students | • Support ICT fairs, fablabs, hackathons and competitions<br>• Promote mentors, role models and networks<br>• Offer awards, grants and other funding mechanisms for studies in ICT-related areas<br>• Organize targeted campaigns to make ICTs attractive to specific segments of the population (e.g. girls and women) | • Organize an international day of girls in ICT<br>• Kenya's AkiraChix, a non-profit organization, encourages girls to embrace technology, and offers them free basic training in web design, mobile applications development, graphic design and entrepreneurship. |

## A. General objective: Develop skills for the digital economy

| Specific objectives | Policy instruments | Examples |
|---|---|---|
| Provide incentives to workers and firms to reskill and upgrade their skills | • Facilitate access to lifelong learning and retraining<br><br>• Provide financial incentives for firms to train workers<br><br>• Promote better work organization and management practices within firms (e.g. training, teamwork, flexible working hours) to encourage workers to learn on the job or outside<br><br>• Facilitate labour mobility across sectors of the economy, academia and government | • Singapore's SkillsFuture offers S$500 grants to pay for training courses at any approved provider<br><br>• Republic of Korea's Employment Insurance Fund provides direct funding for SME workforce training<br><br>• European Commission's e-Leadership Initiative fosters ICT skills among business leaders and promotes e-leadership and digital entrepreneurship<br><br>• Thailand's Talent Mobility programme enables public researchers to spend 20 per cent of their time in industry |

## B. General objective: Match supply of and demand for digital skills

| Specific objectives | Key policy instruments | Examples |
|---|---|---|
| Forecast digital skills needs | • Improve ability to gauge future skills needs (by competency area, level and geographical location) | • South Africa identifies skills needs in priority areas<br><br>• Sri Lanka organizes IT sector surveys |
| Information systems | • Provide guidance on careers in ICT<br><br>• Provide guidance to jobseekers and firms<br><br>• Disseminate information on future skills needs to education and training institutions | • Industry Transformation Maps in Singapore's SkillsFuture initiative |
| Make education and training systems more responsive to market needs | • Improve governance of educational systems: review funding structures for education and improve coordination between industry, government and educational and training institutions<br><br>• Expand industry participation in the design and implementation of digital skills policy/programmes | • Singapore has a Tripartite Council for Skills, Innovation and Productivity (CSIP)<br><br>• Dual education |

*Source:* UNCTAD, based on the following: OECD, 2016b: The Economist, 2017; Santiago, 2010; OECD, 2012; UNCTAD, 2015d; and the following websites: http://www.pmc.gob.mx/; https://www.itu.int/en/ITU-D/Digital-Inclusion/Women-and-Girls/Girls-in-ICT-Portal/Pages/Portal.aspx; http://mhrd.gov.in/ict_awards, http://www.un.org/africarenewal/magazine/special-edition-youth-2017/young-women-breaking-male-dominated-ict-world; http://techmums.co/; http://www.skillsfuture.sg/what-is-skillsfuture.html

## 2. Policies to develop skills for the digital economy

Ensuring that students and workers have the cognitive, technical and socio-emotional skills that are augmented by technology – and not replaced by it – is a priority. This will require reforming teaching methods to promote non-cognitive skills. So far, few countries have developed strategies to foster the acquisition of these skills in formal education (OECD, 2016b). In addition to reviewing teaching methods, governments and individual training institutions should encourage other learning activities (e.g. through work placement, and participation in technology competitions and extracurricular activities) that promote non-cognitive skills.

The traditional phases of learning and working are likely to change: rather than having one long initial learning period followed by a traditional working life and career, the future is likely to necessitate many alternative periods of learning and job or career change. Individuals will need to be flexible and aware of the need for lifelong learning in the age of increased automation and digitalization. A key soft skill or competence for lifelong learning is "learning to learn", or the ability to learn something new.[15] This will be critical for people, in addition to acquiring basic cognitive skills (such as in reading, writing, mathematics and problem-solving), as they will need over time to upgrade their skills or retrain in new areas.

With some level of basic digital skills being required for more jobs, governments should progressively incorporate ICTs into national curricula at an early stage of education. Many developing countries now include specific objectives or courses on basic computer skills or computing in their national curricula, particularly at the secondary level. Others, particularly in sub-Saharan Africa, do not have any such objectives, nor do they offer such courses at the primary or secondary level (UNESCO, 2015). Indeed, in many countries, the development of basic literacy skills requires attention.[16] Moreover, digital literacy programmes targeting specific groups (such as older workers who need to upgrade their ICT skills, or certain groups of women if they are unfamiliar with ICTs) may be needed to ensure that all citizens are equipped with the basic ICT skills. For example, Mexico has a network of "digital inclusion centres" that offer digital literacy programmes.[17]

Enhancing the offer of, and enrolment in, ICT programmes remains important at both the vocational and higher educational levels. In addition to offering courses in new technology areas, such as big data analytics or bioinformatics, the curricula of existing ICT educational programmes' need to be continually updated in step with developments in relevant industrial sectors and activities. UNCTAD's research[18] has found that ICT firms in developing countries often face difficulties finding computer graduates with the right skills because ICT curricula in higher education are out of date. In some instances, to provide training in ICT, in general, and highly demanded ICT skills, in particular (such as basic programming), it is useful to involve the private sector. This may relate to computing boot camps and short, intensive web development courses that can help fill a pressing demand for coders. In this context, the role of public institutions would be to assess the quality of private (and public) training institutions, and financially support students and/or educational programmes.

In addition, there is likely to be a need for broader teacher training and selection strategies. Non-ICT teachers should be trained in the use of digital technologies in teaching, and the relevant ICT infrastructure and Internet access would have to be provided in schools and in institutions of higher education. The private sector can also help to upgrade the ICT skills of teachers and improve the quality of ICT training.

Another challenge is to make ICT skills and careers more attractive. Events that showcase ICTs – such as ICT fairs, hackathons or fablabs – can offer possibilities to experiment with ICTs, interact with experts and practice ICT skills. Many of these experiences promote collaboration, learning through experimentation, and non-cognitive skills that are relevant for the digital economy.

Other measures to attract people to ICT careers include the provision of financial support, as well as encouraging ICT mentors, role models and networks. These measures are particularly useful to attract specific segments of the population, such as girls and women, who are underrepresented in computer education and in ICT-related jobs. Expanding girls' and women's participation in ICT studies and careers benefits not only women, but also the ICT industry, which is in need of computer engineers. It can also generate economy-wide benefits. For instance, a 2013 study found that bringing more women into the digital sector in the EU would boost GDP by €9 billion annually.[19] In Guatemala, special efforts are undertaken

---

**Box VI.3.  Programa Valentina**

In Guatemala, an expanding technology sector is generating new employment opportunities. More than 30,000 tech jobs have been created since 2005, and another 100,000 are expected to emerge in the coming years. However, tech companies are struggling to find sufficient qualified talent to fill vacancies. At the same time, many young and vulnerable people are unaware of the growing technology industry and the employment opportunities it offers. Thus appropriate training and placement programmes have become very important.

Programa Valentina of the Sergio Paiz Andrade Foundation, FUNSEPA, (funsepa.org/programa-valentina) was founded in 2014 to help change perceptions and expand the pool of qualified talent in the country. It aims at training disadvantaged young Guatemalans for employment in the technology sector. It has secured funds to start five new training programmes in rural regions, allowing trainees to be placed in formal jobs with monthly salaries of $730–$1,100, representing two or three times the minimum wage in Guatemala.

The main goal of the programme is to increase the employability of participants. It has been developed with employers' needs in mind, and seeks to emulate the experience of working in technology companies. It defines employability in terms of five characteristics that it seeks to develop in participants: correct, cooperative, proactive, prepared and "techie". In addition, participants have learnt how to use digital tools and widely used business software. All certified participants would be well-equipped for entry level jobs as, for example, junior designers, data processors or content creators.

Programa Valentina's goal is to become the leading open-source training-and-placement programme for the tech industry in Latin America by 2025.

*Source:* UNCTAD, based on information provided by FUNSEPA.

---

to help disadvantaged youth find opportunities in the technology sector (box VI.3).

Governments can facilitate skills development by providing incentives to workers and firms to reskill or upgrade their skills. For instance, as noted earlier, Singapore's SkillsFuture, offers a grant of 500 Singapore dollars to every worker for training courses delivered by approved providers. In addition to obtaining financial support, workers also need to make time available to be trained. Expanding the provision of short training courses that can eventually lead to certifications and diplomas, as well as work organization and management practices within firms (such as flexible working arrangements and time off from work for training purposes), may enable more workers to be retrained. One possibility is to facilitate the use of, and recognize new, digitally enabled ways of delivering education and training, including remotely, such as through massive open online courses (MOOCs), which can make teaching available to those who might otherwise not be able to access it (Commission on Science, Technology and Development, 2016).

Labour mobility is important for skills upgrading. For instance, when computer engineers move between firms, or when computer teachers or university researchers spend time working for a private firm, they acquire new knowledge and skills. However, mobility is often hampered by institutional constraints (e.g.

lack of recognition of time spent in the private sector for the researcher's career progression) or by labour market regulations (e.g. restrictions on the portability of pensions), taxation and social protection systems. Multi-employer plans – an employee benefit plan covering health insurance, pensions, unemployment insurance and vacation benefits to which more than one employer contributes – and the portability of social contracts can support labour mobility and, equally important, provide enhanced social protection to the increasing numbers of citizens working as freelancers or independent contractors in the digital economy (Hill, 2015).

## 3.  Policies to match the supply of and demand for digital skills

Three distinct and complementary sets of actions are important to ensure that the skills supplied match the skills demanded (table VI.1). The first is to improve the ability to forecast the needs for future skills, for example by competency area, at different levels of complexity and in different geographical areas. Businesses can play a key role in identifying current and potential skill shortages. Surveys of firm or focus groups can help identify skills shortages in order to inform national, industry or regional skills development strategies.

One way of collecting information on needs for specialist ICT skills is to include questions on human resources and skills needs in surveys that IT sector associations often carry out among their members (UNCTAD, 2012). In Sri Lanka, for example, the public administration makes continuous efforts to identify the state of the national IT services industry and coordinate with that sector. Surveys and publications on the sector and its workforce are made publicly available, and the public sector has formal and informal interactions with multiple industry associations. A good understanding of its workforce has been one key element in supporting the development of the domestic IT sector in the country (UNCTAD, 2013b).

A second option is to disseminate information on digital skills needs as widely as possible, providing guidance to students on careers in ICT-related areas and to jobseekers and workers who are considering upgrading or adding new skills that are expected to become in great demand. Findings on future skills needs should be shared with education and training providers. Lessons can be learned from Singapore's SkillsFuture initiative, which asks employers to detail the changes they expect will occur in the next 3 to 5 years, by industry, and to identify the skills that they will need. This information is then used to draw Industry Transformation Maps that help guide individuals on future skill requirements (*The Economist*, 2017).

Thirdly, governments can make education and training systems more responsive to market needs by improving the governance of educational systems. Funding structures for education can be reviewed, for example, by basing the funding on skills forecasts to help set the number of places at different educational levels, and putting in place robust coordination mechanisms[20] between the labour market and the education and training system. Rapidly changing skills requirements underscore the need for interaction between businesses, government and educational institutions. Singapore, which is considered a role model in terms of coordinating country strategies for investment in education and industrial development strategies (Kuruvilla et al., 2002; ILO, 2011), has set up a Tripartite Council for Skills, Innovation and Productivity.[21] It is chaired by the Deputy Prime Minister and Coordinating Minister for Economic and Social Policies, and comprises members from government, industry, education and training institutions, and trade unions. It aims to identify skills needs for the future and supports productivity-led economic growth.

Developing digital skills in line with an economy's short- and long-term needs requires the participation of industry players in designing skills development strategies and ICT curricula. Industry associations, trade unions and individual private firms can play a critical role in the implementation of skills development strategies. The private sector can contribute by engaging in training activities, participating in various forms of dual education that provide opportunities for internships and job placements. Indeed, many firms, especially large players in the ICT sector, including in developing countries, have been investing in the development of digital skills among their existing and potential employees. In the Netherlands, for example, educational institutions, employers, employees, the private sector and governments at the regional and central levels have formed a national technology pact to satisfy the need for highly skilled technology workers.[22] The pact has three lines of action up to 2020: (i) increasing the number of learners deciding to study technology-related subjects; (ii) increasing the number of people with a technical qualification taking technology-related jobs; and (iii) ensuring that technology workers who are at risk of losing their jobs or marginalization are kept working in the sector.

## 4.  The time to act is now

Regardless of the speed at which transformations occur, all countries will need to adjust their education and training systems to deliver the skills required in the digital economy. This is vital not only for young people entering the labour market, but also for the stock of existing workers and those who need to be retrained and prepared for a future of lifelong learning with jobs and skills flexibility and adaptability. It is important to start these changes today to prepare for future disruptions.

Digitally induced transformations will need proactive policies that provide the necessary education and training to enable citizens to acquire the basic ICT skills required to work, that make available adequate numbers of ICT-related specialists with relevant skills, and that build the complementary non-cognitive skills, attitudes and values. All countries, whatever their level of development, should pay due attention to the promotion of digital skills. However, priorities may vary by country. LDCs need to focus on promoting digital literacy among a growing number of students and workers, as well as on building a base of ICT specialists. More advanced countries may aim to build full digital literacy and expand their supply of ICT specialists.

Developing the relevant skills involves more than incorporating new disciplines or studies into existing educational curricula. It also requires increasing the opportunities for workers and teachers to upgrade their skills, promoting alternative opportunities to develop non-cognitive skills, reforming teaching methodologies and upgrading teaching capabilities, developing targeted training programmes for specific groups, and making future skills more attractive to students and workers. In addition, a major effort is needed to increase the availability of trained teachers for basic education. Strategies are also needed to improve the matching of skills supply with demand. Implementation of all this will require significant investment, as well as government coordination at the highest level (across educational, industrial and labour bodies) and collaboration with the private sector.

Finally, in order to cope with the transformation of the labour market, policymakers will need to consider ways of supporting companies and workers to adapt. Policies may have to focus on skilling, reskilling and skills upgrading, as well as on changes to labour regulations in ways that can facilitate, rather than impede, jobs and skills transitions. In addition, more attention should be devoted to the social and political dimensions of technological change, innovation and job creation (Nübler, 2016). This includes analysing how social protection systems can best support workers when they are between jobs or not working regularly. Such systems are available at an adequate level to only about a quarter of the world's population at present (ILO, 2015). Finally, redistribution policies will be essential to address the risk of increased polarization and income inequality. The ultimate impact is not a given. There is scope for policymakers to influence the outcome based on informed analysis and a clear idea of the direction in which society wants to move.

# E. GOVERNING CROSS-BORDER DATA FLOWS

The digital economy relies increasingly on data flows within and across national boundaries (chapter I). Data are becoming an essential input in decision-making, production processes, transactions and relationship management across an ever-increasing swath of the agricultural, manufacturing and services sectors. As the digital economy evolves further, data will become even more inextricably interwoven with all aspects of the world economy, including the functioning of the Internet, GVCs and international trade. But to be an effective catalyst for change, the data must be able to flow across national borders. A deep understanding among governments and stakeholders of the role of data flows is therefore becoming increasingly important.

Issues relating to cross-border data flows (CBDFs) have been discussed since the 1970s, but they have recently become more controversial in international policy and trade discussions. Prior to the public Internet era of proprietary platforms, many MNEs began to use international private networks to transfer data across national frontiers in pursuit of new organizational efficiencies and competitive advantages. Recognition of this trend gave rise to concerns among governments that their national policy frameworks relating to privacy protection and economic regulation could be bypassed as data moved out of their national jurisdictions to other countries where they would be subject to different laws and policies (box VI.4).

Policymakers have to balance companies' needs to collect and analyse data for innovation and efficiency gains, on the one hand, and the concerns of various stakeholders over security, privacy, movement and ownership of data on the other (UNCTAD, 2016a). Governments have adopted different strategies to address these and other concerns, ranging from various restrictions on cross-border data flows to entering into international agreements to facilitate such flows.

A growing number of countries have contemplated or adopted measures that create disincentives or barriers to CBDF. The reasons vary and include national security, protecting personal privacy and data, ensuring access to information related to law enforcement, preventing flows that are deemed to challenge national public order, or protecting and promoting economic activity within a national territory (Castro and McQuinn, 2015). In some countries, policies may be part of a wider government strategy to ensure "cyber-sovereign" control over the digital economy and society. In such cases, CBDF barriers have at times been coupled with data localization policies requiring that data be retained within a given jurisdiction and processed there (Chander and Lê, 2015; Drake et al., 2016).

**Box VI.4. The evolution of policy discussions on cross-border data flows**

In 1974, an OECD expert group meeting coined the term "transborder data flow (TDF)". The OECD subsequently established a working party on TDFs which spent the next decade assessing the potential effects of such flows on countries' economic, legal, social and technological independence of action (Drake, 1993). These issues were then taken up by the Intergovernmental Bureau of Informatics (IBI), an organization comprising representatives from 43 member governments mostly from developing countries. At IBI World Conferences in 1980 and 1984, TDFs were cited as a potential threat to national sovereignty. Some countries called for the creation of a new international regime to regulate data flows and related practices (Intergovernmental Bureau of Informatics, 1984). These efforts were complemented by analytical and empirical investigations conducted by the United Nations Centre on Transnational Corporations (1982).

After much debate, three new international instruments were established to deal with the TDF issue. In 1980, the OECD adopted voluntary Guidelines on the Protection of Privacy and Transborder Flows of Personal Data (revised in 2013). In 1981, the Council of Europe adopted a Convention for the Protection of Individuals with Regard to Automatic Processing of Personal Data. Both these initiatives formulated general principles regarding the handling of personally identifiable information (PII) that have since been echoed and built upon in other international privacy instruments (UNCTAD, 2016c). And in 1985, the OECD adopted a Declaration on Transborder Data Flows, which addressed non-privacy issues (OECD, 1985).

Subsequently, concerns among some governments about the potential negative effects of TDFs dissipated, and the term generally disappeared, except with reference to the protection of PII. This issue was accorded firmer legal treatment by, for example, the EU's Data Protection Directive in 1995 and the related Safe Harbor Agreement with the United States in 2000, and again with the EU's General Data Protection Regulation (GDPR) and the Privacy Shield Agreement with the United States in 2016. With the pervasive spread of e-commerce and the advent of cloud computing, the core question of how governments should treat personal and non-personal data flows has surfaced once more.

*Source:* UNCTAD.

Excessively stringent limitations on data flows can have negative effects by stifling trade and innovation. Data privacy and localization requirements that discriminate against foreign suppliers of data and providers of downstream goods and services may raise the costs of doing business (van der Marel et al., 2014). Forced localization of servers can also raise the cost of doing business (Bauer et al., 2016). For example, requirements to store or process data within a country may mean that manufacturers of IoT devices have to build or contract local data operations in multiple countries, which can be a prohibitively expensive endeavour.

In both developing and developed countries, enforcement of privacy and security obligations is often inadequate, as authorities seek to catch up with the latest technological advances. Moreover, many developing countries still lack data protection and privacy legislation altogether (table VI.2). In Africa, for example, less than 40 per cent of countries have adopted such legislation, and in Oceania, only one economy has data privacy legislation in place.

Some governments have begun to grapple with the security implications of IoT (see box I.1). For example, in Germany, government officials banned an Internet-enabled doll because a possible vulnerability to hacking could render it a "concealed transmitting device."[23] The United States Federal Trade Commission has sued smart object maker D-Link, alleging that the company failed to provide the "advanced network security" it advertised for its wireless routers and Internet cameras, thus exposing consumers to the risk of being hacked.[24] The EU's new General Data Protection Regulation (GDPR), which takes effect in May 2018, will require IoT manufacturers serving the EU market "to ensure a level of security appropriate to the risk."[25] And China's new Cyber Security Law, effective as of June 2017, requires pre-market certification of critical network equipment and specialized security products, as well as national security reviews of critical information infrastructure.[26]

Again, the challenge is to find an appropriate balance between supporting processes that allow the transfer of data, on the one hand, and addressing concerns related to issues such as privacy and security on the other. The current system for data protection is fragmented, with varying global, regional and national regulatory approaches. Instead of pursuing multiple initiatives, it would be preferable for global and regional organizations to concentrate on one unifying initiative or a smaller number of initiatives that are internationally

**Table VI.2. Share of economies with relevant e-commerce legislation, by region, 2017 (per cent)**

| Region | Number of economies | Share in e-transaction laws | Share in consumer protection laws | Share in privacy and data protection laws | Share in cybercrime laws |
|---|---|---|---|---|---|
| **Developed economies** | **42** | **97.6** | **85.7** | **97.6** | **97.6** |
| **Developing economies** | | | | | |
| **Africa** | **54** | **51.9** | **33.3** | **38.9** | **50.0** |
| East Africa | 18 | 44.4 | 22.2 | 27.8 | 61.1 |
| Middle Africa | 9 | 22.2 | 11.1 | 44.4 | 11.1 |
| North Africa | 6 | 83.3 | 33.3 | 33.3 | 83.3 |
| Southern Africa | 5 | 60.0 | 40.0 | 40.0 | 40.0 |
| West Africa | 16 | 62.5 | 56.3 | 50.0 | 50.0 |
| **Asia and Oceania** | **50** | **70.8** | **41.7** | **37.5** | **66.7** |
| East Asia | 4 | 75.0 | 50.0 | 50.0 | 75.0 |
| South Asia | 9 | 77.8 | 33.3 | 44.4 | 77.8 |
| South-East Asia | 11 | 81.8 | 72.7 | 45.5 | 72.7 |
| West Asia | 12 | 91.7 | 41.7 | 58.3 | 66.7 |
| Oceania | 14 | 42.9 | 14.3 | 7.1 | 42.9 |
| **Latin America and the Caribbean** | **33** | **87.9** | **63.6** | **48.5** | **72.7** |
| Central America | 8 | 87.5 | 87.5 | 37.5 | 62.5 |
| South America | 12 | 83.3 | 83.3 | 58.3 | 83.3 |
| Caribbean | 13 | 92.3 | 30.8 | 46.2 | 69.2 |
| **Transition economies** | **17** | **100.0** | **17.6** | **88.2** | **100.0** |
| **All economies** | **196** | **77.0** | **50.0** | **57.1** | **71.9** |

*Source:* UNCTAD *Cyberlaw Tracker*, July 2017.

---

**Box VI.5. Core principles for data protection**

Although different national data protection laws vary considerably, there is greater consensus around the core set of data protection principles at the heart of most national laws and international regimes. Some regimes (so-called omnibus regimes) apply equally to all involved in processing personal data. Others apply different rules to specified sectors (e.g. health industry), types of processing entity (e.g. public authorities) or categories of data (e.g. data about children). In such jurisdictions, other sectors are not subject to regulatory controls at all. A distinction can also be made between regimes that operate primarily through enforcement actions brought by individuals or their representative groups, and those that grant enforcement powers to a specialized supervisory authority, which exercises ongoing oversight over the conduct of those that process personal data.

The following eight principles appear in some form of another in all key international and regional agreements and guidelines on data protection. They could be a useful starting point for interoperability and harmonization efforts:

1. Openness: organizations must be open about their personal data collection and use practices
2. Collection limitations: collection of personal data must be limited, lawful and fair, usually with the knowledge and/or consent of the person concerned
3. Purpose specification: the purpose of collection and disclosure must be specified at the time of the data collection
4. Limitation on use: use or disclosure must be limited to specific purposes or closely related purposes
5. Security: personal data must be subject to appropriate security safeguards
6. Data quality: personal data must be relevant, accurate and up-to-date
7. Access and correction: data subjects must have appropriate rights to access and correct their personal data
8. Accountability: data controllers must take responsibility for ensuring compliance with the data protection principles

*Source:* UNCTAD, 2016a.

compatible. Where possible, similarities in underlying principles should be leveraged to develop mechanisms for recognition and compatibility between different frameworks (box VI.5) (UNCTAD, 2016a). In this context, it will be useful to explore ways to ensure an effective dialogue between the trade policy and Internet policy communities (chapter V).

Some analysts argue that governments' existing laws as well as their national commitments under the WTO General Agreement on Trade in Services (GATS) already require the liberal treatment of computer and information services, such as those involved in CBDF and data localization (Burri, 2016; Crosby, 2016). Rules that hinder CBDFs may appear to be discriminatory against foreign providers of data services, and may therefore potentially violate commitments to liberalize trade in goods and services. In particular, data localization obligations can raise issues concerning compliance with trade liberalization commitments under the GATS (box VI.6).

# F. SCALING UP SUPPORT TO DEVELOPING COUNTRIES

The speed at which the digital economy is unfolding, and the significant gaps that exist in terms of the ability and readiness of countries, enterprises and individuals to engage in it, underlines the urgency of scaling up global support for capacity-building and technical assistance to developing countries, and especially the LDCs. A particular challenge for many LDCs is that they have to address a large number of policy areas in parallel and in a coordinated manner, often without reliable statistics and other information to inform the policymaking process.

The international community can provide various forms of assistance which should be tailored to the specific needs of each country. This may include the provision of training, policy advice and strategy formulation. At the country level, development partners may help such activities as e-commerce readiness assessments, financing of infrastructure investment, support for the development of legal and regulatory frameworks, and capacity-building for diverse stakeholder groups.

The current trend is not encouraging. One of the SDG targets (8.11) relates to the need for more Aid-for-Trade support for developing countries, in particular

the LDCs. Despite the growing importance of the digital economy for the achievement of the SDGs and the huge divides, the share of ICT in total Aid for Trade declined from 3 per cent during the period 2002–2005 to only 1.2 per cent in 2015 (OECD and WTO, 2017). As highlighted in the 2017 *WTO Aid for Trade Global Review*, aid disbursements for trade-related infrastructure in 2015 amounted to $23.3 billion, of which only $0.5 billion was devoted to ICT disbursements, mostly in the form of technical assistance for regulatory reform (ibid.).

In the years ahead, priorities will need to change, and synergies be sought between public and private sector investment in digital infrastructure. For developing countries, and especially the LDCs, to catch up, more attention should be given to Internet connectivity, broadband access, computerization and, where it is still insufficient, electricity supply. The Review found that ICT is a priority area in the development strategy of two thirds of the donors, many of whom also give emphasis to e-government and e-commerce (58 per cent and 50 per cent respectively) (ibid.). Hopefully, this growing awareness among the development partners of the need for ratcheting up the level of support in this field will translate into additional resources.

Increasing the contribution of digitalization to sustainable development requires a concerted, holistic, cross-sectoral and multi-stakeholder approach. Numerous organizations, foundations and private sector actors already offer models for expanding connectivity, lowering costs and addressing regulatory issues. These can help unlock the development potential of digital trade. However, these efforts generally target specific policy areas rather than aiming at facilitating e-commerce or the digital economy in general. A greater and more concerted effort is therefore needed to ensure that the shift towards a more digital economy does not leave any person, enterprise or country behind.

One way to capitalize on existing knowledge and maximize synergies with partners is to tap into the *eTrade for all* initiative (box VI.7). It seeks to improve the ability of developing countries to use e-commerce by involving both the public and private sectors in efforts to raise awareness, enhance synergies, scale up existing efforts and undertake new efforts in seven policy areas. The main tool of the initiative is a dynamic, online platform that enables developing countries and donors to navigate more easily the supply of technical and financial support available to foster development gains from e-commerce.

## Box VI.6. GATS and cross-border data flows

Under the WTO General Agreement on Trade in Services (GATS), many countries have committed to according national treatment and market access for providers of data processing services that are based abroad (cross-border or "Mode 1" suppliers). This means that the same rules should be applied to foreign providers as to domestic ones, and that they cannot be designed to disadvantage foreign providers.

There is some jurisprudence in this area. In China – Electronic Payment Systems, a WTO dispute settlement panel held that Chinese rules requiring financial transactions to be processed through a Chinese company disfavoured foreign providers of such services, which were "precluded from providing their services on a cross-border basis to consumers … that are based in China."[a] The panel recognized the services at issue as including "the processing infrastructure, network, and rules and procedures that facilitate, manage, and enable transaction information and payment flows and which provide system integrity, stability and financial risk reduction."[b]

However, GATS national treatment and market access obligations apply only if a country has made a commitment with respect to that service for the relevant mode of service delivery. Furthermore, obligations made can be subject to a public policy or public morals exception, as well as exceptions for measures "necessary to secure compliance with laws or regulations which are not inconsistent with the provisions of this Agreement including those relating to: … the protection of the privacy of individuals in relation to the processing and dissemination of personal data and the protection of confidentiality of individual records and accounts…"[c] Thus, trade rules do not override government efforts to protect privacy.

On the other hand, while GATS members can determine their own level of privacy protection, they cannot apply them in a manner that results in "arbitrary or unjustifiable discrimination between countries where like conditions prevail, or a disguised restriction on trade in services."[d] What this means in practice is not always clear. A country whose companies are denied access to a market on the grounds of privacy protection may complain to the WTO that such restrictions were objectively unnecessary because the country's privacy concerns could be satisfied by a reasonably available alternative, such as strong and enforceable privacy protections applied by those companies globally.[e]

*Source:* UNCTAD.

[a] China – Electronic Payment Systems, para. 7.667. The panel concluded, nevertheless, that China had explicitly excluded market access for such services, and that therefore China's measures did not violate its Mode-1 commitments, though it held that the Chinese measures did violate its Mode-3 commercial presence commitments.

[b] China – Electronic Payment Systems, para. 7.41.

[c] GATS art. XIV(c).

[d] GATS art. XIV.

[e] US – Gambling, Appellate Body, para. 133–134.

On the back of *eTrade for all*, UNCTAD has also launched a project to help the LDCs assess their readiness to engage in and benefit from e-commerce. Such assessments are important to enable targeted support to those areas where assistance is needed the most. They focus on the seven policy areas of *eTrade for all*, and generate a set of tentative recommendations for LDC governments to improve their readiness for e-trade. By June 2017, two such assessments had been completed, for Bhutan and Cambodia respectively (UNCTAD, 2017h, 2017i).The next in line are Liberia, Nepal, Burundi and Samoa, for which the assessments will be funded by the Enhanced Integrated Framework, a multi-donor programme which helps LDCs participate more actively in the global trading system. Many more LDCs can expect to benefit from similar assessments

in 2017–2018 thanks to funding by Germany and Sweden. Discussions with other donors and development banks are under way to extend similar assistance to developing countries that are not LDCs.

Beyond ICT infrastructure, a wider challenge is to address the other policy areas of *eTrade for all*, including improving the legal and regulatory framework, building the right skills for the digital economy, enabling online payments and more efficient trade logistics, as well as creating environments that are supportive of innovation and digital economy start-ups. For example, to help SMEs overcome barriers to e-commerce, the ITC has developed a comprehensive package of technical and advisory services, collectively referred to as E-Solutions.[27] It offers training modules together with technologies that allow MSMEs to list and manage products

## Box VI.7.  eTrade for all: Connecting the dots for inclusive e-commerce

This global initiative was launched in July 2016, during UNCTAD 14 with the aim of helping developing countries engage in and benefit from e-commerce. It is organized around seven key policy areas of particular relevance to e-commerce development, including e-commerce assessments to ICT infrastructure and services, payments and logistics, legal and regulatory frameworks, skills development and financing for e-commerce (box figure VI.1).

It is a truly collaborative effort to enhance cooperation, transparency and aid efficiency in support of more inclusive e-commerce. Through its online platform (etradeforall.org), all stakeholders can find information and assistance to enable more businesses and people to benefit from e-commerce.

The *eTrade for all* initiative is expanding. By July 2017, it had 25 members from international and regional organizations, national entities and development banks.[a] With its aim of fostering dialogue with the private sector, the initiative works in close cooperation with Business for eTrade Development, an advisory council comprising representatives from more than 30 large and small corporations from both developed and developing countries.[b]

During its first month, etradeforall.org generated more than 2,000 visits (an average of 80 daily visits), which stayed on the platform for an average of more than 4 minutes, and more than 60 per cent were returning visitors. About 25 per cent of the visitors accessed the platform through mobile phones and tablets.

The launch of etradeforall.org is just the beginning; continuous collaboration and support will be needed from partners and donors to further improve the platform and to make the partnership as effective as possible. There are plans to add new functions for increased collaboration through a dedicated private space, provide full information in more languages than the three (English, French and Spanish) being used at present, as well as providing constant updates on new programmes, data and publications, and upcoming events pertaining to e-commerce and the digital economy.

**Box figure VI.1.  The seven policy areas of eTrade for all**

E-commerce assessments · ICT infrastructure and services · Payments · Trade logistics · Legal and regulatory frameworks · Skills development · Financing for e-commerce · E-commerce

*Source:* UNCTAD and etradeforall.org.

a   The African Development Bank, Consumers International, Diplo Foundation, Enhanced Integrated Framework, E-residency (Estonia), International Association of Prosecutors/Global Prosecutors Network, International Civil Society Aviation Organization, Internet Society, Inter-American Development Bank, International Islamic Trade Finance Corporation, International Trade Centre, International Telecommunication Union, United Nations Commission on International Trade Law, UNCTAD, United Nations Economic Commission for Africa, United Nations Economic Commission for Europe,  United Nations Economic Commission for Latin America and the Caribbean, United Nations Economic and Social Commission for Asia and the Pacific, United Nations Economic and Social Commission for West Africa, United Nations Social Impact Fund, Universal Postal Union, World Bank Group, World Customs Organization, World Economic Forum and World Trade Organization.

b   See http://business4etrade.org/.

on multiple websites and integrate international payments and logistics solutions. The programme facilitates access to international legal and fiscal support, and assists in raising awareness among international customers.

There is also a huge need to build the capacity of developing countries to measure the evolving digital economy in order to produce the data needed for evidence-based policymaking (chapter II). The way forward needs to include efforts aimed at supporting developing countries in adopting and disseminating statistics according to existing international measurement frameworks and guidelines. There is growing awareness of this challenge. It has been addressed in several sessions of the UNCTAD E-Commerce Week

and highlighted in discussions of the G-20. It is likely to be addressed in the context of the new UNCTAD Intergovernmental Group of Experts on E-Commerce and the Digital Economy. Moreover, collaborative efforts are under way among international organizations to improve measurement of cross-border e-commerce, trade in ICT-enabled services, the gender dimension and various other aspects of the digital economy.[28]

Overall, smart partnerships will be required involving donor countries, development banks, international organizations, the private sector and civil society. The *eTrade for all* initiative should be effectively leveraged to help forge such partnerships. This will be necessary to ensure that no one is left behind in the evolving digital economy.

# NOTES

1   These issues are being analysed by UNCTAD, and discussed at meetings of the UNCTAD Intergovernmental Groups of Expert on Competition Law and Policy and on Consumer Protection Law and Policy, respectively.

2   See, for example, "President Kagame highlights private sector role in digital connectivity at WEF", *Rwandaupdates.com*, 20 January 2017 (http://rwandaupdates.com/president-kagame-highlights-private-sector-role-in-digital-connectivity-at-wef/).

3   "Working group set up to develop e-commerce," *Dawn*, 4 December 2015.

4   Government of Chile, Agenda Digital 2020 (http://www.agendadigital.gob.cl/#/).

5   See http://www.intracen.org/itc/market-info-tools/voluntary-standards/t4sd-principles-and-signatories/.

6   For a summary of the 2016 TPO Network World Conference and Awards organized by the ITC, see http://itceventscms.event2mobile.com/write/Resources/2479435d-92b9-4279-a991-76f989af2b21.pdf.

7   See ProMéxico website at: http://www.promexico.gob.mx/en/mx/desarrollo-estrategia-e-commerce-marketing-digital/_rid/9?language=en&lng_act=lng_step2 (accessed 15 January 2016).

8   See "PROCOMER de Costa Rica presentó un nuevo servicio para exportar a través de e-commerce," *legiscomex.com*, 24 February 2016.

9   See "The World Bank and the ITC partner to support SMEs in Tunisia, Morocco, and Jordan enter one of the world's largest virtual market places", *ITC News*, 29 September 2015 (http://www.intracen.org/news/The-World-Bank-and-the-ITC-partner-to-support-SMEs-in-Tunisia-Morocco-and-Jordan-enter-one-of-the-worlds-largest-Virtual-Market-Places/).

10  See "Pakistan partners up with Alibaba for SMEs", *MIT Technology Review Pakistan*, 16 May 2017 (http://www.technologyreview.pk/pakistan-partners-alibaba-smes/).

11  See UNCTAD, 2015b, box VI.3.

12  For example, UPS, an express delivery company, is transforming some of its existing warehouses at airports into mini-factories where the company uses 3D printing to produce and deliver customized parts to customers, so that they no longer need to keep large inventories. See "The 3D printing revolution", *Harvard Business Review*, 1 May 2015 (https://hbr.org/2015/05/the-3-d-printing-revolution).

13  See e.g. Suominen (2016b).

14  See "Amazon delivered its first customer package by drone", *USA Today*, 14 December 2016 (https://www.usatoday.com/story/tech/news/2016/12/14/amazon-delivered-its-first-customer-package-drone/95401366/).

15  For a more detailed explanation of learning-to-learn competence, see: http://publications.jrc.ec.europa.eu/repository/bitstream/JRC46532/learning%20to%20learn%20what%20is%20it%20and%20can%20it%20be%20measured%20final.pdf.

16  According to UNESCO, at least 758 million youth and adults cannot read and write, and 250 million children are not acquiring basic literacy skills (see: http://en.unesco.org/themes/literacy-all ).

17  See www.pmc.gob.mx/.

18  Information collected from interviews with leading ICT firms while conducting national Science, Technology and Innovation Policy reviews.

19  See http://europa.eu/rapid/press-release_IP-13-905_en.htm .

20  See, for instance, UNCTAD's Training Course on STI Policies, Participant's handbook, module 4: Developing human resources for science, technology and innovation (unpublished).

21  See http://www.skillsfuture.sg/what-is-skillsfuture.html.

22  See www.cedefop.europa.eu/files/9115_en.pdf.

23  See "German officials order parents to execute a spy – Cayla the doll", *Wall Street Journal*, 14 April 2017 (http://www.npr.org/2017/02/20/516292295/germany-bans-my-friend-cayla-doll-over-spying-concerns). The hacking concern stemmed in part from reports that a "bluetooth-enabled device could connect to [the doll's] speaker and microphone system within a radius of 10m (33ft)" (http://www.bbc.com/news/world-europe-39002142).

24  See https://www.ftc.gov/news-events/press-releases/2017/01/ftc-charges-d-link-put-consumers-privacy-risk-due-inadequate.

25  GDPR Art. 32.

26  See http://www.chinalawtranslate.com/cybersecuritylaw/?lang=en.

27  For more details about the programme, see http://www.intracen.org/uploadedFiles/intracenorg/Content/Exporters/Sectors/Service_exports/Trade_in_services/eSolutions-brochure-optimized.pdf.

28  Such efforts involve organizations such as the International Monetary Fund, ITU, OECD, UNCTAD, UPU, the World Customs Organization, WTO and other members of the Partnership on Measuring ICT for Development.

# REFERENCES

Abeliansky AL and Hilbert M (2017). Digital technology and international trade: Is it the quantity of subscriptions or the quality of data speed that matters? *Telecommunications Policy*, 41(1): 35–48.

Acemoglu D and Restrepo P (2017). Robots and jobs: Evidence from US labor markets. Working Paper No. 23285, National Bureau of Economic Research, Cambridge, MA.

Ahsan K and Azeem A (2010). Insights of apparel supply chain operations: A case study. *International Journal of Integrated Supply Management*, 5(4): 322–343.

Aker JC (2010). Information from markets near and far: Mobile phones and agricultural markets in Niger. *American Economic Journal: Applied Economics*, 2(3): 46–59.

Armstrong LJ, Diepeveen DA and Gandhi N (2011). Effective ICTs in agricultural value chains to improve food security: An international perspective. In: *Report of the 2011 World Congress on Information and Communication Technologies*, Mumbai, 11–14 December 2011: 1217–1222.

Arntz M, Gregory T and Zierahn U (2016). The risk of automation for jobs in OECD countries. OECD Social, Employment and Migration Working Papers. Organisation for Economic Co-operation and Development, Paris.

Ashraf N, Giné X and Karlan D (2009). Finding missing markets (and a disturbing epilogue): Evidence from an export crop adoption and marketing intervention in Kenya. *American Journal of Agricultural Economics*, 91(4): 973–990.

Asian Development Bank (2014). *Information and Communication Technologies for Women Entrepreneurs*. Manila.

Asian Development Bank (2015). *Aid for Trade in Asia and the Pacific: Thinking Forward About Trade Costs and the Digital Economy*. Manila.

Autor DH, Levy F and Murnane RJ (2003). The skill content of recent technological change: An empirical exploration. *The Quarterly Journal of Economics*, 118(4): 1279–1333.

Azimi P, Zhao D, Pouzet C, Crain NE and Stephens B (2016). Emissions of ultrafine particles and volatile organic compounds from commercially available desktop three-dimensional printers with multiple filaments. *Environmental Science & Technology*, 50(3): 1260–1268.

Bagazonzya H et al. (2011). ICT in agriculture : Connecting smallholders to knowledge, networks, and institutions. Report no. 64605, International Bank for Reconstruction and Development/World Bank, Washington, DC.

Bankole FO, Osei-Bryson K-M and Brown I (2015). The impacts of telecommunications infrastructure and institutional quality on trade efficiency in Africa. *Information Technology for Development*, 21(1): 29–43.

Bauer M, Ferracane MF and van der Marel E (2016). Tracing the economic impact of regulations on the free flow of data and data localization. GCIG Paper No. 30, Centre for International Governance Innovation, Waterloo, ON.

Baumüller H (2015). Assessing the role of mobile phones in offering price information and market linkages: The case of M-Farm in Kenya. *The Electronic Journal of Information Systems in Developing Countries*, 68(6): 1–16.

Bean C (2016). Independent review of UK economic statistics. Chancellor of the Exchequer, London.

Bechtold S (2015). 3D printing and the intellectual property system. Economic Research Working Paper No. 28, World Intellectual Property Organization, Geneva.

Beerepoot N and Lambregts B (2015). Competition in online job marketplaces: Towards a global labour market for outsourcing services? *Global Networks*, 15(2): 236–255.

Berg J (2016). Income security in the on-demand economy: Findings and policy lessons from a survey of crowdworkers. Conditions of work and employment Series No. 74, ILO, Geneva.

Broadband Commission (2016). *The State of Broadband 2016: Broadband Catalyzing Sustainable Development*. ITU and UNESCO, Geneva and Paris.

Broadband Commission (2017). *Connecting the Unconnected: Working Together to Achieve Connect 2020 Agenda Targets*. ITU and UNESCO, Geneva and Paris.

Brugger F (2011). Mobile applications in agriculture. Available at: http://www.gsma.com/mobilefordevelopment/wp-content/uploads/2011/12/Syngenta_Report_on_mAgriculture_abridged_web_version.pdf.

Brynjolfsson E (2016). How IoT changes decision making, security and public policy. Available at: http://mitsloanexperts.mit.edu/how-iot-changes-decision-making-security-and-public-policy/.

Bukht R and Heeks R (2017). Defining, conceptualizing and measuring the digital economy. Development Informatics Working Paper No. 68. Centre for Development Informatics, University of Manchester, Manchester.

Burrell J and Oreglia E (2013). The myth of market price information: Mobile phones and the application of economic knowledge in ICTD. *Economy and Society*, 44(2): 271–292. Available at: http://markets.ischool.berkeley.edu/about/.

Burri M (2016). The World Trade Organization as an actor in global Internet governance. SSRN Scholarly Paper No. ID 2792219, Social Science Research Network, Rochester, NY.

Castro D and McQuinn A (2015). Cross-border data flows enable growth in all industries. Information Technology and Innovation Foundation, Washington, DC

Chander A and Lê UP (2015). Data nationalism. *Emory Law Journal*, 3(64): 677–739.

Chui M, Manyika J and Miremadi M (2016). Where machines could replace humans – and where they can't (yet). *McKinsey Quarterly*, July.

Clarke GRG, Qiang CZ and Xu LC (2015). The Internet as a general-purpose technology: Firm-level evidence from around the world. Policy Research Working Paper, No. 7192, World Bank, Washington, DC.

Clarke GRG and Wallsten SJ (2006). Has the Internet increased trade? Developed and developing country evidence. *Economic Inquiry*, 44(3): 465–484.

Cohen D, Sargeant M and Somers K (2014). 3-D printing takes shape. *McKinsey Quarterly*. January.

Commission on Science, Technology and Development (2016). Foresight for digital development. E/CN.16/2016/3. United Nations Economic and Social Council, New York.

Cornell ILR School (2013). Employment & Sustainability. Report of the Cornell ILR School 2013 Roundtable on Employment and Technology. Cornell University, Ithaca, NY.

Cornell ILR School (2014). Technology and Employment Sustainability Initiative: 2014 European Commission Roundtable on Information Technologies and Labour Market Disruptions: A Cross-Atlantic Dialogue. Cornell University, Ithaca, NY.

Craviotti C (2012). Producer relationships and local development in fresh fruit commodity chains: An analysis of blueberry production in Entre Ríos, Argentina. *Regional Studies*, 46(2): 203–215.

Crosby D (2016). Analysis of data localization measures under WTO services trade rules and commitments. E15 Policy Brief, ICTSD and World Economic Forum, Geneva.

David H, Magnus W, Ted L and Göran B (2003). What does it cost to make a payment? *Review of Network Economics*, 2(2): 1–16.

D'Cruz P and Noronha E (2016). Positives outweighing negatives: The experiences of Indian crowdsourced workers. *Work Organisation, Labour & Globalisation*, 10(1): 44–63.

del Carmen Vásquez Callo Müller M (2014). The regulation of trade in information and communication technology services in Chile, Colombia and Peru. A comparative analysis of the rules contained in regional trade agreements. SECO/WTI Academic Cooperation Project, Working Paper Series 2014/16. Berne.

De Stefano V (2016). The rise of the "just-in-time workforce": On-demand work, crowdwork and labour protection in the "gig-economy". Conditions of work and employment Series No. 71, ILO, Geneva.

Degryse C (2016). Digitalisation of the economy and its impact on labour markets. European Trade Union Institute, Brussels.

Deloitte (2014). The Internet of Things ecosystem: Unlocking the business value of connected devices. New York.

Deloitte (2016). Cyber risk in advanced manufacturing: Getting ahead of cyber risk. Available at: https://www2.deloitte.com/us/en/pages/manufacturing/articles/cyber-risk-in-advanced-manufacturing.html#.

Deming DJ (2015). The growing importance of social skills in the labor market. Working Paper No. 21473, National Bureau of Economic Research, Cambridge, MA.

de Silva H and Ratnadiwakara D (2008). Using ICT to reduce transaction costs in agriculture through better communication: A case-study from Sri Lanka. Available at: http://www.lirneasia.net/wp-content/uploads/2008/11/transactioncosts.pdf.

Dicken P (2011). *Global Shift, Sixth Edition: Mapping the Changing Contours of the World Economy*. The Guilford Press, New York and London.

Donner J (2004). Microentrepreneurs and mobiles: An exploration of the uses of mobile phones by small business owners in Rwanda. *Information Technologies & International Development*, 2(1): 1–21.

Donner J and Escobari MX (2010). A review of evidence on mobile use by micro and small enterprises in developing countries. *Journal of International Development*, 22(5): 641–658.

Drahokoupil J and Fabo B (2016). The platform economy and the disruption of the employment relationship. Available at: http://www.etui.org/Publications2/Policy-Briefs/European-Economic-Employment-and-Social-Policy/The-platform-economy-and-the-disruption-of-the-employment-relationship.

Drake WJ (1993). Territoriality and intangibility: Transborder data flows and national sovereignty. In: Nordenstreng K, and Schiller H I, eds. *Beyond National Sovereignty: International Communications in the 1990s*. Ablex Publishing, Norwood, NJ: 259–313.

Drake WJ (2017). Data localization and barriers to cross-border data flows: Toward a multi-track solution. World Economic Forum, Geneva.

Drake WJ, Cerf VG and Kleinwächter W (2016). *Internet Fragmentation: An Overview*. World Economic Forum, Geneva.

Duckworth AL and Yeager DS (2015). Measurement matters: Assessing personal qualities other than cognitive ability for educational purposes. *Educational Researcher,* 44(4): 237–251.

Duncombe R (2016). Mobile phones for agricultural and rural development: A literature review and suggestions for future research. *The European Journal of Development Research*, 28(2): 213–235.

eBay (2013). Commerce 3.0 for development: The promise of the global empowerment network. eBay. San Francisco, CA.

eBay (2016). Small online business growth report: Towards an inclusive global economy. San Francisco, CA.

Esselaar S, Stork C, Ndiwalana A and Deen-Swarray M (2007). ICT usage and its impact on profitability of SMEs in 13 African countries. *Information and Communication Technologies and Development,* 4(1): 87–100.

EuropeAid (2012). Agricultural markets and small-scale producers: Access and risk management tools. Available at: https://ec.europa.eu/europeaid/sites/devco/files/study-agricultural-markets-small-scale-producers-201205_en_5.pdf.

European Commission (2014). E-skills for Europe: Towards 2010 and beyond. European E-Skills Forum Synthesis Report, Brussels.

Fold N (2001). Restructuring of the European chocolate industry and its impact on cocoa production in West Africa. *Journal of Economic Geography*, 1(4): 405–420.

Foster C and Graham M (2015a). The Internet and tourism in Rwanda. Oxford Internet Institute Report, University of Oxford, Oxford.

Foster C and Graham M (2015b). Connectivity and the tea sector in Rwanda. Oxford Internet Institute Report, University of Oxford, Oxford.

Foster CG and Azmeh S (2016). Digital latecomer economies and national internet policy: The case of Chinese platforms. University of Oxford, Oxford.

Foster CG, Graham M, Mann L, Waema T and Friederici N (2017). Digital control in value chains: Challenges of connectivity for East African firms. *Economic Geography* (forthcoming).

Franz M, Felix M and Trebbin A (2014) Framing smallholder inclusion in global value chains: Case Studies from India and West Africa. *Geographica Helvetica*, 69(4): 239–247.

Frey CB and Osborne MA (2017). The future of employment: How susceptible are jobs to computerisation? *Technological Forecasting and Social Change*, 114(C): 254–280.

Galperin H and Viecens MF (2014). Connected for development? Theory and evidence about the impact of Internet technologies on poverty alleviation. SSRN Scholarly Paper No. ID 2397394, Social Science Research Network, Rochester, NY.

GEMS4 (2016). Facilitating commodity trading through technology platforms for farmers and traders. Available at: http://www.gems4nigeria.com/assets/11.-commodity-trading-platform.pdf.

Gereffi G (1999). A commodity chains framework for analyzing global industries. Available at: https://www.ids.ac.uk/ids/global/pdfs/gereffi.pdf.

Gereffi G (2014). Global value chains in a post-Washington Consensus world. *Review of International Political Economy*, 21(1): 9–37.

Gereffi G, Humphrey J and Sturgeon T (2005). The governance of global value chains. *Review of International Political Economy*, 12(1): 78–104.

Gereffi G and Lee J (2012). Why the world suddenly cares about global supply chains. *Journal of Supply Chain Management*, 48(3): 24–32.

Global Commission on Internet Governance (2016). One Internet. Centre for International Governance Innovation and The Royal Institute for International Affairs, London.

Global Connectivity Index (2017). Harnessing the power of connectivity. Huawei.

Global Express Association (2016). Policies to promote international MSME trade: Tapping the full potential of global e-commerce. Available at: http://www.global-express.org/assets/files/Whats%20new%20section/GEA-MSME-(F).pdf.

Goos M, Manning A and Salomons A (2014). Explaining job polarization: Routine-biased technological change and offshoring. *American Economic Review*, 104(8): 2509–2526.

Gordon RB and Suominen K (2014). Going global: Promoting the internationalization of small and mid-size enterprises in Latin America and the Caribbean: Executive summary. Inter-American Development Bank, Washington, DC.

Goyal A (2010). Information, direct access to farmers, and rural market performance in Central India. *American Economic Journal: Applied Economics*, 2(3): 22–45.

Graetz G and Michaels G (2015). Robots at work. IZA Discussion Paper no. 8938. Institute for the Study of Labor (IZA), Bonn.

Graham M, Lehdonvirta V, Wood A, Barnard H, Simon D. P. and Hjorth I. (2017). The risks and rewards of online gig work at the global margins. Oxford Internet Institute, Oxford.

Graham M, Hjorth I and Lehdonvirta V (2017). Digital labour and development: Impacts of global digital labour platforms and the gig economy on worker livelihoods. *Transfer: European Review of Labour and Research,* 23(2): 135–162.

Grimm AN (2016). Trends in U.S. trade in ICT Services and in ICT-enabled services, Survey of current business, May. United States Bureau of Economic Analysis, Washington, DC.

Hampson FO and Jardine E (2016). *Look Who's Watching,* Centre for International Governance Innovation, Waterloo, ON Canada.

Hill S (2015). *Raw Deal: How the "Uber Economy" and Runaway Capitalism Are Screwing American Workers*. St. Martin's Press, New York.

Hinson R (2010). The value chain and e-business in exporting: Case studies from Ghana's non-traditional export (NTE) sector. *Telematics and Informatics*, 27(3): 323–340.

Humphrey J, Mansell R, Paré D and Schmitz H (2003). Reality of e-commerce with developing countries. London School of Economics, London.

IFDC (2015). Sorghum soars in Kenya. International Fertilizer Development Center, Alabama. Available at: https://ifdc.org/sorghum-soars-in-kenya/.

IG Metall (2016). Frankfurt paper on platform-based work. Available at: http://crowdwork-igmetall.de/.

Ihedigbo S (2014). COLEACP supports Nigerian fresh produce to access EU market. Available at: https://www.feedingknowledge.net/home?p_p_id=1_WAR_feeding_knowledgeportlet&p_p_lifecycle=2&p_p_state=maximized&p_p_mode=view&p_p_cacheability=cacheLevelPage&_1_WAR_feeding_knowledgeportlet_cmd=serveAttachment&_1_WAR_feeding_knowledgeportlet_stepAttachmentId=15946&_1_WAR_feeding_

knowledgeportlet_callId=6011&_1_WAR_feeding_knowledgeportlet_mvcPath=%2Fcalls%2Fview_all_steps. jsp&_1_WAR_feeding_knowledgeportlet_languageId=en_GB.

ILO (2011a). Formulating a national policy on skills development. Skills for employment policy brief. Geneva. Available at: http://www.ilo.org/wcmsp5/groups/public/---ed_emp/---ifp_skills/documents/publication/wcms_167172.pdf.

ILO (2014). Issues in the development of internationally harmonized measures of employment related to information and communications technology (unpublished), Geneva.

ILO (2015). *Report of the ILO's Director-general: The Future of Work Centenary Initiative*. ILC.104/DG/Itest data, Geneva.

ILO (2016). ASEAN in transformation: How technology is changing jobs and enterprises. Geneva.

Intel (2015). SDG ICT Playbook: From innovation to impact. Available at: https://www.intel.com/content/www/us/en/ corporate-responsibility/sdgictplaybook.html.

Intergovernmental Bureau of Informatics (1984). Second World Conference on Transborder Data Flow Policies.Working document. UNESCO, Paris.

International Post Corporation (2017). Cross-border e-commerce shopper survey 2016. Brussels.

Internet Society (2015a). The Internet and sustainable development. Contribution to the United Nations discussion on the Sustainable Development Goals and on the 10-year Review of the World Summit on the Information Society. Reston, VA and Geneva.

Internet Society (2015b). The Internet of Things: An overview. Internet Society. Reston, VA and Geneva.

Irani LC and Silberman MS (2015). Turkopticon: Interrupting worker invisibility in Amazon Mechanical Turk. eScholarship.

ITC (2015). International e-commerce in Africa: The way forward. Geneva.

ITC (2016). Bringing SMEs onto the e-commerce highway. Available at: http://www.intracen.org/uploadedFiles/ intracenorg/Content/Publications/Bringing%20SMEs%20onto%20the%20e-Commerce%20Highway_ final_250516_Low-res.pdf.

ITC (2016). E-Commerce in China: Opportunities for Asian firms. Geneva.

ITU (2015). *ICT Facts and Figures. The World in 2015*. Geneva.

ITU (2016). *Measuring the Information Society Report 2016*. Geneva.

ITU and CISCO (2016). *Harnessing the Internet of Things for Global Development*. Geneva.

Kaplinsky R and Morris M (2002). *A Handbook for Value Chain Research*. Institute of Development Studies, Brighton.

Kässi O and Lehdonvirta V (2016). Online labour index: Measuring the online gig economy for policy and research. MPRA Paper. University Library of Munich, Munich.

Kassi O, Lehdonvirta V, Graham M, Barnard H and Hjorth I (2016). "Not a lot of people know where it is": Liabilities of origin in online contract work. Oxford Internet Institute, University of Oxford, Oxford.

Kende M (2015). The Mobile app divide. Internet Society, Geneva.

Kenney M and Zysman J (2015). Choosing a future in the platform economy: The implications and consequences of digital platforms. Discussion paper, Kauffman Foundation New Entrepreneurial Growth Conference, Amelia Island, Florida, 18–19 June 2015.

Kuek SC, Paradi-Guilford CM, Fayomi T, Imaizumi S and Ipeirotis P (2015). The global opportunity in online outsourcing. No. ACS14228, World Bank, Washington, DC.

Kshetri N (2017). The economics of the Internet of Things in the global South. *Third World Quarterly*, 38(2): 311–339.

Kshetri N, Fredriksson T and Torres DCR (2017). *Big Data and Cloud Computing for Development: Lessons from Key Industries and Economies in the Global South*. Routledge, Oxford.

Kumar R (2014). Elusive empowerment: Price information and disintermediation in soybean markets in Malwa, India. *Development and Change*, 45(6): 1332–1360.

Kuruvilla S, Erickson CL and Hwang A (2002). An assessment of the Singapore skills development system: Does it constitute a viable model for other developing nations? *World Development*, 30(8): 1461–1476.

Lai P-H and Shafer S (2005). Marketing ecotourism through the Internet: An evaluation of selected ecolodges in Latin America and the Caribbean. *Journal of Ecotourism*, 4(3): 143–160.

Lanier J (2014). *Who Owns the Future?* Simon & Schuster, New York.

Laplume AO, Petersen B and Pearce JM (2016). Global value chains from a 3D printing perspective. *Journal of International Business Studies*, 47(5): 595–609.

Lee J, Gereffi G and Beauvais J (2012). Global value chains and agrifood standards: Challenges and possibilities for smallholders in developing countries. *Proceedings of the National Academy of Sciences*, 109(31): 12326–12331.

Lehdonvirta V, Barnard H, Graham M and Hjorth I (2014). Online labour markets: Levelling the playing field for international service markets? Paper presented at IPP 2014: Crowdsourcing for Politics and Policy, 25-26 September 2014, Oxford.

Levy F and Murnane RJ (2013). Dancing with robots: Human skills for computerized work. Third way, Cambridge, MA

Liyanage H (2015). Nations forgotten by e-commerce giants. Discussion paper. eNovation4D.

Loebbecke C and Picot A (2015). Reflections on societal and business model transformation arising from digitization and big data analytics: A research agenda. *The Journal of Strategic Information Systems*, 24(3): 149–157.

McAfee A. and Brynjolfsson E (2016). Human work in the robotic future. *Foreign Affairs,* 95(4): 139–150.

Mai NTT and Tuan NP (2012). Competition in Vietnamese e-marketplace: A case study of Alibaba in Vietnam. *International Journal of Business and Social Science*, 3(10): 60–67.

Mandel M (2015). Vietnam and the app economy. Progressive Policy Institute, Washington DC.

Manyika J, Lund S, Robinson K, Valentino J and Dobbs R (2015). Connecting talent with opportunity in the digital age. McKinsey Global Institute.

McKinsey Global Institute (2015). The Internet of things: Mapping the value beyond the hype.

McNamara K (2008). The global textile and garments industry : The role of information and communication technologies (ICTs) in exploiting the value chain. Working Paper No. 47488, World Bank, Washington, DC.

Meijers H (2014). Does the Internet generate growth, international trade, or both? *International Economics and Economic Policy*, 11(1–2): 137–163.

Melguizo Á and Perea JR (2016). Mind the skills gap! Regional and industry patterns in emerging economies. OECD Development Centre Working Papers, No. 329, OECD, Paris.

Melitz MJ (2003). The impact of trade on intra-industry reallocations and aggregate industry productivity. *Econometrica*, 71(6): 1695–1725.

Meltzer JP (2016). Maximizing the opportunities of the Internet for international trade. SSRN Scholarly Paper No. ID 2841913, Social Science Research Network. Rochester, NY.

Michaels G, Natraj A and Reenen JV (2010). Has ICT polarized skill demand? Evidence from Eleven Countries over 25 years. Working Paper No. 16138, National Bureau of Economic Research, Cambridge, MA.

Minges M (2016). Exploring the relationship between broadband and economic growth. Background Paper for the *World Development Report 2016*, World Bank, Washington, DC.

Molla A and Heeks R (2007). Exploring e-commerce benefits for businesses in a developing country. *The Information Society*, 23(2): 95–108.

Moodley S (2002). Global market access in the Internet era: South Africa's wood furniture industry. *Internet Research*, 12(1): 31–42.

Moodley S, Morris M and Velia M (2003). E-commerce for exporting garments from South Africa. Institute for Development Studies, University of Sussex, Brighton.

Murphy JT (2013). Transforming small, medium, and microscale enterprises? Information-communication technologies (ICTs) and industrial change in Tanzania. *Environment and Planning A*, 45(7): 1753–1772.

Murphy JT and Carmody P (2015). *Africa's Information Revolution: Technical Regimes and Production Networks in South Africa and Tanzania*. Wiley-Blackwell, Oxford.

Murphy JT, Carmody P and Surborg B (2014). Industrial transformation or business as usual? Information and communication technologies and Africa's place in the global information economy. *Review of African Political Economy*, 41(140): 264–283.

Murray J and van Welsum D (2014). Technology's triple threat (blog, October). Available at: http://www.adamalthus.com/blog/2014/10/05/technologys-triple-threat/ (accessed 15 June 2017).

Muto M and Yamano T (2009). The impact of mobile phone coverage expansion on market participation: Panel data evidence from Uganda. *World Development*, 37(12): 1887–1896.

Nayak R, Singh A, Padhye R and Wang L (2015). RFID in textile and clothing manufacturing: technology and challenges. *Fashion and Textiles*, 2(9):1–16.

Nübler I (2016). New technologies: A jobless future or golden age of job creation? Working Paper No. 13, ILO, Geneva.

OECD (1985). OECD Declaration on Transborder Data Flows. OECD Digital Economy Papers. Paris.

OECD (2011). *OECD Guide to Measuring the Information Society 2011*. Paris.

OECD (2012). *OECD Science, Technology and Industry Outlook 2012*. Paris.

OECD (2014a). *Focus on Inequality and Growth*. Paris. Available at: https://www.oecd.org/social/Focus-Inequality-and-Growth-2014.pdf.

OECD (2014b). *Measuring the Digital Economy: A New Perspective*. Paris.

OECD (2015). *OECD Digital Economy Outlook 2015*. Paris.

OECD (2016a). *OECD Science, Technology and Innovation Outlook 2016*. Paris.

OECD (2016b). Skills for a digital world. Background report for the 2016 Ministerial Meeting on the Digital Economy. Digital Economy Papers No. 250, OECD Publishing, Paris. Available at: http://www.oecd-ilibrary.org/science-and-technology/skills-for-a-digital-world_5jlwz83z3wnw-en.

OECD (2017a). *The Next Production Revolution: Implications for Governments and Business*. OECD Publishing. Paris.

OECD (2017b). OECD Going Digital Project: State of play. No. DSTI/CDEP/GD(2017)1/REV1. Paris.

OECD and WTO (2017). *Aid for Trade at a Glance 2017: Promoting Trade, Inclusiveness and Connectivity for Sustainable Development*. WTO and OECD publishing. Geneva and Paris.

Ojanpera S (2016). Mapping the availability of online labour. Available at: https://www.oii.ox.ac.uk/blog/mapping-the-availability-of-online-labour/.

Osnago A and Tan SW (2016). Disaggregating the impact of the Internet on international trade. Policy Research Working Paper, No. 7785, World Bank, Washington DC.

Paré DJ (2002). B2B e-commerce services and developing countries: Disentangling myth from reality. Available at: http://www.academia.edu/download/30689019/R7930a.pdf.

Parikh TS, Patel N and Schwartzman Y (2007). A survey of information systems reaching small producers in global agricultural value chains. In: Proceedings of the IEEE Conference on Information and Communication Technologies and Development (ICTD 2007): 1–11.

Parker GG, Alstyne MWV and Choudary SP (2016). *Platform Revolution: How Networked Markets are Transforming the Economy –And How to Make Them Work for You*. W. W. Norton & Company. New York and London.

Paunov C and Rollo V (2016). Has the Internet fostered inclusive innovation in the developing world? *World Development*, 78(C): 587–609.

Peppet SR (2014). Regulating the Internet of Things: First steps toward managing discrimination, privacy, security & consent. SSRN Scholarly Paper No. ID 2409074, Social Science Research Network, Rochester, NY.

Pilat D (2005). The ICT productivity paradox: Insights from micro data. *OECD Economic Studies*, 2004(1): 37–65.

Ponte S and Gibbon P (2005). Quality standards, conventions and the governance of global value chains. *Economy and Society*, 34(1): 1–31.

Porter ME (1998). *Competitive Advantage of Nations*. Free Press, New York.

Poulton C and Macartney J (2012). Can public-private partnerships leverage private investment in agricultural value chains in Africa? A preliminary review. *World Development*, 40(1): 96–109.

Qiang C (2009). Telecommunications and economic growth (unpublished paper). World Bank, Washington, DC.

Rammohan S (2010). The Shea Value Chain Reinforcement Initiative in Ghana. Paper presented at the Stanford Global Supply Chain Management Forum, December.

Rey-Moreno C (2017). Supporting the creation and scalability of affordable access solutions: Understanding community networks in Africa. Internet Society, Geneva.

Sachs JD et al. (2015). ICTs & SDGs: How information and communications technology can achieve the Sustainable Development Goals. The Earth Institute, Columbia University and Ericsson, New York.

Santiago F (2010). Human resource management practices and learning for innovation in developing countries: Pharmaceutical firms in Mexico. (Doctoral thesis) UNU-MERIT, University of Maastricht. *Innovation and Development,* 1(2).

Schmidt FA (2017). Digital labour markets in the platform economy : Mapping the political challenges of crowd work and gig work. Friedrich-Ebert Stiftung. Bonn.

Scholz T and Schneider N, eds. (2017). *Ours to Hack and to Own: The Rise of Platform Cooperativism, A New Vision for the Future of Work and a Fairer Internet.* OR Books, New York.

Shackelford SJ et al. (2017). When toasters attack: A polycentric approach to enhancing the security of things. *University of Illinois Law Review,*2017: 415–474.

Shiller B (2014). First degree price discrimination using big data. Working Paper No. 58. Brandeis University, Department of Economics and International Business School, Waltham, MA.

Stanford Graduate School of Business (2016). U.S.-to-China B2C e-commerce: Improving logistics to grow trade. White paper, Stanford Graduate School of Business. Stanford, CA.

Stewart S (2014). Is this the end of work? Information technologies and labor market disruption: A cross-Atlantic conversation. Executive Action Report No. 431, The Conference Board, New York.

Sturgeon TJ (2002). Modular production networks: A new American model of industrial organization. *Industrial and Corporate Change*, 11(3): 451–496.

Suominen K (2015). Fueling the online trade revolution a new customs security framework to secure and facilitate small business e-commerce. Center for Strategic & International Studies, Washington, DC.

Suominen K (2016a). How the Global Fund for Ecommerce is helping entrepreneurs in developing countries enter the digital era. Available at: http://www.gereports.com/kati-suominen-how-to-help-entrepreneurs-in-developing-countries-enter-the-ecommerce-era/.

Suominen K (2016b). Next big roadblock to trade – congested cities. 18 February. Available at: http://www.gereports.com/kati-suominen-next-big-roadblock-to-trade-congested-cities/ (accessed 26 May 2017).

Suominen K (2017). Accelerating digital trade in Latin America and the Caribbean. Working paper, Inter-American Development Bank, Washington, DC.

Technical Centre for Agricultural and Rural Cooperation (CTA) (2015). ICT uptake and usage in agricultural value chains in the Caribbean: A regional synthesis. Available at:  http://www.cta.int/en/article/2015-06-17/ict-uptake-and-usage-in-agricultural-value-chains-in-the-caribbean.html.

Technoserve (2016). Assessing the impact of a commercial mobile agriculture (mAgri) solution. TechnoServe, Washington, DC.

Thanh VT, Narjoko D and Oum S (2009). Integrating small and medium enterprises (SMEs) into the more integrated East Asia. Research Project Report 2009 No. 8, Economic Research Institute for ASEAN and East Asia, Jakarta.

*The Economist* (2017). Lifelong education. Special Report. 14 January.

Thun E and Sturgeon T (2017). When global technology meets local standards: Reassessing the China's mobile telecom policy in the age of platform innovation. Working Paper 17-001, MIT Industrial Performance Center, Cambridge MA; and in: Brandt L and Rawski T, eds. *The Impact of Industrial Policy and Regulation on Upgrading and Innovation in Chinese Industry* (forthcoming).

Tiamiyu MA, Bankole AS and Agbonlahor RO (2012). Catalytic mechanisms for promoting ICT investment and use in cassava value chains in south-western Nigeria. *Information Development*, 28(2): 132–148.

Tokatli N (2008). Global sourcing: Insights from the global clothing industry-the case of Zara, a fast fashion retailer. *Journal of Economic Geography*, 8(1): 21–38.

UN Centre on Transnational Corporations (1982). *Transnational Corporations and Transborder Data Flows: A Technical Paper*. United Nations, New York.

UNCTAD (2011). *Information Economy Report 2011: ICTs as an Enabler to Private Sector Development*. United Nations, New York and Geneva.

UNCTAD (2012). *Information Economy Report 2012: The Software Industry and Developing Countries*. United Nations, New York and Geneva.

UNCTAD (2013a). *Information Economy Report 2013: The Cloud Economy and Developing Countries*. United Nations, New York and Geneva.

UNCTAD (2013b). *Promoting Local IT Sector Development through Public Procurement*. United Nations, New York and Geneva.

UNCTAD (2014). *Empowering Women Entrepreneurs through Information and Communications Technologies*. United Nations, New York and Geneva.

UNCTAD (2015a). *Implementing WSIS Outcomes: A Ten-Year Review*. United Nations, New York and Geneva.

UNCTAD (2015b). *Information Economy Report 2015: Unlocking the Potential of E-Commerce for Developing Countries*. United Nations, New York and Geneva.

UNCTAD (2015c). International trade in ICT services and ICT-enabled services. UNCTAD Technical Notes on ICT for Development No. 3, Geneva.

UNCTAD (2015d). *Science, Technology and Innovation Policy Review of Thailand*. Geneva.

UNCTAD (2016a). *Data Protection Regulations and International Data Flows: Implications for Trade and Development*. United Nations, New York and Geneva.

UNCTAD (2016b). *The Least Developed Countries Report 2016: The Path to Graduation and Beyond: Making the Most of the Process*. United Nations, New York and Geneva.

UNCTAD (2017a). *The Role of Science, Technology and Innovation in Ensuring Food Security by 2030*. No. UNCTAD/DTL/STICT/2017/5. United Nations, New York and Geneva.

UNCTAD (2017b). *World Investment Report 2017: Investment and the Digital Economy*. United Nations, New York and Geneva.

UNCTAD (2017c). *Bhutan: Rapid ETrade Readiness Assessment*. United Nations, New York and Geneva.

UNCTAD (2017d). *Cambodia: Rapid ETrade Readiness Assessment*. United Nations, New York and Geneva.

UNCTAD (2017e). The "new" digital economy and development. UNCTAD Technical Notes on ICT for Development No. 8, Geneva.

UNCTAD (2017f). *Trade and Development Report 2017: Beyond Austerity: Towards a Global New Deal*. United Nations, New York and Geneva.

UNCTAD (2017g). UNCTAD E-Commerce Week 2017: Summary report. Available at: http://unctad.org/en/PublicationsLibrary/dtlstict2017d7_en.pdf.

UNCTAD and ILO (2015). Global assessment of sex-disaggregated ICT employment statistics: Data availability and challenges on measurement and compilation. UNCTAD Technical Notes on ICT for Development No. 4, Geneva.

UNESCO (2015). Information and communication technology (ICT) in education in sub-Saharan Africa: A comparative analysis of ICT integration and e-readiness in schools. Information paper No.25, Paris. Available at: http://www.uis.unesco.org/Communication/Documents/ICT-africa.pdf.

UNESCO (2017). *Global Education Monitoring Report 2016: Education for People & Planet: Creating Sustainable Futures for All*. Paris.

United States Federal Trade Commission (2015). Internet of Things: Privacy & security in a connected world. FTC Staff Report. Washington, DC.

Unwin T (2017). *Reclaiming Information and Communication Technologies for Development*. Oxford University Press, Oxford.

UPU (2017). UPU shares new approach to development cooperation. Postal statistics update 2017/No. 1, June. Bern.

Van Alstyne M (2016). Platform shift: How new biz models are changing the shape of industry. 10 May. Available at: https://www.youtube.com/watch?v=8OFRD66pl0Y.

van der Marel E, Lee-Makiyama H and Bauer M (2014). The costs of data localisation: A friendly fire on economic recovery. ECIPE Occassional Papers No. 3, European Centre for International Political Economy, Brussels.

Van Dijk JA (2005). *The Deepening Divide: Inequality in the Information Society*. Sage Publications. Thousand Oaks, CA.

van Welsum D and Lanvin B (2012). E-Leadership skills: Vision report. Prepared for the European Commission. INSEAD, Paris.

van Welsum D, Overmeer W and van Ark B (2013). Unlocking the ICT growth potential in Europe: Enabling people and businesses. European Commission, Brussels.

Vodafone (2011). Connected agriculture: The role of mobile in driving efficiency and sustainability in the food and agriculture value chain. Available at: http://www.vodafone.com/content/dam/vodafone/about/sustainability/2011/pdf/connected_agriculture.pdf.

Volpe Martincus C and Carballo J (2008). Survival of new exporters in developing countries: Does it matter how they diversify? Working paper, Inter-American Development Bank, Washington, DC.

Waema T and Katua C (2014). The promises of fibre-optic broadband in tourism and tea sectors: A pipeline for economic development in East Africa. School of Computing and Informatics, University of Nairobi, Nairobi.

Weber RH (2015). The expansion of e-commerce in Asia-Pacific trade agreements. The e15 initiative, Geneva. Available at: http://e15initiative.org/blogs/the-expansion-of-e-commerce-in-asia-pacific-trade-agreements/.

Wohlers (2014). *Annual World Wide Progress Report 2014*. Wohlers Associates, Fort Collins, CO.

Wood A (2017). Variation in structural change around the world, 1985–2015: Patterns, causes and implications. WIDER Working Paper No. 2017/34, UNU-WIDER, Helsinki.

World Bank and African Development Bank (2012). *The Transformational Use of Information and Communication Technologies in Africa*. Washington, DC and Tunis.

World Bank (2016). *World Development Report 2016: Digital Dividends*. International Bank for Reconstruction and Development/World Bank, Washington, DC.

WorldPay (2015). Your global guide to alternative payments 2015.

WTO Secretariat (2017). E-commerce, WTO rules and regional trade agreements: Discussion paper for the G20. Available at: https://www.bmwi-registrierung.de/G20-TIWG-February-2017/pdf/G20%20TIWG%20discussion%20paper%20E-commerce%20WTO%20Rules%20and%20RTAs.pdf.

Xu LD, He W and Li S (2014). Internet of Things in industries: A survey. *IEEE Transactions on Industrial Informatics*, 10(4): 2233–2243.

Zanello G, Srinivasan CS and Shankar B (2014). Transaction costs, information technologies, and the choice of marketplace among farmers in Northern Ghana. *The Journal of Development Studies*, 50(9): 1226–1239.

Zwillenberg P, Field D and Dean D (2014). Greasing the wheels of the Internet economy. BCG Perspectives, Boston Consulting Group, Boston, MA. Available at: https://www.bcgperspectives.com/content/articles/digital_economy_telecommunications_greasing_wheels_Internet_economy.